An Introduction to the
POLICY PROCESS

Theories, Concepts,
and Models of
Public Policy Making

THOMAS A. BIRKLAND

M.E. Sharpe
Armonk, New York
London, England

Library of Congress Cataloging-in-Publication Data

Birkland, Thomas A.
    An introduction to the policy process : theories, concepts, and models of public policy
making / by Thomas A. Birkland.
      p. cm.
    Includes bibliographical references and index.
    ISBN 0-7656-0417-5 (cloth : alk. paper)—ISBN 0-7656-0418-3 (pbk. : alk. paper)
    1. Political planning—United States. 2. Policy sciences. I. Title.

JK468.P64 B58 2001
320′.6′0973—dc21
                                            00-053157
                                                CIP

Printed in the United States of America

The paper used in this publication meets the minimum requirements of
American National Standard for Information Sciences
Permanence of Paper for Printed Library Materials,
ANSI Z 39.48-1984.

BM (c) 10   9   8   7   6   5   4   3   2
BM (p) 10   9   8   7   6   5   4

An Introduction to the
POLICY
PROCESS

Contents

List of Tables and Figures

Tables

Figures

Preface

It has long been said that one never really gets to know a subject until one has to teach it. If this is true, it's doubly true that one really learns a subject when one writes a book about it. This is not to say, certainly, that this book represents all there is to know about public policy. Rather, I have written this book to be a starting point in what I hope you will find to be an interesting and fruitful lifetime of thinking about and engaging in public policy making.

Most public policy texts tend to de-emphasize theories of public policy in favor of more topic-centered discussions. A common type of textbook in public policy contains one or two chapters on basic theoretical or structural aspects of policy making and devotes the remaining chapters (between half to seven-eighths of the typical book) to particular policy areas, such as "health policy" or "criminal justice policy" or "national security policy." One of my goals in writing this book is to fill in the gap between the end of the theoretical section and the case studies that are staples in these textbooks. Striking the right balance between the theoretical and the substantive or "practical" is a challenge throughout the social sciences, and I hope this book helps teachers balance these two important aspects of the public policy curriculum. To that end, I have included many examples in the book, based on my research or merely on interesting things I've heard from my colleagues, in the newspapers, or en route to learning about something else. Those who find the example of the Turtle Excluder Device interesting may be pleased to know that I stumbled on this example some years ago while researching transportation policy! Such serendipitous discoveries make the study of policy fresh and fascinating, and I hope I've conveyed some of that excitement in this book.

Another motivation for this book was my interest in providing a primer in public policy for advanced undergraduates or graduate students in courses and programs that are not primarily about public policy, but in which an understanding of public policy is particularly useful. I teach in and codirect such a program at the University at Albany. The University's Biodiversity and Conservation Policy program, which is housed in the biological sciences department, is a master of science program that teaches a great deal of conservation biology and a great deal of public policy to its students, including a required course in politics and policy and a course in the policy of biodiversity and environmental conservation. For many students this course is initially quite daunting, as most of our students have a background in biology or other sciences, but little exposure to public policy ideas beyond the introductory undergraduate American politics course. In particular, the "messiness" and indeterminacy of the policy process are often troubling to students with a science background. My goal in writing this book is to provide an overview of the policy process that acknowledges this messiness while showing how policy scholars have developed ways that we can think more systematically about this seemingly chaotic process.

I also hope people who are returning to policy studies or are seeking to teach themselves about the process will find this book useful. Students who are returning to graduate work after some years of professional experience will find that the policy studies field grows and changes quite quickly. This book is intended to help students, both those in a formal educational institution and those studying on their own, to become current with some important ideas in the study of policy. I urge all my audiences to think of this book as a beginning, or a supplement, and certainly not the final word on public policy.

I've attempted to write this book in a somewhat more conversational style than most textbooks. My goal is to provide you with a readable text and a useful reference that you can use to supplement or clarify concepts learned in classes, textbooks, and in daily contact with the policy process, including personal experience, the news media, and your own participation in policy making. The book includes an extensive glossary of terms used in policy studies and an annotated reference section, which contains short descriptions of many of the materials cited here, to serve as a guide to some of the classic works in the field of public policy. I hope you have the chance to read the materials that interest you and to continue your engagement with this material.

What's Ahead

This book starts with a reflective chapter on the idea of policy studies as a scientific endeavor that has much in common with other social science disciplines and with science more broadly. I've included this chapter because many students, particularly from outside political science, want to understand how social sciences in general, and policy studies in particular, can be "scientific" in the same way as the "hard" or "natural" sciences. Clearly, there are very important differences between natural and social sciences. The methods, the assumptions, and the way hypotheses are derived, tested, and reported differ considerably between social and natural sciences and to some extent among all disciplines. In Chapter 1, I review my thinking on what makes policy studies an appropriate endeavor for scientific study, even when the subject of study seems to be irrational and even when *we* are the subject of the discipline itself!

Chapter 2 focuses on the historical and structural features of American politics that influence public policy. This historical development helps to explain unique features of the American political experience and sets the foundation for other elements of the policy process. This discussion is particularly important because most political scientists and policy scholars acknowledge the importance of the structure and rules under which the game, if you will, of politics is played. Students are often taught—or at least are allowed to conclude—that the rules and structure are neutral and that anyone who wants to play the game can get involved in politics and "make a difference" in their community. Chapter 2 paints a rather less sanguine picture of the structure of politics and policy. I argue, following the lead of key experts in the field of politics, that the founders of our constitutional order purposefully designed our system to favor commercial interests and property holders and to make it difficult for mass publics to mobilize and seek a share of the wealth. For those interested in progressive policy change, the structure is troubling, for it suggests that mass movements and participatory democracy are not likely to carry the day in policy debates. But, as highlighted throughout this book, there are circumstances under which policy can change, and sometimes policy changes quite rapidly. Indeed, one of the most fascinating aspects of politics comes in understanding when, against the odds, policy change based on mass mobilization is possible.

The various institutions and people that make public policy are described in Chapters 3 and 4. Chapter 3 describes the official or institutional actors in the process—the legislative, executive, and judiciary.

Chapter 4 discusses the unofficial actors, such as interest groups and media, and then outlines the ways in which we think about how all the actors come together—in "iron triangles," subgovernments, and issue networks—to debate and negotiate policy alternatives.

Groups, power, and agenda setting are reviewed in Chapter 5. These are discussed at some length, since agenda setting is perhaps the most important stage of the policy process at which groups exercise political power to achieve their goals, either by promoting change or blocking it. The use of power in politics is subtle and complex, particularly in our political system. An understanding of what power is, how it is acquired, and how it is used to prevent issues from gaining attention is key to understanding why any political system does some things while not doing other things, even in the face of obvious needs or logic that would seem to compel a "superior" course of action.

Chapter 6 then describes several different ways one can categorize the substance of policies and how the various actors make decisions about which policies to pursue. Like so much in public policy studies, these descriptions of policy types are not final—they are sometimes illogical and often make the process of categorizing policies so confusing that it does not seem worth the analytic payoff. But the policy types that I review in Chapter 6 are, I believe, primarily useful as a way of stimulating thinking about what sorts of things governments do and what sorts of things we ask governments to do.

The type of policy in question often influences the design of policies intended to address policy problems. Thus, Chapter 7 considers issues of policy design and the nature of the various policy tools or instruments that we can use to mitigate or solve society's problems.

Closely related to policy design and tool choice is policy implementation and arguments of failure, which I discuss in Chapter 8. Policy implementation is a well-studied aspect of the policy process, which considers the oft-forgotten work that must come after the excitement of policy enactment has passed. Implementation—putting a program into effect—is often as difficult and contentious as policy design and enactment and in some cases is more difficult to manage. Because of the difficulties inherent in policy design and implementation, many people claim that policies have failed to meet their goals. In Chapter 8, I examine policy failure by outlining the various ways in which any policy can be said to be a failure. The complexity of policy making, with interconnectedness of policy impacts but disjointed policy design, makes real or claimed failure almost inevitable, depending on how one defines failure.

Chapter 9 puts all of these elements of policy making together. By thinking of the policy process as a "system," we can summarize and discuss the inputs to and outputs from the political system in terms of their relationship to the political system, or what is often called "the black box" in systems models. The second half of the chapter discusses four different and complementary ways of looking inside the black box; most of these models of policy making are at the forefront of current policy theory.

* * *

Affixing one's name to a book on policy and politics indicates a willingness to set forth one's particular view of the world. One must be particularly prepared to accept responsibility for the inevitable gaps and lapses, both in fact and logic, which often become clearer after the manuscript is set into type and bound between covers. Fortunately, writing and research need not be utterly solitary endeavors, and I am blessed with many friends, students, and colleagues who have been willing to take time from their busy schedules and pressing projects to review and comment on this book and on work that relates to this book. These include Scott Barclay, Brian Davis, Mark Donovan, Ben Fordham, Jennifer Krausnick, Regina Lawrence, Peter May, Henrik Minassians, Bob Nakamura, and Beryl Radin. A special debt of gratitude is owed to my students at the University at Albany, State University of New York, particularly students in the Master of Arts in Public Policy (MPP), Political Science, and Biodiversity and Conservation Policy programs, who have always challenged me to be clear in my communication of often complex and sometimes obscure concepts. I've learned as much from them as they have from me, and I am grateful to them. Patricia Kolb and Elizabeth Granda at M.E. Sharpe have been particularly helpful and even more patient in shepherding me and this project through the sometimes daunting publishing process. Thanks also to the graduate assistants and staff of the Graduate School of Public Affairs—including Dori Brown and Ellie Leggieri—for their help in producing the manuscript. Of course, the lapses in analysis or presentation remain mine.

Finally, I dedicate this book to Molly, who came into my life while this book was being written and has endured the considerable ups and occasional downs of writing and the academic life. She has been my most persistent and patient editor and critic, and she represents the audience of motivated, concerned citizens whom I hope to reach with this book.

An Introduction to the
POLICY
PROCESS

1

The Study and Practice of Public Policy

This chapter introduces readers to the science of policy studies and the origins of this enterprise in the academic and theoretical study of politics. Many readers may feel an urge to skip this chapter, deciding instead to get to what might be considered the "meat" of this book. But it is important to understand the intellectual and historic foundation of the enterprise—the study of public policy making—in which you are now a participant. Indeed, you may find that this historical context, and an explanation of how the study of public policy fits with more familiar disciplines such as political science, sociology, and economics, helps you to think about the concepts discussed later in the book.

Some readers may have trouble believing that the study of something that is as chaotic as public policy making can be treated as a "science" and can employ the scientific method. For those readers, I hope this discussion of policy "science" will serve as a confidence builder in the face of the almost inevitable claim that the research policy scholars do "isn't really science." While the study of public policy is different from the study of the "natural" or "hard" sciences, I hope to explain how those of us who study policy believe it can be a scientific and rigorous endeavor that yields important hypotheses and allows these ideas to be tested and refined.

The study of public policy is firmly grounded in the study of politics, which is as ancient, perhaps, as human civilization itself.[1] Most of the ancients tended to look at politics in general, theoretical ways. While the Koran, the Bible, and other early religious texts set down political suggestions as well as religious guidelines, they clearly do not have as

3

their primary focus the study of politics in order to better understand how it works.

The modern era of political theory begins in the fifteenth century with Niccolò Machiavelli, who wrote *The Prince* for his patron, "Magnificent Lorenzo, Son of Piero de' Medici." Machiavelli sought to show us that if we understand and plan the political actions we take in pursuit of our goals, we are better prepared to seize the political opportunities that arise in the normal course of political life. While *The Prince* remains a controversial work, it marks the beginning of modern political thought that seeks to lay out postulates and consider them in the context of real-world politics. Such thinking accelerated during a period of history known as the *Enlightenment*, in which a host of brilliant thinkers turned their focus to understanding the use of power—a basic element of politics—in social settings. Many readers are familiar with the works of these thinkers, including Hobbes, Locke, Rousseau, Hegel, Marx, Weber, and Durkheim. These theorists laid the groundwork for how we understand politics and our social interactions. They focused upon the exercise of power between individuals, families, groups, communities, and the various levels of government. Their ideas help us to understand the historic and modern ways of thinking about the relationships between our governments and ourselves. To this day, we continue to explore the functioning of politics and the role of government in our ever-changing societies.

While the study of politics has a long history, the systematic study of *public policy*, on the other hand, can be said to be a twentieth-century creation. It dates, according to Daniel McCool, to 1922, when political scientist Charles Merriam sought to connect the theory and practice of politics to understanding the actual activities of government, that is, public policy. While McCool argues that "the study of public policy did not suddenly spring into existence in the 1950s and 1960s," he notes that the classic literature—including much that is discussed in this book—is only about fifty years old, beginning with Harold Lasswell's call for the development of a distinctive policy science.[2] Because the field is so new, many of the fundamentals of the policy sciences have begun to be well understood only in the last twenty years or so. Considerable debate remains over whether there is one coherent set of principles that can govern the study and understanding of what we call the public policy process.[3]

The study of politics is the attempt to explain the various ways in which power is exercised in the everyday world and how that power is used to allocate resources and benefits to some people and groups, and costs and burdens to other people and groups. The study of public policy is the examination of the creation, by the government, of the rules, laws, goals, and standards that determine what government does or does not do to create resources, benefits, costs, and burdens. In studying public policy, we focus upon those decisions made (or implicitly accepted) by government and nongovernmental actors to address a problem that a significant number of people and groups consider to be important and in need of a solution. In other words, we study individual, group, organizational, or governmental activities that, for better or worse, influence our lives through the creation and implementation of public policy.

A major element of studying and teaching public policy—and one of the reasons this subject is so fascinating—is the reliance of policy studies on a broad range of the social sciences. I am a political scientist and tend to approach the questions raised in public policy as a political scientist; I consider the interplay of interest groups, the institutions that make policy, and the rules under which they make policy. But one can also approach these questions by adopting the insights of many other disciplines. Many programs, particularly in political science, but also in sociology, economics, public administration, law, and other disciplines, offer bachelor's, master's and doctoral degrees in these disciplines but allow students to specialize in the study of public policy. Dozens of universities now offer master's degrees in public policy (MPP degrees), and others offer bachelor's or doctoral degrees in public policy that draw from multiple disciplines to provide training in policy studies.[4] Most of these programs are interdisciplinary and draw their faculties from across the social, behavioral, and natural science disciplines. This interdisciplinary background is both a strength and a weakness that has perennially faced policy studies. It is a strength because the discipline draws upon the best insights from the natural sciences, social sciences, and the humanities. To some people, however, it is a weakness because, not having a distinctive discipline, students of policy often study and discuss the subject in terms of their own training and their discipline's language, not necessarily in terms of a shared language in policy studies. Programs that are influenced by economics will focus on concepts such as *efficiency*, optimization, marginal cost, and marginal utility. Public policy programs or courses offered in political science often incorporate economic methods and ideas, but they are also much more consciously "political" in their approach and interpretation of the policy process. Political scientists and sociologists think in terms of "policy communities" and "power relationships" to try to describe the sometimes confusing "systems" under which public policies are made. Where public policy is taught as part of a law school curriculum, the emphasis is more on legal practice and on the underlying theories of law, litigation, and the search for legal meaning and legitimacy. A summary of some of the disciplines that are involved in the study of public policy is shown in Table 1.1.

Because the public policy field is so new and because of its interdisciplinary variation, the field has yet to coalesce around a shared set of principles, theories, and priorities. I will alert you to some of these differences without making too much of them, because most of you reading this book are likely to be more interested in how these ideas can help you understand policy making, regardless of how unified the study of public policy appears to be.

For the study of public policy to be useful to you, your community, and to society as a whole, a particularly important problem that academics must address is bridging the gap between what academics know and how practitioners and citizens use what we have learned to make better policy or, at least, better *arguments* in favor of a particular policy option. This problem reflects the oft-cited tensions between what is sometimes called "pure" versus "applied" science. This is also reflected in student comments that some public policy courses are too "theoretical" and lack "practicality" or "relevance." In schools of public policy, the connection between academic research and the practical application of this knowledge to current problems is sometimes unclear to students, who have not yet had an opportunity to apply the tools we teach in these programs. One of my goals in writing this book is to show how one could apply ideas to gain greater understanding of public policy issues. The ability to apply these ideas is one of any scholar's or practitioner's most important tools. A great deal of our research and the publications resulting from that research do help to clarify the real world, and, in this overview of this field, I hope to show you how you can use the traditional public policy literature to better understand issues and problems that most concern you.

Policy Science As Applied Science

Many readers of this book are students in political science courses, perhaps an introductory public policy course or a broader course on American politics or government (although some of the examples and ideas here do translate to, and derive from, other Western democracies). Others may be reading this book in a particular course, such as environmental policy or health policy, to quickly learn the basics of policy studies so that they can be applied to particular fields. And many may simply be brushing up on what you learned years ago, getting caught up on new ideas, or simply reading for your own curiosity. Whatever your motivation, I hope, in this book, to highlight the advances in our understanding of public policy—and, yes, the things we do not know—by drawing on the literature in what we now call the policy sciences.

Many of you may react a particular way to the term *science* in this context. After all, maybe you or your friends, family or colleagues have chuckled at the idea of "political *science*" or "social *science*" more generally. "That's not real science," you or they may say. "Science is practiced by *scientists* who do things like discover planets around distant stars or unlock the mysteries of the cell or the atom, or who predict the weather, or design computers." Implicit in this assumption is the idea that *science* is something that one does in a laboratory, wearing a white lab coat or carrying a clipboard, using highly technical and seemingly exotic equipment while engaging in careful experimentation or observation. Or science is done in the field, by archaeologists who study ancient civilizations, or geologists who study landforms, or biologists who spend months on fieldwork. Indeed, in the elementary and high schools, the natural sciences are lumped into the "science" category, while history, politics, sociology, economics, and other subjects are considered "social *studies*." In colleges and universities, we think of these disciplines as *social sciences*, with a particular method of gaining knowledge, instead of just endless and directionless social *studies*.

Those of us who study social interactions—how economic transactions take place, how communities coalesce, how families get along, how policy decisions are made, why there are wars, how people developed language—do not practice our science the same way as natural scientists. But we share with scientists the desire to broaden human *knowledge*, which is ultimately what the word "science" means. And we all seek to apply the best methods to our work—to ensure that our data and conclusions are reliable, valid, and, ultimately, useful in advancing knowledge.

After all, according to the *Merriam-Webster's Collegiate Dictionary*, the word *science* is derived from the Latin word *scientia*, meaning, "having knowledge." The dictionary thus defines *science* as "the state of

Table 1.1

Selected Disciplines That Sudy Public Policy

Discipline	Description	Relationship to public policy	Some important journals
Political science	The study of political relationships; that is, the study of the processes by which societies seek to allocate political power and the benefits of such power.	The political process is the process through which policies are made and enforced.	*American Political Science Review, American Journal of Political Science, Journal of Politics, Policy, Political Research Quarterly, Public Opinion Quarterly*
Sociology	"Sociology is the study of social life, social change, and the social causes and consequences of human behavior. Sociologists investigate the structure of groups, organizations, and societies, and how people interact within these contexts" (*Source:* American Sociological Association, http://www.asanet.org/public/what.html).	Community and group activities are an important part of policy making, because groups of people often form to make demands.	*American Sociological Review, Contemporary Sociology, American Journal of Sociology*
Economics	The study of the allocation of resources in a community, however defined. Economists study markets and exchanges. Welfare economists seek to understand the extent to which an overall community's welfare can be maximized.	There are many economic factors that influence public policy, such as economic growth, productivity, employment, and the like. The tools of economics are often used to promote policies or to explain why policies succeed or fail.	*American Economic Review, Econometrica, Journal of Applied Economics, Journal of Political Economy*

| Public administration | The study of the management of government and nonprofit organizations, including the management of information, money, and personnel in order to achieve goals developed through the democratic process. | The management of public programs is an integral part of the policy process. PA scholars study the motivation of program implementers and targets and help research innovations to improve service delivery. | *Public Administration Review, Journal of Public Administration Research and Teaching* |
| Public policy | The study of what governments choose to do or not to do, including studies of the policy process, policy implementation and impact, and evaluation. | We give this label to the highly interdisciplinary study of the public policy process. Policy scholars develop theories about how the policy process works and develop tools and methods to analyze how policy is made and implemented. | *Journal of Policy Analysis and Management, Journal of Public Policy, Policy Studies Review, Policy Studies Journal, Journal of Policy History* |

knowing: knowledge as distinguished from ignorance or misunderstanding." This is what all of us engaged in science, both natural and social, are doing—trying to *know* why something happens instead of simply believing it happens or basing our belief in an outcome on faith or human nature. Some examples will illustrate what this means.

When I was in junior high school, one of our science teachers explained the differences between the ancient Greek and modern methods of pursuing scientific knowledge. He said that there was once a debate in Greece over whether men had more teeth than women. All sorts of reasons were given for men having the most teeth: larger jaw and overall body size, bigger appetites, the supposed physical superiority of men over women. The Greeks, our teacher told us, failed to do what to us is the most obvious thing: look in the mouths of men and women and count up how many teeth they have. This seems obvious to us because all of us are steeped in the logic of the Enlightenment. One of the outgrowths of the Enlightenment was the development of *empirical science*; that is, science based on the observation of a phenomenon or the collection of data about a phenomenon. Since we are so steeped in this tradition, it seems absurd to argue about the number of teeth in men and women's mouths. Of course, this story itself may be an anecdote told simply to make a point about the difference between the scientific method and other, less successful ways of knowing things. But the story makes a useful point.

Here's an example of a less useful way to use anecdotes. In my public policy courses, I will often start by asking students if they have ever worked in grocery stores or convenience stores. Often, several students have had such experiences, so then I ask if they ever had customers who used food stamps to buy food. Many have, and then I ask what kinds of foods those people bought. Almost without fail, a student or two will describe, in detail, with a measure of annoyance, how they saw a customer "buy steaks with food stamps." After all, why should poor people use our tax dollars to buy fancy foods like steaks? Others often chime in: poor people should buy juice, not soda pop, they say. Others question purchases of sugary breakfast cereals or "junk foods" like tortilla chips or microwave popcorn. When the hubbub this generates in class dies down (with students agreeing or disagreeing with each speaker), I ask the class, "Is the food stamp program a failure?" Not all claim that it is, because some students may have direct or indirect experience of the use of food stamps. Some students rely on their experiences to argue that most people buy nutritious food with their food stamps and that the abusers are unrepresentative of the broader group of food stamp recipients. Others claim that the perceived abuse of food stamps is enough to document its failure as a program.

I use this example to illustrate the difference between the scientific (or, at least, the careful) analysis of public policies and the careless, unscientific, or pseudoscientific analysis of policies. The stories people (and, quite often, their elected officials and journalists) tell are known as *anecdotes*, and the collection of anecdotes constitutes what we call *anecdotal evidence*. Anecdotes are quite powerful in the debate over policies. President Ronald Reagan was particularly fond of using anecdotes to illustrate policy problems, and presidents and other elected officials before and since Mr. Reagan have told stories to great rhetorical effect. The problem with anecdotes is that they are little tidbits of information that are unsystematically gathered and that reflect the biases of the person relating the story. A political conservative is likely to tell stories extolling the virtues of individual initiative and limited government, while her liberal counterpart will often spin tales of the proper role and function of government in ensuring our quality of life. The differences between evidence and anecdote are outlined in Table 1.2.

Let us be more systematic, then, by looking at some research on the food stamp program. Research that looks at the outcomes of public policies is called *evaluation*, so I set out to find some evaluation research on the food stamp program. In browsing the databases available at my library, I found an article that documents the positive outcomes of the food stamp program. As the authors note, the United States Department of Agriculture (the agency that administers the food stamp program) reviewed seventeen studies of the program and found that these studies overall concluded that, compared with the poor who do *not* get food stamps:

1. Participants spend a larger portion of their total expenditures on all food items.
2. Foods used at home by recipients have a greater monetary value per person and more nutrients per dollar.
3. Recipients are more likely to shop for food on a monthly basis, resulting in better planning and lower transportation costs.
4. The availability of twelve essential nutrients (including Vitamin C, calcium, and iron) in the diet is higher for recipients.

These investigations also show that a dollar increase in food stamp benefits increases food expenditures by between 17 cents and 47 cents,

Table 1.2

Anecdotes and Evidence

	Description	How it is used	Strengths/rationale
Anecdotes	Stories told to illustrate a problem or the failure of a policy, such as "I saw someone buy a steak with food stamps" or "welfare queen" stories.	To justify starting or stopping programs by providing an easily understood story with obvious conclusions and underlying normative or moral principles.	Anecdotes are good for staking out a position on an issue or for motivating people to believe a certain way. They are less useful as part of serious analysis, because they do not delve deeply into how programs work.
Evidence from scientific study	Conclusions reached through scientific study of a problem or of the outcomes of a policy.	To justify starting or stopping programs by providing the most scientifically sound information that policy makers can use to make decisions.	Scientific evidence is much stronger than anecdotes in understanding how and why things work the way they do. However, the results of scientific study are often controversial and unpopular and sometimes run counter to popular expectations.

whereas a dollar increase in income only raises expenditures by between 5 cents and 10 cents. Furthermore, the size of the benefit is correlated positively with the availability of most nutrients studied. Nonetheless, 24% of recipients report not having adequate supplies of food on a regular basis. This statistic is not surprising, because average benefits equal only 76 cents per meal, which requires extraordinary planning, nutrition knowledge, and cooking skills to fulfill dietary requirements.[5]

There are several things to notice about this passage. First, and most important for our discussion, is that the conclusions reached in the study are derived from actual research. Because it is likely that the USDA reviewed what we call *peer-reviewed* research, we can assume that this is quality scientific research, not a collection of anecdotes. Second, the results are presented in *aggregate* form—that is, the results are a description of the entire population of food stamp recipients rather than separate, disconnected stories. Third, some of the research runs counter to the "common wisdom" dispensed in anecdotes. In particular, the second and fourth points above suggest that people are, overall, buying highly nutritious foods and that the amount of nutrition per dollar is higher than in the foods bought by the poor who do not receive food stamps.

Can we conclude, then, from this evidence, that the food stamp program "works"? Not necessarily. As you will learn in your studies and reading, in this book and elsewhere, the definition of whether a program "works" is entirely dependent on one's definition, before the program is even put into effect, of what it means for the program to work. The opponent of food stamps might argue that the gains in nutrition are not worth the cost of the program or that the gains are too small. Opponents might also argue that the program has other costs in other policy areas that make the program difficult to justify. In both of these arguments, analysis (such as a form of cost benefit analysis) is employed, but *normative* assumptions are also inherent in these judgments. Others may dispense with the analysis and go right to the normative argument: They may argue that any abuse of food stamps or any public program is bad and that the extent of the abuse overwhelms any benefit from the program. On the other hand, supporters of food stamps may argue that helping the poor is so important that any but the most extreme act of abuse is acceptable. Yet proponents of food stamps may claim that the program has failed, perhaps because it does limit people's food choices (why not use food stamps in restaurants?) or that it does not serve all the poor people that could benefit from it (after all, who are all these poor people who do not get food stamps?).

How do we answer these questions? This book will not provide you with the answers; rather, it is an overview of the *tools* we can use to understand and promote our preferred policy ideas. You will have your own ideas about what programs should be promoted, what the standards for judging success and failure will be. These decisions are often *normative* decisions, rather than *positive* or scientific decisions. Throughout this book, I will argue that the tools we review here will be useful to you in helping you make decisions about what the "best" policies should be. But, because this book is about decision making in nominally democratic societies in general, and the United States in particular, it is clear that argument and persuasion are an important part of policy advocacy. My role is to provide some ideas that help you relate what we know about the policy process to policy advocacy.

Policy Studies As a Science

We can say that the careful study of public policy is "scientific" because it contributes to knowledge by relying on methodological rigor. Regardless of our disciplinary backgrounds, students of public policy have begun to develop a new discipline because we share a set of values and assumptions regarding *how* policy is most profitably studied. In other words, policy scholars share a commitment to *methodology*, but not to any one particular method. Rather, the most influential policy scholars value analytic precision, economy, and rigor, seeking to promote them in their work.

Harold Lasswell, reflecting the *behaviorist* nature of social sciences that began in earnest in the 1950s, argued that quantitative analysis and the *scientific method* were important elements of any policy science. To many new students of politics and the policy process, this promotion of science and method is a bit puzzling. The term "the scientific method" conjures in some minds the idea that an endeavor will be strictly quantitative, with a lot of numeric data, number crunching, and esoteric statistical analysis, yielding results about exotic phenomena that are hard to apply to real-world situations. Indeed, Thomas Kuhn argues that basic science often generates as many questions as it answers and that some of the results are puzzling or, at least, not immediately applicable to the production of goods or services.

It is true that many policy scholars rely on quantitative methods, for good reason; such methods are remarkably useful and, in the information age, relatively inexpensive. And more important, these tools are a small part of the analytic techniques that students of policy use to study practical problems in governance and politics. Indeed, Harold Lasswell was not a statistician and understood that policy research could not be solely quantitative. A great deal of qualitative evidence has to be brought to bear as well, such as the evidence that we can gather from interviewing key participants, reading journalistic accounts or agency reports, and gathering other information that is not strictly "quantifiable." In essence, each type of data requires different analytic techniques, but these techniques are all grounded in the "real world" of policy making.

Thus, Lasswell's prescriptions for an empirically driven, methodologically rigorous, yet flexible style of policy research have served as the basis of policy studies in the late twentieth century. But Lasswell's call for a science of public policy was also very much driven by a desire to solve problems. Lasswell, like many social scientists and reformers of the 1940s through the 1960s, felt that the increasingly sophisticated research techniques available to social scientists would allow them to study public problems and to propose solutions to them. While one use of science is to inform social decision making on a range of issues, from nuclear war to medicine to mass transit, a great deal of scientific endeavor is not solely or simply driven by the desire to learn about individual problems and their solutions, but is also a function of a desire to gain knowledge of the social world. Many of the scholars reviewed in this book are interested in public policy because they can apply the tools of their disciplines to social problems, thereby gaining greater understanding of society and politics as a whole and, perhaps, in the process, contributing to the change for the better.

Policy studies, like many social sciences, are sometimes said to lag behind the natural sciences because we still have not developed what McCool calls a "dominant theoretical tradition," or what Thomas Kuhn would call a "paradigm."[6] For example, McCool notes that Thomas Dye's text, *Understanding Public Policy*, lists and discusses eight theoretical traditions in policy study.[7] All eight are treated as equally useful, even though some of them may actually conflict with each other, such as the theories that support pluralism versus those that suggest a more elitist model of government. Most other introductory public policy texts do the same thing, providing little guidance for adopting or developing theory. While it is not the role of these texts to exalt one tradition or disparage another, it is clear that the basic works in our field—the ones that introduce students to the key concepts—do not share one single theoretical foundation. They therefore reflect the current state of the field.

This is not to say that the state of the field is viewed positively by all who work in it. The proliferation of theory building without testing and refinement of something that looks like a paradigm or at least a set of principles for the study of public policy led George Greenberg and his colleagues to assert that the explosion of modeling needed to yield to actual empirical testing of theories. These tests would allow policy scholars to gain a better sense of which theories work better than others.[8] Paul Sabatier, echoing this sentiment, promotes a research agenda to improve the making *and testing* of policy theories.[9]

To a considerable extent, these calls for testing theories have been heeded. Sabatier and Jenkins-Smith, in their 1993 text *Policy Change and Learning: An Advocacy Coalition Approach*, further refine Paul Sabatier's "*Advocacy Coalition Framework*" and invite other policy scholars to help test this framework. The authors then provide a reassessment of the advocacy coalition framework and of theory building in general.[10] Frank Baumgartner and Bryan Jones, in *Agendas and Instability in American Politics*, extensively study how issues gain or lose prominence in American politics by analyzing congressional hearings and news coverage of key policy areas. Their research yields two important insights. First, using a considerable amount of evidence derived from congressional hearings and media coverage of issues, Baumgartner and Jones find that American politics is characterized by long periods of policy stability followed by sudden change in the agenda and in policy. Second, Baumgartner and Jones show how congressional hearing data can be used to track how much attention is being paid to particular issues. This methodological contribution may be as important as the main conclusions of the study, because it shows how one can use congressional data to study the public policy process and how one can build a fairly sophisticated model or at least a story of why policy making seems so slow or even static at one moment and highly dynamic the next.[11]

But why is all this theorizing important, particularly when many of us seek practical answers to solve daily, real-world problems? Theories are important because, by helping to make sense of this ambiguity, they allow us to develop general concepts that apply to more than one case or problem. In creating these general concepts or "rules," we can structure our thinking about the policy process and its application to real-world situations. Understanding and teaching theory can be very difficult, however, because of the wide variation in terminology in the various texts and policy studies. Daniel McCool, in his excellent introductory essay to an anthology of classic policy texts, lists three different definitions of *policy science* taken from the policy literature, two definitions of policy studies, three definitions of policy evaluation, and four definitions of policy analysis. "The conceptual distinction between these terms," he argues, "is indistinct."[12] McCool also lists five definitions of the term "theory" and four each of "model" and "concept," the definitions of which overlap considerably.

With all these overlapping and sometimes confusing definitions, it is understandable that theory seems so complex and unhelpful, particularly in a book like this one. But theories of public policy making are very important because they are the very tools that help us to understand the broader questions of public policy. This book does not create new theories, but relies on existing theories to illustrate the tools we need to understand public policy. My goal is to provide you with additional or alternative explanation of the theories you may be learning now, or have learned before, in order to clarify their features and reinforce their practical importance in policy studies.

Science, Rationality, and the Policy Process

Those who apply the most rigorous qualitative and quantitative techniques to their work are sometimes called policy scientists, and their field of study *policy sciences*. These researchers practice in the analytic tradition of policy studies. An important part of the policy sciences is the study of policy analysis. This importance of policy analysis is reflected in the existence and importance of respected and successful consulting firms and policy research organizations like RAND and Mathematica. Policy analysis is taught in many textbooks, such as classics by Weimer and Vining, and Stokey and Zeckhauser, which borrow heavily from literature on economics and decision making.[13]

This book tends to follow the research tradition that focuses on the policy process. Policy process studies go beyond what is called the rationalist analysis of policy.[14] Students of the policy process view rational, scientific, and often quantitative policy analysis as *evidence* for various participants in policy making to use to *advocate* for their preferred policies. Thus, while students of the process should not discount or ignore the contributions of economically based rational analysis, students would do well to keep such analysis in its broader context, particularly when considering policy issues, such as abortion, prayer in schools, and welfare policy, that transcend economic or statistical analysis. The interplay of this evidence, the values and belief systems of the participants in the process, the structure of the process itself, and the distribution of power within the structure all have an important influence on public policy.

For years, political scientists have known that government is neither monolithic—that is, one single-minded body that speaks with one voice and works toward just one set of goals—nor a neutral referee that dispassionately judges between policy alternatives by weighing their costs and benefits, however defined. The participants in the policy process— whether they are considered policy entrepreneurs, brokers, analysts, interest groups, or association leaders—are not all or even primarily neutral participants in the policy process. Along the same lines, as Clarke Cochran and his colleagues argue in their book, there are few "neutral" policy analysts and by definition no neutral advocates of particular policy alternatives.[15] Thus, as Giandomenico Majone and Deborah Stone note,[16] analysis is often undertaken in the name of advocacy. Policy analysis is an important part, but only one part, of the overall rhetorical arsenal employed by partisans in political debate. Indeed, the results of policy analysis are often abandoned when it generates negative or contrary results, or when other rhetorical tools seem to work better. Indeed, as discussed later in this book, the actual act of identifying a problem is as much a normative judgment as it is an objective statement of fact; thus, if analysis proceeds from the identification of a problem, and the problem is defined normatively, then one cannot say that any subsequent analysis is strictly neutral.

As I write this chapter, my introductory public policy course is giving its group presentations on issues related to the apparent outbreak of school violence incidents in places like Springfield, Oregon, and Littleton, Colorado. One of the groups chose to organize their presentations by looking at pending federal legislation, alternative policy choices (following John Kingdon's book, *Agendas, Alternatives and Public Policies*), and their conclusions on the desirability of alternative solutions to the school violence problem. The group argued that armed guards, cameras in classrooms, metal detectors, and other measures seemed too severe. These security techniques would make schools look like prisons and thereby damage the educational environment, in turn reducing academic performance.

During the question and answer period, I asked the group whether they had any information that showed that there is a link between these stern security measures and a poorer educational environment. They answered that they did not; I followed up by asking, "Does it matter that you have no evidence?" After some discussion, we concluded that evidence is useful in policy debate, but is not always necessary. Sometimes, the imagery and symbolism one associates with a policy—the image of a school that looks and in some ways works like a jail, in this case—are sufficient to carry an argument. Thus, while one can gather considerable information on the relationship between school security and the educational environment, one need not necessarily have all the evidence in hand if one's argument strikes a chord with the public and decision makers. This means, more bluntly, that one needs relatively little evidence to make an argument if one can appeal to popular prejudices and common misconceptions, or to common values or interests that are not too far outside the mainstream of current thought. This sounds cynical, but there are abundant examples in American history and world history of emotion overcoming rationality in policy making, such as the imposition of Jim Crow laws on black Americans based on a scientifically unfounded belief that blacks are genetically inferior in some way to whites. Because neither facts nor emotions are solely decisive, evidence *and* emotion play important roles in policy making, and sometimes emotion gets the upper hand.

What Is Public Policy?

We now know that the study of public policy can be approached in a scientific way, although all participants in the policy process may not universally adopt that evidence derived from the scientific method. But at this point we do not have a working definition of *public policy* itself. There are many possible ways to define public policy; this section provides some reasons to pick a particular definition over another.

In academic studies of policy, we offer definitions of public policy to understand the shape of the field we seek to study. For many people, defining public policy helps them define their own roles in policy making, as well as that of the organization they work for. As I was writing this chapter, a member of the policy analysis office of a New York State agency called me. The agency was engaging in a strategic planning initiative; to do so it needed to establish its mission—that is, its very reason for existing. Because this agency has a major influence on state taxation, spending, and government performance assessment—that is, on public policy in the broad sense—the caller was particularly interested in defining the term *public policy*, so that her agency could know better how public policy relates to its work. The analyst ran through a list of the classic public policy texts, and asked if these were good sources of a definition of public policy.

There are many good sources for such a definition, and I urged her to look at these sources because of scholars' lack of a consensus definition of public policy. Thomas Dye argues that this search for a definition of public policy can degenerate into a word game. It may be fruitless to look for one particular definition of public policy, and it is certainly not useful to continue to develop yet more definitions. I suggested to my caller that she review the texts and adopt a definition that the agency feels makes the most sense in its particular context. Table 1.3 provides some examples of the definitions of public policy that my caller could draw from.

You may recognize one of these definitions from a current or past textbook. The value of reviewing these definitions is in deriving certain attributes that define public policy:

- The policy is made in the "public's" name.
- Policy is generally made or initiated by government.
- Policy is interpreted and implemented by public and private actors.
- Policy is what the government intends to do.
- Policy is what the government chooses *not* to do.

While reaching a consensus on the precise definition of public policy has been impossible, all the variants of the definition suggest that public policy making is *public*—it affects a greater variety of people and interests than do private decisions, and this is why government and the policies made by government are sometimes so controversial, frustrating, and at the same time very important. But because the public is the source of political authority—that is, the authority to act on the public's behalf—it is clear that government is at the center of efforts to make *public* policy.

Finally, it is important to define what a *policy* is, because this is sometimes not obvious. You might argue that a policy is a law, or a regulation, or the set of all the laws and regulations that govern a particular issue area or problem. This would be a sound but incomplete answer. Anne Schneider and Helen Ingram provide a more extensive definition of policy: "Policies are revealed through texts, practices, symbols, and discourses that define and deliver values including goods and services as well as regulations, income, status, and other positively or negatively valued attributes."[17] This definition means that policies are not just contained in laws and regulations; once a law or rule is made, policies continue to be made as the people who *implement* policy—that is, those who put policies into effect—make decisions about who will benefit from policies and who will shoulder burdens as a result. In studying policy, then, we look at the broader sweep of politics, not simply the written laws and rules themselves.

Table 1.3

Defining "Public Policy"

Definition	Author
"The term *public policy* always refers to the actions of government and the intentions that determine those actions."	Clarke E. Cochran, et al.*
"Public policy is the outcome of the struggle in government over who gets what."	Clarke E. Cochran, et al.
"Whatever governments choose to do or not to do."	Thomas Dye[†]
"Public policy consists of political decisions for implementing programs to achieve societal goals."	Charles L. Cochran and Eloise F. Malone[‡]
"Stated most simply, public policy is the sum of government activities, whether acting directly or through agents, as it has an influence on the life of citizens."	B. Guy Peters[§]

* Clarke E Cochran, et al., *American Pubic Policy: An Introduction*. 6th ed. (New York, St. Martin's Press, 1999).

† Thomas R. Dye, *Understanding Public Policy*. 7th ed. (Englewood Cliffs, N.J.: Prentice-Hall, 1992).

‡ Charles L. Cochran and Eloise F. Malone, *Public Policy: Perspectives and Choices*. (New York: McGraw Hill, 1995).

§ B. Guy Peters, *American Public Policy: Promise and Performance* (Chappaqua, N.Y.: Chatham House/Seven Rivers, 1999).

What Makes Public Policy Public

The dominant ideological foundation of our constitutional system (and that of other countries, such as Canada, Australia, and Great Britain, for example) is known as *classical liberalism*. One of the best expressions of this ideology is provided in John Locke's *Second Treatise of Civil Government* (1690). Among the many beliefs of liberalism is the belief that power derives from the consent of the governed, and that "we the people" are the governed who provide our consent to the government. Thus, when policy advocates seek to induce the government to make policy (by taking an action or refusing to do so), proponents of the new policy will claim that the government does so in the "public interest."

Often, however, controversies arise because there is disagreement over what constitutes "the public interest." For example, agencies that regulate public utilities, such as electric companies, claim to regulate in the public interest by limiting rates or assuring service. Some policy advocates claim that laws that relieve tax burdens on the rich are in the public interest because they create overall public wealth. Those who argue that the rich should be taxed at a higher rate than the poor claim that taxation based on ability to pay is more in the spirit of the public interest. Another example of disputes over what policies should be made in the broader public interest involves a rather esoteric issue: the protection of sea turtles. The National Marine Fisheries Service of the National Oceanic and Atmospheric Administration requires shrimp fishers to use devices called "Turtle Excluder Devices," so that turtles are not caught in shrimp nets. This effort may hurt the shrimp fishers somewhat by reducing the amount of shrimp they catch, but the policy is claimed to support a broader public good: in this case, the protection of an endangered species. Indeed, many states have groups called "Public Interest Research Groups" or PIRGs, which promote their interpretation of the public interest. By arguing for a particular interpretation of the public interest or the "national interest," one is making a normative claim for what we might call the "public good." Clearly, the public interest is then highly variable depending on who is defining it.

For example, in our shrimp example, how would you define the public interest? If you were a shrimp fisher or a member of a fisher's family, you would likely define it in a much different way than would a representative of an environmental or conservation group. You might say that the public really has no clearly stated interest in turtles, but they do display a preference for lower costing shrimp based on an economic analysis, or that the public interest *in your community* is in seeing a strong and economically viable shrimp industry. Environmentalists, on the other hand, could argue that the public, given a choice, would be willing to pay a little more to save an endangered species. These different arguments reflect the difficulty of defining a universal, agreed-upon public interest.

Many inhabitants of Pacific Northwest logging communities display signs on their homes saying, "This home supported by the timber industry."[18] When enough houses display such signs, or people display such sentiments, one may gain a sense of what that community defines as its public interest. Yet the public interest is often more broadly defined than by the interests of a town or region's fishers or loggers. This is the problem inherent in defining the public or a set of publics, and deriving interests from them. There are multiple public interests at the local, regional, national, and even international levels. A policy restricting logging may cost us our livelihood or a few hundred dollars more on a new house, depending on which public we belong to. When different groups or communities define differing interests, conflict is likely to ensue.

Public policy is related to the public interest because it in some way affects all of us. But we are not all affected by the same policies in exactly the same way, nor is one's intensity of feeling about an issue necessarily equal to others.' Most of us do not care too much about the day-to-day workings of government because we are busy with the day-to-day workings of our lives and because the activities of government seem removed from our daily interests and needs. Still, the government plays an important role in every aspect of our lives, from the nutrition labeling on our breakfast cereal to the federal standards for fire-retardant kids' clothing. As oppressive as government is claimed to be by some interests, at least some government activities are benign and beneficial to most people, and we tend not to dwell on those policies until something goes very wrong with them.

Presumably, you are interested in public policy because you care intensely about a particular area of public policy—the environment, maybe, or civil rights, or economic freedom, or the promotion of personal morality. But even the most intensely interested participants in the policy process are not concerned with every issue. There is a considerable division of labor in democratic politics—different people have different constitutional responsibilities, and the vast array of issues that government handles on our behalf requires that even members of legislatures need to be specialists in fairly narrow fields.

We delegate the power to make policies in *our* name (or, more precisely, the system is designed this way) because it's *our* government. Because we cannot all concern ourselves with the day-to-day panoply of issues that government must address, we have delegated our decision making to people who specialize in making the complex decisions that modern government must face. By delegating our power, we do not abandon our interest in what the government does or how it does it (and sometimes the procedures government uses are at least as important as the goals to be achieved), nor our right to promote our own ideas of what constitutes the public interest when we are sufficiently motivated. Indeed, nearly every reader of this book probably has some reason for studying public policy—many of the readers have, in their minds, a definition of "the public interest" that is likely to differ from others.

Why Do We Study Public Policy?

While the image of the public interest varies from person to person, and one person's individual interests are likely to differ in some ways from their neighbors' interests, most people are interested in the impact of policies on their lives: how many services they receive or how much they have to pay in taxes, for example. That said, why do you want to study the *process* that leads to the decisions to make these policies? Since you are reading this book, you probably already have an idea of why you are studying or working in public policy.

Two texts in particular, by Clarke E. Cochran and his colleagues, and by James Anderson,[19] provide reasons for the study of public policy. The first of these is what Cochran calls a theoretical reason and what Anderson calls a scientific reason. They argue that one studies public policy so that one can know more about the process, both in pursuit of knowledge for its own sake and to inform practitioners. One might compare the pursuit of knowledge to "pure" science and the practitioner orientation to "applied" science. The practical and applied study of public policy takes its cues from theory, but seeks more actively to apply those theoretical insights to actual cases of public policy formation, thereby helping theorists improve their theories. In a course on public policy, theory may be applied to particular cases or policy areas, as often seen in the later chapters of introductory public policy texts. As knowledge filters from the more abstract to the more applied, insights from the theoretical world are employed, knowingly or not, by practitioners. Conversely, students of public policy derive theory by observing the collective activity of the practitioners of public policy.

Related to the practical reasons for studying policy are political reasons. This is the ultimate in practicality: people with political goals study public policy to learn how to promote their preferred policy options. I hope you find this book useful in understanding the political process so that you can work toward reaching your policy goals while at the same time understanding why your best efforts may be thwarted.

How Does Theory Help You?

A key reason for this book is to provide you with conceptual tools to understand policy making—as a student of the process, as a citizen, and as a potential actor in the policy process.

If you are a student, you may be reading this book because you want to understand the policy process quickly. While this book is not a shortcut, it is designed to enhance your understanding by reviewing concepts raised in current-day texts on public policy and relating them to broader theories and trends in public policy. I also and sincerely hope that you find this book more than a supplement to a course you are merely enduring. Rather, I hope that this book, and any courses you are taking and other books you are studying, will enrich your understanding and spark some intellectual curiosity. Indeed, your teachers and I will have truly succeeded if we make you want to continue your study of public policy.

Beyond simply assisting you in your studies, I also hope that this book will reach students in school, recent graduates, not-so-recent graduates, and people who have not had any formal education in politics or policy making at all. I hope to reach people in all these categories because civic education is an important foundation of any democracy. This assertion is based as much on a sense of community spirit as it is on rational self-interest. You may share my dismay at a political system dominated by sound bites and sketchy policy ideas developed simply to curry favor with interest groups. You may also respond to my claim about democracy by responding, "The United States really isn't a democracy, it's run by wealthy insiders and elites" or "What difference can one person make anyway?"

I hope that this book will highlight what social scientists and practitioners know about the policy process and, in particular, how individuals and groups can work to significantly affect public policy. Healthy criticism of the obstacles that prevent the public interest from being addressed is a good thing, but paralyzing cynicism about the process is not.

Some of you will become actual participants in the policy process. Some will become elected officials, appointed officials, or agency managers and staff. Others will lead interest groups, work in the news media, or provide scientific and technical information for others. Many of you, never thinking you're involved in the process, will go on to successful careers in business, the arts, or other endeavors. But some day, when you least expect it, you may get involved in policy making. Perhaps you will become active when you and your neighbors oppose building a new shopping mall in your neighborhood. Perhaps you will join with your neighbors in volunteering for a political campaign. Or your business may ask you to work with others to promote a policy or to prevent one from being adopted. In short, chances are good that you will become interested in the policy process at some time in your career, and I hope that this book will help you become a more thoughtful and effective participant.

2

The Historical and Structural Context of Public Policy Making

The history of American politics and policy making is characterized by considerable change. Were George Washington, James Madison, and Thomas Jefferson to find themselves in the United States at the beginning of the twenty-first century, they would find much that has changed in the size, nature, and scope of government, particularly the federal government, since their day. Yet they would also, I think, recognize some of the more enduring features of American government and political life that date from their time.

This chapter is about both the changes and the enduring features of American politics that influence policy making. To understand the policy environment, it is important to understand the history of the United States from a policy perspective. A particularly useful summary of this history is provided by David Robertson and Dennis Judd,[1] and is reviewed in the first section of this chapter. We then turn the environmental factors that help shape public policy. These factors are largely influenced by the history and structure of the United States, and the decisions that were made at the founding still resonate today; some of those decisions have proven wise, others apparently less so.

The Historical Development of Public Policy

In their second chapter, "The Legacy of Constitutional Design," Robertson and Judd lay out a history of the United States characterized by what they call "policy restraint." This history is divided into four eras: a period of divided power, an era of state activism, an era of national activism, and, finally, an era of national standards. In all these eras, some degree of policy restraint has historically prevented government from taking action on issues when, in many cases, such action may have been warranted. In many cases, such policy restraint in policies like housing and health care has distinguished the United States from other industrialized states, which have much more actively pursued policies that provide more services for citizens but that also involve greater government action.

Divided Power

In the first era, the era of "divided policy making power" (1787–1870), the major task facing the nation was to divide policy making power between the states and the national government.

After the United States won its independence from Great Britain, many thought that the newly free states would experience a period of peacetime prosperity; instead, an economic *depression* ensued. The economic crisis was worsened by the weakness of the national government under the Articles of Confederation. The national government could barely raise taxes or armies, and often too few states sent representatives to the seat of government to discuss policies. In the states, the farming interests sought loose money policies to alleviate the damage done by deflation; this meant the printing of paper money. The most radical act—and the one that most clearly illustrated the shortcomings of the national government—was Shays' Rebellion. Daniel Shays was a farmer in western Massachusetts who led a group of about a thousand men to intimidate the courts to delay foreclosures and debt collections; his band also sought to attack a federal arsenal. While Massachusetts responded by providing relief for debtors, the event awakened other states to their need for strong national action to provide protection against insurrection.

The Constitution, finalized in 1787, is widely considered to place limits on the scope of the federal government, but the resulting federal government was still considerably more powerful than the skeleton government established under the Articles of Confederation. In light of economic instability and episodes like Shays' rebellion, both of which stemmed from federal weakness and the inability to persuade or compel states to act in their joint interests, the framers drafted provisions to protect property and the political standing of the moneyed classes against popular uprisings. Robertson and Judd call these features "structural impediments to radical policy." There are many such features in the Constitution. The federal structure itself and the division of power among the three branches of government provide structural barriers to rapid and radical policy change. But the most important feature of the early Constitution was its relatively limited grant of power to the federal government, and the reservation, under the Tenth Amendment, of a great deal of power to the states, thereby, Judd and Robertson argue, "sort[ing] political conflicts into different jurisdictions" (p. 30). The result is that "one of the enduring consequences of the American federal structure is that policy conflicts tend to turn as much on jurisdictional questions as on the merits of policy alternatives" (p. 31). In other words, many debates are as much over which level of government should do something as over whether something should be done.

Because the federal government assumed regulation of interstate commerce and because economic growth was considered vital to the young nation's prospects, Congress's role was largely focused on promoting commerce. Congress, however, had many other powers as well, as shown in Table 2.1, which reproduces Article I, Section 8, of the Constitution, listing all the things Congress had the power to do.

Clearly, some of these clauses seem dated to us (such as the regulation of commerce with the Indian tribes in Clause 3, the *Commerce Clause*), or appear obscure (such as Clause 17, which declares federal authority to establish a capital at what was to become known as Washington in the District of Columbia). But most of these powers are as current and important today as they were over 200 years ago.

The powers granted to Congress fall into two broad and overlapping duties: the management of national responsibilities, such as defense and immigration policy, and commercial responsibilities, such as coining money, setting bankruptcy rules, and building roads and post offices. The latter function was particularly important, since federal efforts to encourage communication and transportation established links between states so as to forge a new *nation* from separate and often distant states.

The powers of Congress are broader in practice than those listed in Article I, Section 8, because Clause 18, also called the "elastic clause," grants Congress power to do things not explicitly listed in Article 1, Section 8, to advance the goals outlined in the Constitution. For instance, Congress in this period funded canal and road building for much more general purposes than simply moving mail. Congress, in establishing

Table 2.1

Article 1, Section 8 of the Constitution

Perhaps the most important passage of the Constitution, particularly for students of public policy, is Article 1, Section 8. If, as we discussed in Chapter 1, a viable definition of "public policy" is what the government does or chooses not to do, it is worthwhile to outline what the founders had in mind:

Clause 1: The Congress shall have Power To lay and collect Taxes, Duties, Imposts and Excises, to pay the Debts and provide for the common Defense and general Welfare of the United States; but all Duties, Imposts and Excises shall be uniform throughout the United States;

Clause 2: To borrow Money on the credit of the United States;

Clause 3: To regulate Commerce with foreign Nations, and among the several States, and with the Indian Tribes;

Clause 4: To establish an uniform Rule of Naturalization, and uniform Laws on the subject of Bankruptcies throughout the United States;

Clause 5: To coin Money, regulate the Value thereof, and of foreign Coin, and fix the Standard of Weights and Measures;

Clause 6: To provide for the Punishment of counterfeiting the Securities and current Coin of the United States;

Clause 7: To establish Post Offices and post Roads;

Clause 8: To promote the Progress of Science and useful Arts, by securing for limited Times to Authors and Inventors the exclusive Right to their respective Writings and Discoveries;

Clause 9: To constitute Tribunals inferior to the supreme Court;

Clause 10: To define and punish Piracies and Felonies committed on the high Seas, and Offences against the Law of Nations;

Clause 11: To declare War, grant Letters of Marque and Reprisal, and make Rules concerning Captures on Land and Water;

Clause 12: To raise and support Armies, but no Appropriation of Money to that Use shall be for a longer Term than two Years;

Clause 13: To provide and maintain a Navy;

Clause 14: To make Rules for the Government and Regulation of the land and naval Forces;

Clause 15: To provide for calling forth the Militia to execute the Laws of the Union, suppress Insurrections and repel Invasions;

Clause 16: To provide for organizing, arming, and disciplining the Militia, and for governing such Part of them as may be employed in the Service of the United States, reserving to the States respectively, the Appointment of the Officers, and the Authority of training the Militia according to the discipline prescribed by Congress;

Clause 17: To exercise exclusive Legislation in all Cases whatsoever, over such District (not exceeding ten Miles square) as may, by Cession of particular States, and the Acceptance of Congress, become the Seat of the Government of the United States, and to exercise like Authority over all Places purchased by the Consent of the Legislature of the State in which the Same shall be, for the Erection of Forts, Magazines, Arsenals, dock-Yards, and other needful Buildings;—And

Clause 18: To make all Laws which shall be necessary and proper for carrying into Execution the foregoing Powers, and all other Powers vested by this Constitution in the Government of the United States, or in any Department or Officer thereof.

and funding the army, also funded the process of westward expansion by providing military protection for westward expansion.

In general, however, from the perspective of the average citizen, the federal government was not the most important official participant in policy making in the early days of the United States. The structure of the Constitution and the founders' understanding of the role of the new federal government help explain this. However, other factors are important, including the mostly rural nature of the nation; its sparse and generally homogeneous population,[2] a political philosophy based on limited government, individual liberty, and the protection of private property rights; and the fact that the industrial revolution had not yet taken hold in the United States. Indeed, Thomas Jefferson was the strongest proponent of a largely rural, agricultural America populated by a virtuous class of farmers, an ideal that stood in sharp contrast with Alexander Hamilton's vision of a more industrial and mercantile America. In the end, Hamilton's vision won out over Jefferson's: with growing industry and national systems of production and distribution of manufactured and agricultural goods came greater demands on government to create policy that would foster greater uniformity throughout what was to become a great industrial nation.

State Activism

The next era—state activism—spans the period from the 1870s to 1933. This was a period of great changes and turmoil as the nation shifted from a predominantly rural, farming-based economy to a modern urban, industrial economy, powered both by native and immigrant labor. This urbanization led to great wealth for some people, and great poverty for others, particularly those living in the urban ethnic ghettoes as well as in the "company towns" set up and run by large mining and industrial monopolies. The presence of disease and crime in these newly industrialized cities, the regularity of mass popular uprisings in the cities, such as the Haymarket Riot in Chicago in 1886, severe labor strife, such as the Pullman Strike of 1893–94, and the ongoing problem of large industrial disasters prompted the states to seek solutions to some of the most overt ills wrought by the rapid industrialization and social change of this era.

Many states sought to regulate industry in general and to rein in the excessive power exercised by many of the largest industrial monopolies. Yet the fact that these monopolies existed across state boundaries made regulation by individual states difficult, if not impossible. Because these firms were engaged in interstate commerce, many people felt that the federal government needed to step in and regulate business. Congress had the power to regulate interstate commerce under the commerce clause of the Constitution (Article 1, Section 8, Clause 3), one of the most important clauses in the Constitution.

As the industrial revolution continued, Congress reacted to the problems of railroad rate setting by establishing the Interstate Commerce Commission (a body that was recently dissolved by Congress). And in 1890, Congress passed the Sherman Antitrust Act, which, combined with later efforts by Theodore Roosevelt and others, led to the breakup of the trusts, most notably the Standard Oil trust, which was the parent firm of what we now know as Exxon, Mobil, Chevron, and others. Ironically, as this book was being written, Exxon and Mobil have merged into Exxon Mobil, bringing together two old members of the Standard Oil Trust.

On the social front, the federal government began to tackle the problems of integrating former slaves into the political community—problems that vexed those who wanted to see former slaves rapidly enjoy the fruits of equal citizenship with whites, and those who wanted blacks to remain servile and uninvolved in deciding their and their nation's fate. The primary step in addressing these problems was the enforcement of the recently passed "Civil War Amendments"—the Thirteenth, Fourteenth, and Fifteenth Amendments to the Constitution. In addition, Congress passed several comprehensive Civil Rights laws, including the 1866 and 1875 Civil Rights Acts, intended to grant basic civil rights to African-American men, such as voting, property rights, and the right to equal public accommodations, such as schools or railroad service. For a short period, these acts, enforced by federal agencies such as the Freedman's Bureau and by federal troops occupying much of the South during Reconstruction, created a political system open to the participation of African-Americans.

Federal activity to protect civil rights declined by 1880 as other issues and the political desire to reintegrate the South into the federal union (starting with the presidential election of 1876) rendered civil rights in the South a lower federal law enforcement priority. In keeping with this change in federal priorities, the Supreme Court, in *Plessy v. Ferguson* in 1898, effectively returned the power over civil rights and liberties to the states to do whatever they wanted with such issues. In effect, this decision allowed the southern states to pursue policies of racial segregation in all aspects of social, political, and economic life. Nevertheless, racist and segregationist policies and practices were also evident outside the South and some of the more difficult political battles against racism had to be fought in the North and West.

Similar to the failure of the federal government to ensure civil rights in this era was the federal government's weakness in its efforts to regulate industry. Corporate power was protected from government interference by a conservative judiciary that interpreted constitutional law to protect capital from minimal regulation. Thus, by 1900, public demands for federal and state action focused on industrial safety and labor relations. Federal policy in this area can be defined as purposefully noninterventionist. The federal government was supportive of *laissez-faire economics* and identified the role of the government as allowing states and individuals to conduct their business without government intrusion.

For example, the Supreme Court, in *Lochner v. New York* (1905), ruled that the cities and states could not regulate the wages and hours of workers (in this case, bakers) because such regulation interfered with the workers' right to freely contract their labor with their employers. This decision sparked serious controversy, because the workers, in reality, were *not* very free to negotiate the terms of their labor and were often required to work far more hours in a day than would be best for their health or safety. These employees knew this, but the *Lochner* doctrine ignored their needs, putting a serious damper on workplace regulation for the next three decades. However, the federal courts, under the *Lochner* doctrine, and the Congress, under the sway of corporate power, failed to enact policies that would substantially limit industry's freedom of action, even when this freedom caused hardship and upheaval. Effective regulation of wages and hours did not extend fully to most workers until 1936. Even the most basic child labor laws were often struck down under the *Lochner* logic, as the courts became the ultimate arbiter of what constitutes a reasonable regulation of industry. In most cases, state actions were found to be "unreasonable," leaving business relatively unfettered.

Still, this period was not completely without government action to address the needs of a growing national, industrial economy. Congress established the Federal Reserve System in 1912, establishing the central bank that is vital to a modern economy. In 1914, Congress further regulated monopoly by adding the Clayton Act to the Sherman Act. While both the Sherman and Clayton Acts are quite vague, requiring additional legislation to clarify their meaning, they laid the groundwork for modern antitrust law. Congress also passed, in response to muckraking journalists such as Upton Sinclair, the Pure Food and Drug Act. This act was intended to remedy the severe problems in food packaging revealed by Sinclair in his novel *The Jungle*, about a working-class community and its meatpacking plant, where insects, rodents, and other filth were introduced into canned meat. But even this act was passed with the active support of the major food processing firms, who sought such laws to instill public faith in their products; its fate without their support might have been tenuous. Drugs were regulated when it became clear that many popular remedies were often useless or, sometimes, more harmful than beneficial. However, the Federal Reserve was still dominated by private banking interests, and Congress significantly weakened Woodrow Wilson's proposed antitrust legislation.[3] In sum, the federal and state governments were not moribund between 1905 and 1937, but many of their activities were constrained by an economically and socially conservative federal judiciary that blocked government initiatives while containing the backlash against capitalism.

National Activism

The third era, called "national activism," runs from 1933 to 1961, and was triggered by the demands placed on the national government by the Great Depression. But the *Lochner* doctrine continued to dominate thinking on the Supreme Court. The starkest example of the constraints on federal and state action created by the letter and spirit of *Lochner* is seen in the early years of President's Roosevelt's *New Deal* programs. Upon Franklin Roosevelt's inauguration in March 1933, the president called Congress into session and presented sweeping proposals to end the Depression and to maintain confidence in business, industry, and finance. These ideas, most of which became law, included greater regulation of banking and securities, the National Industrial Recovery Act (NIRA), and the Civilian Conservation Corps. The conservative Supreme Court, operating under the *Lochner* doctrine, struck down the NIRA.[4]

The Supreme Court's restraining influence on policy was so great that, after his 1936 reelection, President Roosevelt attempted to break this constraint by proposing a new way of organizing the Supreme Court, that would add one justice to the Court for every justice who was seventy or older. This would have resulted in a fifteen-member court at the time, dominated by Roosevelt appointees, who presumably would be more favorable to the president's plans. But the scheme was wildly unpopular across the board, becoming known as Roosevelt's court-packing plan. Roosevelt's enthusiasm for the plan was further diminished after two swing justices seemed to change their philosophy toward New Deal legislation, in what became known as the "switch in time that saved nine," and the Court, starting with a case dealing with issues similar to *Lochner—West Coast Hotel Co. v. Parrish*[5]—began to abandon the conservative *Lochner* standard. By 1940, the Supreme Court became more amenable to Roosevelt's program, in no small part because of the addition of justices that he appointed.

Perhaps the most important outcome of the New Deal history is its creation of the modern system of active federal involvement in national policy making. And not all of the actions of the Roosevelt administration were struck down. Thus, by 1937, the New Deal had created a vast system of governmental regulatory bodies, including but not limited to the Federal Communications Commission, the Civil Aeronautics Administration (later the Civil Aeronautics Board), the Securities and Exchange Commission, the Federal Deposit Insurance Corporation (FDIC), and the Federal Home Administration (FHA). The government got into businesses that were traditionally private, such as power generation, with the creation of the Tennessee Valley Authority (TVA) and the Bonneville Power Authority. Indeed, the TVA had a broader goal of fostering economic development in the once-isolated Tennessee Valley. These agencies had a profound influence on American policy and politics during and after the New Deal.

World War II-era programs such as price controls and the GI Bill further enhanced the influence of the federal government. Taken together, the GI Bill (which funded many servicemen's and -women's postwar educations), the FHA (which made mortgage loans easier to obtain), and the FDIC (which guaranteed the safety of bank deposits) laid the groundwork for the postwar economic boom. And other programs, such as Social Security, became so entrenched in the national psyche that even leading Republicans, by the 1950s, realized that they could not resist their popularity. The result was a bipartisan consensus on the sanctity of Social Security, even though the way the system was funded sparked debate that continues to this day.

After World War II, the United States' foreign and defense policy establishments grew significantly, setting the tone for the United States' postwar foreign policy. The defense establishment of the United States was substantially reorganized in 1947, and NATO was formed in 1949. Fears of communist subversion led to ethically questionable congressional actions to root out subversion, such as the creation of the House Un-American Activities Committee (HUAC) and the crusade against communism led by Senator Joseph McCarthy (R-Wisc.). At the same time, the expansion of the federal role in defense policy slowed under the Eisenhower administration because of Americans' desire for a somewhat slower pace of change. Still, the seeds of important federal initiatives, such as the space program and the construction of the Interstate Highway System, were planted in the late 1950s.

National Standards

The final period in Robertson and Judd's formulation, the era of "national standards," runs from 1961 to the present. The 1960s were a very fertile period for domestic policy making, akin to the New Deal era. John F. Kennedy's election as president led to slow movement on the civil rights front, which accelerated after his assassination in 1963. Indeed, under President Lyndon Johnson's *Great Society* program, federal efforts to address policy problems again accelerated. Great Society programs addressed poverty, racial discrimination, educational problems, barriers to access to health care for the poor and elderly, mass transportation, urban renewal, environmental problems, and myriad other problems. It is not a coincidence that the 1960s also saw the birth of the scientific study of public policy and public problems, as researchers asked, first, what are the problems; second, what causes the problems; and third, do the policies we have to address the problems work? This scientific study was impelled, in large part, because the federal government was starting to set national standards for the states and other actors to follow in the pursuit of policy goals. At the same time, the states' capacity to make and enforce policy grew rapidly, particularly in leading states like New York and California.

Much of the research on these new national programs revealed mixed results. Efforts to foster a renewal of the urban core were not widely successful,[6] while the Elementary and Secondary Education Act (ESEA), and, in particular, the Head Start program were considered successes by some while others found at best mixed results.[7]

Richard Nixon's election in 1968 was viewed by some as a return to

more conservative federal policy making; indeed, many of Nixon's proposals and programs were intended to cut back federal activities in various problem areas. But the Nixon administration was not afraid to use
federal power and policy making to address national programs. The
Environmental Protection Agency and the National Environmental Policy
Act were passed under the Nixon administration, although the Trans-
Alaska Pipeline, opposed by many environmentalists, was also approved.
Nixon attempted to stem inflation through wage and price freezes. On
the other hand, Nixon's programs of New Federalism and block grants
were attempts to move power from the federal level to the state level.

From a policy making perspective, the Nixon years were also important because this period witnessed major changes and reforms in Congress. President Nixon often angered Congress by not spending funds
that were appropriated for particular uses—this is called "impoundment,"
and the Congress prohibited the practice, while reforming the budget
process, in the 1974 Budget and Impoundment Act. The president's ability
to commit troops to overseas actions was somewhat constrained by the
1973 War Powers Resolution. And the power and prestige of the executive branch in general were dulled by the Watergate scandal and
Congress's investigations into the activities of the Federal Bureau of
Investigation and Central Intelligence Agency. From a policy perspective, the important change here is the reassertion of congressional power
in its relationship with the presidency.

The End of Big Government?

Perhaps the most important demarcation between the New Deal period
and today is 1980, with the election of Ronald Reagan as president. His
perceived mandate was to cut back on "big government," and in some
ways he aggressively did so.

But it is important to remember that the move to shrink government
and decentralize it was also undertaken by President Jimmy Carter. He
even foreshadowed his desire to make the federal government smaller
and more efficient in his inauguration speech, in which he declared,
"We have learned that 'more' is not necessarily 'better,' that even our
great nation has its recognized limits, and that we can neither answer all
questions nor solve all problems. We cannot afford to do everything, nor
can we afford to lack boldness as we meet the future." And in his 1979
State of the Union speech, after listing the challenges faced by the na-

tion, Carter said, "At home, we are recognizing ever more clearly that government alone cannot solve these problems." Later in his speech, Carter, in language sounding very familiar to Reagan supporters, claimed:

> We must begin to scrutinize the overall effect of regulation in our economy. Through deregulation of the airline industry we've increased profits, cut prices for all Americans, and begun—for one of the few times in the history of our nation—to actually dismantle a major federal bureaucracy. This year, we must begin the effort to reform our regulatory processes for the railroad, bus, and the trucking industries.
>
> America has the greatest economic system in the world. Let's reduce government interference and give it a chance to work.

The deregulation of the airline industry is perhaps the most-remembered action taken by the Carter administration, as it opened airlines to price competition and allowed people of modest means to fly.

President Carter's efforts to shrink the federal government were similar, although perhaps not as strong, as Reagan's efforts. Indeed, some people viewed some of Reagan's decisions as extreme, as reflected in his appointments to cabinet posts, such as the controversial interior secretary, James Watt. By the mid-1980s, an aroused Congress was tempering the Reagan cutbacks, and Reagan suffered a major setback in his prestige during the Iran-Contra scandal. This loss of prestige also cost him support in his failed attempt to appoint Robert Bork to the Supreme Court. Before then, however, Reagan had substantially increased American military spending, signaling a return to American willingness to project military power overseas, such as in Grenada, Panama, and the Gulf War. This tendency continued in the Bush and Clinton administrations, which have used the military in Iraq, Somalia, Bosnia-Herzegovina, and Kosovo.

The Reagan legacy—at a minimum, the legacy of distrust of government and the exaltation of free enterprise—loomed over the Clinton administration and will likely influence policy for many more years. The "Reagan Revolution" may have laid the groundwork for the Republican takeover of the Congress in 1994. Even more, the rhetoric and the actual policies made by Reagan have created an America in which Bill Clinton could remark in his 1996 State of the Union speech, driven possibly by his party's stinging defeat in the 1994 congressional elections and his failure to pass major health care reform, that "the era of big government is over." This sentiment may be changing, as federal government spending grew somewhat in the late 1990s, while the federal *budget deficit* has become a *budget surplus*. Still, we continue to live in an era in which the federal government is mistrusted and in which the state governments, while for the most part not able to develop vast new programs, are still better positioned to address local needs and appear to be more responsive to citizens' needs.[8]

This brief history of policy making in America reflects the flexibility of our constitutional system and its stability. Flexibility is important, or the constitutional order itself might not be able to endure; the Civil War, however, demonstrated the ability of the Constitution to bend but not break in the face of major upheavals. Given the importance of stability in the American political system, the discussion now turns to this important aspect of American politics.

Stability in American Politics and Policy Making

Since our nation's founding in its current form in 1789, the United States has been one of the most stable nations in the world. James Anderson, author of *Public Policymaking*, argues that the United States has four kinds of stability: ideological stability, political stability, policy stability, and stability in power.[9] These features of our stability are summarized in Table 2.2.

Ideological stability means that Americans and their representatives have not been quick to shift their basic political beliefs. Since the founding and even before, Americans have believed in personal liberty and equality (except for those considered outside the mainstream of citizenship, such as women and slaves), a generally limited government, "popular sovereignty," or the belief that the highest power in government is held by the people, the rule of law, and respect for market economics, free enterprise, and private property. While attitudes have changed considerably since the founding on things such as slavery and racial discrimination, the rights of women and children, voting rights, and the role of religion in society, the core beliefs on which the nation were founded are durable, adaptable to new problems and conditions, and rarely threatened by those who seek policy change.

The acceptable range of ideology—and therefore, the range of policy preferences—in the United States is considerably narrower than the range of ideologies represented in political institutions in Europe, ranging from the extreme right of the French National Front to the German Greens or the pre-Tony Blair British Labour Party on the left. Because our system of

Table 2.2

Elements of American Stability

	What this means	Examples in action
Ideological stability	Americans tend not to stray from a set of ideological precepts based largely on our national experience.	The United States hasn't had a labor party or workers' movement like European nations, because our ideological stability includes some suspicion of "class warfare."
Political stability	Politics in the United States tends to be fairly stable.	Our constitutional structure has changed little since 1789, although practices under it have changed. In 1800, Thomas Jefferson, whose views were quite different from his predecessor's, took office.
Policy stability	Policies tend to change very little over time.	Policies such as laws governing business practices, social welfare (Social Security, aid to the poor), environmental protection, and many others remain stable over time.
Stability in power	Changes in power tend not to cause major policy, political, or social upheavals.	The transition from one president to another, or the transition in party dominance in a house of Congress, is generally smooth, democratically accepted, and results in little sweeping, immediate change.

Source: Derived from James E. Anderson, *Public Policymaking*, 4th ed. (Boston: Houghton Mifflin, 2000).

representation is based on the single member district and the winner of the majority or plurality of the votes wins the seat, the prospect for more extreme parties winning elections is remote. Thus, the two political parties in the United States have both tended to accommodate a relatively broad (in American terms) range of opinion because only two parties can reasonably contest elections in the United States. This broad accommodation of ideologies has changed in recent years, as more politically conservative people, including many former southern Democrats, have shifted to the Republican Party, while, to a lesser extent, more moderate to liberal Republicans have gone to the Democratic Party.

Of course, some of these beliefs can be contradictory:[10] for example, equality and capitalism often clash, depending on one's definition of "equality," and battles over workers' rights versus owners' prerogatives have been fought, mostly politically but sometimes violently, in the United States. However, even what we might call "working-class" people often evince attitudes that generally support American notions of capitalism, business, and success. This agreement on basic ideology across social classes may explain the lack of as powerful a *political* labor movement as one sees in Western Europe.

Political stability is a key element of our overall national stability. The United States has operated under the same constitutional structure since 1789, thereby claiming the title of the oldest continuously operating system with a written constitution. While that structure has certainly been altered, as new groups of people gained the right to vote and hold office and as new demands have been placed on government, the general outline of the rules remains, including a structure that promotes a two-party system, the method of electing the president through the electoral college, a Senate based on state representation and a House based on apportionment by population, and so on. Beyond the structural features, since our basic beliefs have remained remarkably stable, our political preferences have only varied in a narrow range.

Because of our political stability, American history is characterized by a considerable degree of *policy stability*. Policies tend not to change very quickly, for several reasons. First, the American governmental and constitutional system is not designed to be quickly responsive to national needs or desires. The three branches of government were not designed to foster rapid, coordinated action among the branches; rather, they were intended to serve as checks on each other's power. Two historical examples illustrate this. The first is the Supreme Court's consistent blocking of policies intended to regulate industry and working conditions, culminating with the Court's blocking of Franklin Roosevelt's New Deal programs. Roosevelt's and the states' policy changes to address the problems of the Great Depression were only accepted by the

.irt when President Roosevelt, in his second term, was able to appoint .ore ideologically friendly justices and when some justices began to change their positions. In the end, considerable policy change did occur, but it took many years before the full strength of Roosevelt's plans went into effect.

A second example is President Clinton's failure to get his health care reform proposals passed by Congress.[11] The reform package failed to pass partially because it was very complex and because many interests—insurers, employers, health maintenance organizations, many individual citizens—mobilized to aggressively oppose the Clinton proposals. This is a particularly stark example of how policy change is stymied when the president and Congress cannot agree. In this case, the dominant coalition in Congress did not even agree with the president that there was a problem requiring congressional action. Because the founders designed the constitutional system to delay policy change, not to expedite it, one can say that the failure of the health care reforms was predictable simply because of the structure of American politics. Had the United States been established as a parliamentary system, in which the chief executive was the prime minister, health reform and other legislation would likely be easier to pass because prime ministers are the leaders of a cohesive majority party or coalition until their party loses or the coalition collapses.

The federal system also operates to delay policy change. As James Madison explained in *Federalist* 10, a primary benefit of federalism is that it contains policy fads or fast-moving popular movements in one or a few states, thus preventing the growth or expansion of conflict to the national level. Many students of federalism cite the system as advantageous because it fosters state innovation and induces states to improve their capacity to address problems that the federal government does not address.[12] This has induced many students of policy to call states the "laboratories of democracy" because innovations can be developed state by state and then adopted and adapted by other states. For example, California is widely viewed to be the leader in developing policies to reduce the damage caused by earthquakes, for obvious reasons, while New York was long a leader in developing and implementing social welfare policy and is still more active in this area than most other states. Indeed, the *devolution* of federal programs to the states is often justified in terms of the notion that the states are more innovative and responsive than the too-large federal government. As Tallon and Brown note, writing about welfare reform, "If nothing is very new about the stakes of devolution, why not craft a block grant, turn states loose, and record what transpires in the federal system's famous laboratories of democracy?"[13] The problem with this sort of policy making is that it assumes that some or all of the states will make faithful efforts to build capacity to do the things the federal government seeks to accomplish with the block grant. There are no such guarantees, which is why *block grant* programs—that is, programs to give large sums to states with relatively vague rules for how the money is to be spent—are often so strenuously opposed.

While federalism can be justified by the "laboratories for democracy" argument, this is not the justification provided by James Madison, a leading founder, constitutional scholar, and fourth president of the United States. Rather, Madison and the other founders justified the constitutional system to their countrymen because it served to maintain the social and economic status quo, thereby maintaining *stability in power.*[14] The status quo that Madison sought to preserve revolved around the interests of wealthy property owners and other men (this was 1787, after all) of means. These interests are clearly different from those of the mass public, much of which had few political rights, such as office holding and voting, and relatively little influence on the drafting or ratification of the Constitution. Of course, women and most black Americans had no political rights at all.

Because of this status-quo orientation, one of the enduring features, benefits, or problems—depending on your perspective—of the federal system is its structure that preserves the status quo. The interests that have the most advantages and are in power are most interested in maintaining the status quo and are well organized to do so.[15] The status-quo orientation of the Constitution, coupled with its inherent protections of private wealth and property, advantages these groups over, for example, the poor and racial minorities. While Harrell Rodgers notes this point in the *Journal of Black Studies*, what he found applies to any interest seeking to overcome the disadvantages of being in the pro-change position. I quote him directly because his explanation is quite clear:

> The realities of the power structure in America severely limit the ability of some groups to exercise influence. To have power in Washington a group must be organized, active, well financed, politically sophisticated, and well represented by elected and appointed officials. Washington is loaded with groups that meet these standards, but mostly they represent interests dedicated to the preservation of the status quo. Minority groups

do not have the organization, staffs, funds, expertise or connections of groups that represent big business and the wealthy.

Additionally, given the separation of powers in the American government and the decentralization of power in Congress, it is much easier to defeat than to pass legislation. Thus, minorities who need to pass legislation are disadvantaged compared to groups that desire primarily only to maintain the status quo.[16]

Indeed, this orientation toward the status quo and the denial of political power to many people has led many historians and social scientists to conclude that the American "revolution" was far less "revolutionary" than the changes wrought by the Civil War.[17] The Civil War, after all, was fought over fundamental national questions such as states' rights and the civil and equal rights of individuals. The federal Constitution, on the other hand, was in many ways a counterrevolutionary document, drafted in the wake of domestic insurrection and the obvious failures of the Articles of Confederation to protect the interests of the dominant classes of the day.[18]

All this being said, one must recognize the obvious brilliance of the constitutional design. The constitutional design provides for *deliberative* government—that is, government that takes the time to consider the various aspects and affected interests in any legislation. The founders sought, by providing a two-house legislature, to provide both a voice of the popular will (the House of Representatives) and a means of restraint against policy fads or flash-in-the-pan social movements (the Senate). And to some extent the courts provide another restraint against popular passions or the tyranny of the majority.[19] From this structure comes the considerable policy moderation and restraint that is an essential part of American political stability. Others, however, have concluded that structural features of American politics create so much restraint that the system prevents government from addressing some of the key problems of the day through means supported by a majority of citizens.[20]

Policy Restraint and Barriers to Change

One should not conclude from this review that policy stability is solely a result of the constitutional structure. Nor should one conclude that policy change does not happen. As we will see throughout this book, policy change can and does happen under the proper conditions. But in the end, anything more than incremental policy change is difficult, if not impossible, to achieve in the United States.

Ideological and Political Stability

The United States' ideological and political stability prevents sudden shifts in ideas or the hasty adoption of policy fads. The founders designed our system this way. The federal system, in which the national and state governments share power, also slows change. Under Article V of the Constitution, three-quarters of the states (thirty-eight states today) must approve amendments to the Constitution. The separation of powers between the executive and legislative branches also limits change—if the legislature makes policy the president cannot support, the president can veto it, and it takes two-thirds of each body in the Congress to override the veto. Moreover, even if the president and Congress agree, the Supreme Court can exercise the power of judicial review to declare a law or other act of another branch unconstitutional.

Basic Rules and Norms

James Anderson notes that political actors and institutions operate both under the Constitution and under a system of "basic rules and norms" that go beyond the very broad guidelines set out in the Constitution. For example, in the United States Senate, one senator can *filibuster*, holding the floor and speaking nonstop, tying up the body for hours or days until enough senators vote for *cloture* to stop the filibuster. A good if maybe too melodramatic example of this is Senator Smith's (James Stewart's) filibuster scene in the film *Mr. Smith Goes to Washington.* In many cases, filibusters are successful in allowing one or relatively few senators to thwart the legislative preferences of a majority of the Senate. (The House of Representatives operates under different rules, and the filibuster is not allowed there.)

The norm of seniority in Congress meant that, for years, committee chairmanships were held by conservative southern Democrats, who tended to stymie legislation proposed by their liberal colleagues from both parties. Today, seniority is more evenly distributed nationally, so this norm is still important, but not as important as it was before major congressional reforms were instituted in the early 1970s. Congress's procedural rules, intended to preserve decorum and order in the legislature, have been highly successful in maintaining at least some level of collegiality in the Congress, but at the cost of making legislating a slow and sometimes frustrating process.

Open Government and Policy Restraint

In the past three decades, laws such as *open public meetings laws*, the *Administrative Procedure Act*, and the *Freedom of Information Act* have opened up government to considerable scrutiny. These laws allow people greater access to government. They have helped to root out some unseemly practices in government, since the participants in a policy arena know that their actions are on the public record. On the other hand, these benefits come with the cost of slowing down policy change as agencies and policy proponents must seek and address public comment, scrutiny, and sometimes opposition. In other words, an agency cannot simply regulate without any public scrutiny, and that scrutiny can sometimes lead to conflict and delay. In our system, as in many democracies, citizens and policy makers must seek a broadly accepted balance between legislative speed and efficiency, on the one hand, and a respect for democracy and the rights of all citizens to participate, on the other.

A Rationale for Stability

Indeed, it is important to recognize that other goals—such as deliberation and public participation—are at least as important as rapid and efficient policy making action. Lest we think the American system is entirely hamstrung, however, it is important to remember that rapid policy making is possible during, for example, wars and other serious national crises. But during normal periods of policy making, the political and constitutional order makes it possible and quite common for a minority of citizens to thwart the apparent will of the majority in seeking policy change—this blocking is accommodated by the constitutional structure and the norms of the legislative process. Furthermore, this blocking is entirely healthy and justified if it prevents the passage and implementation of dangerous, unconstitutional, or unfair policies.

Policy does not change radically because much of the public does not support such rapid change—rather, years of electoral experience and public opinion data suggest that Americans value political and policy stability and are rather unwilling to see the government take large steps towards certain goals. Starting in the late 1970s and early 1980s, there was a diffuse public sense that the government had grown too big and that the Reagan administration was justified in dismantling a great deal of it. At the same time, public opinion also registered disapproval of

President Reagan's attempts to significantly reduce federal commitments to environmental protection. This was most clearly demonstrated when he appointed administrators to the Department of Interior and the Environmental Protection Agency with an obvious anti-environmental agenda.[21] In short, change is often welcomed by the public, so long as it is not radical change.

When a social movement or a crisis sweeps the nation, change can be remarkably swift, as we have seen during the Civil War, the New Deal, the Great Society era, and the movement to shrink government that began under President Carter and accelerated under the Reagan administration.

Fragmentation

The fragmentation of the American political system is a feature that is underappreciated by most Americans and, perhaps, overstated by those who argue that policy change and progress are impossible in the United States. There are two dimensions of fragmentation in American politics: the *separation of powers* among the branches of government, and the division of power between states and the federal government, known as *federalism*.

The separation of powers in the federal government, as well as most state and local governments, was intended to check the power of any one element of the government through the exercise of power by the others. The founders drew upon European political theory that held that there are three major functions of governments: a legislative function, in which the laws are made; an executive function, in which the laws passed by the legislature are implemented, enforced, or *executed*; and a judicial function, in which the laws are interpreted, disputes over matters of fact or law are settled, and meaning given to the enactments of the legislature, as implemented by the executive.

While these powers are separate, they also serve to check each other and to overlap to some extent, as shown in Table 2.3.

When the states disagree with the federal government, considerable delay in the implementation of policies can result.[22] The early years of the civil rights movement are a remarkable example of how states can delay policies thought to be in the national interest. After *Brown v. Board of Education* (1954 and 1955) made it unconstitutional for states and their local school districts to segregate the schools on the basis of race, many southern districts continued to do

Table 2.3

The Balance of Power

	Congress	President	Courts
Legislative	Make laws	Recommend laws; veto laws; make regulations that have the force of law (quasi-legislative powers)	Review laws to determine legislative intent; new interpretations = law making
Executive	Override vetoes; legislative vetoes of regulations	Enforce and implement laws	Review executive acts; restrain executive actions (injunction)
Judicial	Impeach judges and president; call witnesses in hearings	Pardon criminals; nominate judges	Interpret laws

Note: The primary function of each branch is indicated in the double-lined box.

so well into the 1960s. The federal courts continually sought to compel compliance, but there is strong evidence to suggest that it took financial incentives from the federal government, in the form of school aid tied to desegregation, to impel the South to desegregate its schools.[23]

Not all state delay or resistance is bad, however. As Malcolm Goggin and his colleagues argue in their study of intergovernmental policy implementation, sometimes states engage in "strategic delay" in implementing federal mandates, to learn more about the policy and how to implement it to address unique local situations.[24] This ability to shape policy in this way is perhaps a primary strength of federalism.

Discussion of the fragmentation and separation of power in the United States is sometimes met with dismay by students of the process. After all, why does it have to be so slow? Can't we find ways to make the system more efficient so that it can react more quickly to address what we feel are the most pressing problems? But before calling for a more "responsive" government, consider carefully its implications. The founders did, and concluded that deliberation—that is, a reasonably long period of thinking, discussing, and debating issues—is good, and that policies should not be made hastily.

Conclusion

Many structural and historic factors influence the making of public policy and constitute, in part, the environment in which public policy is made. These environmental factors are not fixed in time; rather, they are long-standing features of American politics and daily life that can change—and have changed—over the course of our history. But change in the policy environment is relatively slow compared with the daily give-and-take of politics. Successful actors in policy making will understand and accommodate the enduring features of the policy making environment and the ways in which the environment can change to enhance or retard the possibility of policy change.

3

Official Actors and Their Roles in Public Policy

For years after the establishment of political science as a distinctive discipline, political scientists focused their research on the texts of constitutions, laws, and other written statements of policies and studied the relationships between formal government institutions—the three branches of government and the states, for example. In the 1950s, the tradition of *institutionalism* began to be dominated by a more sophisticated understanding of politics known as *behaviorism*, in which the political motivations of individuals, acting singly or in groups, were analyzed, often through sophisticated polling, game theory, and statistical techniques.

While behaviorism remains the research tradition in which many, if not most political scientists (and other social scientists) practice, the study of institutions and the people that compose them is neither obsolete nor unimportant, and we continue to study the behavior of actors within institutions and the interactions between institutions. Moreover, our definition of an "institution" has moved from the older political science–style definition of discrete, formally created institutions, such as Congress, the Supreme Court, and the presidency, toward a newer definition of institutions both as organizations and as systems in which individuals interact and achieve political and policy goals through explicit or implicit rules and operating procedures. This newer way of studying institutions, called neo-institutionalism, has become more important in political science, and new insights are being derived from it. Indeed, as B. Dan Wood notes, "a series of studies [has examined] the presidency, the Congress, and the courts to make clear that institutions do make a difference when explaining public policy outcomes."[1] In this chapter and the next, I share this neo-institutionalist approach and consider the network of actors, institutions, and rules that is involved in policy making.

Students of the public policy process divide the players in the policy process into two main categories: official and unofficial actors. Official actors are involved in public policy by virtue of their statutory or constitutional responsibilities and have the power to make and enforce policies. The legislative, executive, and judicial branches are clearly official institutions. Unofficial actors include those who play a role in the policy process without any explicit legal authority (or duty) to participate, aside from the usual rights of participants in a democracy. Thus, interest groups are involved in politics not because they are sanctioned in law, but because interest groups are an effective way for many people to collectively express their desires for policy. The media have a constitutional right to freedom of the press because of their implicit roles as provider of political information and watchdog over government, but the news media have no formal, guaranteed role in policy making. Under certain conditions, such as matters of national security or personal privacy, the media can be denied access to policy making information and processes. In this chapter, I review the official actors in the policy process. Chapter 4 discusses the unofficial actors in the policy process.

Legislatures

I begin with the legislative branch because it is the first listed branch in the federal and most state constitutions and was considered, at the time of the founding, to be the most active and perhaps the most important of the three branches. The legislative branch is also the subject of considerable research, and political scientists continue to work to understand how the legislature works, why it does what it does, and, in recent years, why the legislature has been perceived as unresponsive and undemocratic.

Let us first consider what a legislature does. The very name of this branch suggests lawmaking, and this is assumed to be the primary function of the legislative branch. Indeed, this function consumes a considerable amount of the legislative branch's time and energy. If we use the number of bills introduced as a rough measure of the process, we can make a rough guess of how busy Congress is. Some figures for the 105th Congress are shown in Table 3.1.

Table 3.1

Measuring Legislative Activity: Bills, Amendments, Joint Resolutions, and Concurrent Resolutions in the 105th Congress (1997–1998)

	House	Senate
Bills	4,874	2,655
Joint resolutions	140	60
Concurrent resolutions	354	130

Definitions:

Bills: Bills are the most common form of legislation; they may be public or private. Bills have the prefix "H.R." when introduced in the House, "S." when introduced in the Senate, followed by a number assigned sequentially as bills are introduced. Most legislative proposals are in the form of bills, dealing with either domestic or foreign issues. Authorizations (establishing federal programs and agencies) and appropriations (actually providing the money for these programs and agencies) are both in the form of bills.

Public bills deal with issues of a general nature. If approved by both houses of Congress (the House and the Senate) in identical form and signed by the president (or repassed by the Congress over a presidential veto), they become *Public Laws.*

Private bills deal with matters of concern to individuals, such as claims against the Federal government, immigration or naturalization cases, or land titles. They become "Private Laws" if approved by Congress and signed by the president or enacted over his veto.

Joint resolutions: There is little practical difference between bills and joint resolutions, although the latter are not as numerous as bills. Usually joint resolutions concern limited or temporary matters, such as a continuing or emergency appropriation. Like bills, joint resolutions also have the force of law, upon approval of both houses of Congress and the signature of the president.

A joint resolution is the legislative vehicle used for proposing amendments to the Constitution. This type of joint resolution is not presented to the president for his signature, but instead becomes part of the Constitution when three-fourths of the states have ratified it.

Concurrent resolutions: Concurrent resolutions are limited in nature. They are not legislative in character and are not presented to the president for action. They are used to express facts, opinions, principles and purposes of the two houses, such as fixing the time and date for adjournment of a Congress. Annual congressional concurrent resolutions set forth Congress's revenue and spending targets for the coming fiscal year and thus have great impact upon other legislation. Upon approval by both chambers, they are published in a special part of the *Statutes at Large.* They do not require presidential approval and do not have the force of law.

An *amendment* is a proposal of a Member of Congress to alter the language, provisions, or stipulations in a bill or in another amendment. An amendment usually is printed, debated, and voted upon in the same manner as a bill.

Source: Reproduced from the Library of Congress, THOMAS Web Site http://thomas.loc.gov.

With nearly 5,000 bills to consider in the House, and over 2,500 in the Senate, it is easy to imagine that Congress is remarkably busy simply dealing with the volume of legislative work: drafting bills, assigning them to committees, keeping track of them, and so on. Lest we believe that Congress is awash in paper, however, it is important to bear in mind that the 535 members of Congress have ways to lighten this load. Members of Congress have staff people who help them draft, read, sift through, and understand the volume of legislation that they process every year. Other staff members manage the day-to-day workings of Congress, from providing security to maintaining the Capitol and the House and Senate office buildings.[2]

The committee structure helps divide the labor in Congress so that each member need not study every bill that is introduced.[3] The committees serve as gatekeepers for legislation, in both organizational and political senses. Organizationally, the committees help Congress prioritize the legislation that it will hear: The routine but mandatory issues that Congress must address every year, like the budget, are higher priority than less pressing business, and crisis will often overwhelm all other priorities.[4]

The committee chairs wield considerable political power when they decide which bills will be debated and advanced to action by the full House or Senate and make decisions about the committees and Congress's agenda to advance their individual or party's policy agenda. This power is entirely consistent with the way in which Congress is organized, and both parties realize that control over the partisan balance in Congress means control over the legislative agenda.

Although many bills are introduced in each session of Congress, a great number of bills fail to move past their initial introduction and assignment to a committee. Many bills are simply symbolic acts that are introduced at the behest of constituents or some interest, but that languish because their sponsors understand that they will gain relatively little support from many members of Congress. Other symbolic legislation moves through the system because the legislation has relatively little influence on broader, more controversial issues, and because it allows members to support each other's initiatives. This is known as the norm of reciprocity in Congress. For example, H.R. 815 of 1997[5] would "designate the United States courthouse located at 401 South Michigan Street in South Bend, Indiana, as the 'Robert K. Rodibaugh United States Bankruptcy Courthouse.'" This bill made it well through the legislative process with apparently little controversy, but died when the session of Congress ended without action being taken on the bill. Interest groups know that today's seemingly symbolic gesture or courtesy introduction of a bill could spark its rapid movement up the legislative ladder or mark the beginning of a slow but still successful movement to spur policy change.

Of course, the legislative branch does more than simply introduce bills and make laws. Congressional representatives (and state legislators) are remarkably busy people, often maintaining a dawn-to-dusk schedule of meetings, hearings, campaign and fund-raising appearances, news media interviews, communications with constituents, and a host of other activities that make service in the legislative branch a full-time job, even in states where legislators are considered and paid as part-timers. While a full treatment of the legislature's activities is beyond the scope of this book,[6] it is important to consider two other functions that have gained considerable importance in recent years: casework and oversight.

Casework refers to the tasks undertaken by a legislator (or, more commonly, the legislator's staff) to help constituents solve problems with government agencies or to gain a privilege or benefit from the government. Examples include writing letters of recommendation for admission to military academies, resolving immigration or passport problems, and resolving problems with federal benefits, such as Social Security. Casework provides elected officials, particularly members of the House of Representatives, with opportunities to reach out to constituents and demonstrate concern for their needs. Rather than seeing casework as an annoyance, many members even invite their constituents to write or call with their problems. Most members of Congress believe that, when they help an individual constituent resolve a frustrating agency-related problem, the constituent will overlook party and ideological differences and vote for the incumbent.[7]

Oversight has grown far more important since the late 1970s and early 1980s, as overall trust in government and belief in its efficacy have declined. Oversight refers to the process by which Congress oversees the implementation of policies. Congress has a number of methods by which it can oversee the implementation of programs. Congress's investigative arm, the General Accounting Office (GAO) studies public programs and makes recommendations to improve efficiency, effectiveness, and accountability to elected officials. You may have seen newspaper or television news reports of the results of GAO studies that have found management problems, waste, lost money, and other problems with federal programs. By investigating these programs, the GAO helps Congress to fulfill its very important function as a check on the executive branch. Congress also gets information on programs and problems from other sources; in particular, the Congressional Research Service, an arm of the Library of Congress, researches issues and prepares briefings for members of Congress. Members will also get information from their constituents and the media, which can sometimes trigger greater oversight.[8]

Congress also pursues its oversight function by holding public hearings about policy issues and problems. Sometimes these hearings are triggered by sudden, newsworthy events: Congress held hearings very soon after such highly visible events as the *Exxon Valdez* oil spill, various floods, hurricanes, and earthquakes in the 1980s and 1990s, and in the wake of the violence at Columbine High School in Colorado and other school shootings in the late 1990s. Congress also holds hearings when scandal or policy failure is revealed,[9] such as the hearings held in the wake of the Watergate, Whitewater, and Iran-Contra affairs.

These hearings serve at least three functions. First, they help Congress and the public to understand issues by bringing together various interests to testify about the issue; their testimony is often reported in major national news outlets. Second, the hearings reveal shortcomings in current policies. After the *Exxon Valdez* spill, hearings revealed the gaps in federal and state policies relating to oil spill prevention, cleanup, and liability. These hearings paved the way for passage of an improved set of policies contained in the Oil Pollution Act.[10] In another example, in the early 1980s a series of product tampering incidents involving Johnson and Johnson's Tylenol brand of pain reliever, in which the products were tainted with cyanide and people who took the pills died, led to congressional hearings on product safety. This action impelled Johnson and Johnson, which had its own interests at stake, to introduce what became industry standard packaging techniques to thwart tampering.

Finally, oversight hearings can be used by a political party or a set of members to score political points, usually against the executive branch. This strategy is particularly likely if the executive branch is of a different party than the party controlling a particular house of Congress.[11] A particularly useful technique for highlighting an issue is the *field hearing*, in which a committee or subcommittee will hold a hearing in the community where an accident or disaster occurred or where a scandal has had the most impact. Members hear testimony and give speeches expressing their concern and endorsing the complaints of local citizens. These hearings are symbolic, providing local officials and citizens with an opportunity to vent their frustration, but the hearings can also provide useful feedback to legislators and can create and enhance popular pressure for changes in policy.

Organization

Many people who have visited the Senate or House galleries or have watched their proceedings on C-SPAN find the action on the floor slow and dull. Sometimes one member, particularly in the House of Representatives, speaks to a camera that may not reveal that the member is speaking to an empty or near-empty chamber. While "speechifying" seems silly to some, these short speeches, recorded and shown on C-SPAN and other outlets, are an important way in which members communicate their positions on issues to their constituents, each other, and the nation.

The empty chambers and the highly technical and procedural activity that seem so boring when Congress is in session, mask the activity that takes place in the offices and the committee rooms. The bulk of Congress's work is done in the committees, which review legislation, propose and vote on amendments, and, in the end, decide whether a bill will die at the committee level or will be elevated to consideration by the full body. The entire legislative process, which you may have learned as "how a bill becomes a law," is presented with some elements of the regulatory process in Figure 3.1.

A final element of congressional organization is important to consider: the organization of the body along party lines. The assignment of leadership positions in both the House and Senate is subject to the will of the majority of the members of the body. The Speaker of the House, for example, is not the Speaker of only the majority party, but is in many ways the institutional leader and spokesperson for the body as a whole; he is, however, elected along a strict party line ballot. The office of Speaker has become more visible and partisan in recent years, starting with the respectful but often intense rivalry between Speaker Thomas "Tip" O'Neill (D-Mass.) and President Reagan. This continued through the tumultuous tenure of Speaker Newt Gingrich (R-Ga.), although the office has become somewhat less visible during the term of the current (at this writing) Speaker, Dennis Hastert (R-Ill.).

At the committee and subcommittee level, the party division in Congress determines who chairs the committees and how many members of

Figure 3.1 **The Legislative and Regulatory Process**

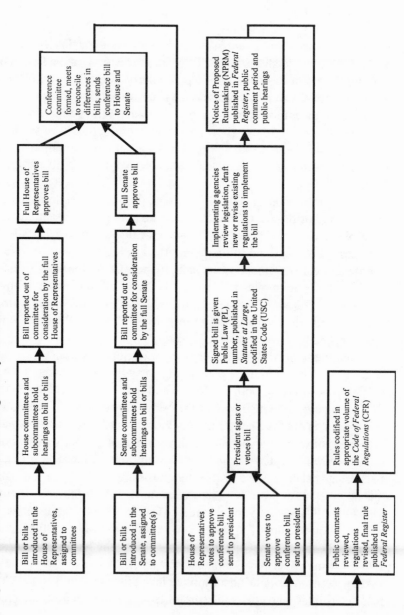

each party serve on each committee. Committee chairs are senior, but not necessarily the most senior, members of the majority party, and more seats on a committee are given to the majority party than the minority party, in a rough approximation of the relative balance of seats in the House or Senate.

For the student of public policy, the legislative branch is an important center of policy making, the institution we most often study when trying to assess what issues are gaining and losing prominence and which alternatives are currently being weighed. This is also true at the state level, although state legislative activities are not as thoroughly tracked and analyzed as federal legislation. The process by which bills become law at the state level is roughly similar to the federal process. A few states, for example, do not have conference committees that coordinate differences between the lower and upper house's version of bills. Many state legislatures have posted, on their Web sites, descriptions of how bills become laws in those states.

Public Policy and Critiques of the Legislative Branch

Many people argue that legislatures, at the state and federal level, are out of touch with the wishes of the people. A recent article in my alumni association magazine, for example, found that substantial majorities of Oregonians favor stricter gun control measures, while the state legislature has failed to pass strict measures, even in the wake of a school-shooting incident in Springfield, Oregon. These sorts of examples frustrate many people. Why, they ask, does the legislature act against what seems to be the clearly stated will of the majority of the people? Why is the legislature so bogged down in partisan squabbling? Why can't the legislature get anything *done*? These critiques and complaints are leveled against both the state and federal legislatures, and because of these problems, many people are becoming remarkably frustrated and alienated from politics and policy making.

To better understand what legislatures do, it is important to understand at least two elements of legislatures: the nature of the members of the body, and organization and the nature of the legislative branch itself. The motivation of members seems very simple: to be reelected. Morris Fiorina, in *Congress: Keystone of the Washington Establishment*, assumes "that the primary goal of the typical congressman is reelection." Why? Because of all the benefits that accrue from being a member of

Congress, including power, fame, job satisfaction (many people simply enjoy the work), and the ability to make better policy. If one assumes this to be true, then many other elements of politics and policy making, such as how election campaigns are financed and run, how legislators and the media interact, and how the labor is divided among committees and congressional leadership, become clearer. Fiorina argues that "even those congressmen genuinely concerned with good public policy must achieve reelection in order to continue their work." Fiorina argues that members enhance electoral success by creating connections with bureaucracies that facilitate "casework." The bureaucracy is usually very happy to respond to representatives prodding for faster or more favorable action, because such action can help cement friendly, mutually supportive relationships between Congress (which controls the purse strings, after all) and the agencies.[12]

Too many voters and commentators, I believe, make too much of the motivation to be reelected, seeing it as distasteful and even contrary to what Americans believe should be the motivations of our elected officials. It is true that the motivation to be reelected is powerful. Nevertheless, in most professions, such as law, medicine, academia, and business, people like their jobs and seek to please their "bosses"—their supervisors, clients, or colleagues—so they can keep their jobs. In Congress's case, the voters are the bosses, and elected officials have challenging jobs because their periodic performance reviews (coming every two or six years) are very public, contentious events in which a large number of people are prepared to critique the incumbent's job performance, often very vocally and personally. That said, many seats, particularly since the 1970s, have become "safe" for a member or his political party, so the pressures of reelection may not always be great for every member, allowing them to take, if they wish, more chances in their legislative choices than other members.

Richard Fenno provides a somewhat more subtle explanation of members' motivations in his classic book *Homestyle*.[13] Fenno argues that the primary goal of members may not be reelection. Certainly, he argues, they do fight to be reelected, but this is usually in pursuit of other goals that depend on their reelection, such as making public policy. Furthermore, different members have different styles of working, both at home and in Congress itself—this reflects the old saying in Congress that there are workhorses (those who enjoy the give-and-take of legislating) and show horses (those who like the more public aspects of the job).

Congress As a Decentralized Institution

The decentralized nature of Congress helps explain the decisions made by the legislative branch. There are 535 members of Congress—435 members of the House of Representatives, and 100 senators—with different ambitions, goals, and interests. One can argue that for every member there is a separate agenda, and trying to reach consensus among even half of these legislators, all with their own agendas, is difficult even in the best of circumstances. This may explain why many members, as Fenno notes, run for Congress by running against it. Fenno notes that Americans "hate Congress and love their Congressmen," because there are things that individual members seem to do for our district and us that Congress as a whole seemingly does not. When a member brings federal money to our individual districts, it is hailed as a boon, but when Congress as a body approves spending on local projects, it simply reflects Congress's predilection for wasteful pork-barrel spending. These members, of course, are not entirely free to do whatever they want; the body is organized into committees, and the two political parties serve as an organizing force. However, as party influence weakens and as members find that taking independent stances sometimes gains more points at home than does cooperation and consensus building, agreement on policy becomes even more difficult to achieve.

Before about 1974, power in Congress was rather more centralized in the hands of legendary party leaders like Sam Rayburn in the House of Representatives and Lyndon Johnson in the Senate. But a number of events—Watergate, Vietnam, and the eroding faith in government and its leaders—combined with and contributed to the frustrations of junior and rank-and-file members of Congress. Many of the members of Congress elected in the historic 1974 elections—following President Nixon's resignation by just three months—were deeply committed to reforming government in general as well as the Congress. They sought, in many ways successfully, to reduce the influence of seniority in the selection of committee chairs, to gain power for subcommittees, and to provide a voice for junior members of the body. These new members were much less patient than their senior colleagues with the old norms that junior members should quietly serve an apprenticeship period before speaking out on substantive issues.

In the 1990s, however, as the two political parties have become polarized, some power has returned to the top party leadership. This was most dramatically demonstrated during the term of Speaker Newt Gingrich, who created a remarkably high degree of party discipline in the House, particularly in 1995 and 1996. The tumultuous events of late 1998, with the impeachment of President Clinton and the resignation of Gingrich and his successor, Robert Livingston (R-La.), changed the personalities in the leadership of the House to some extent. Speaker Dennis Hastert (R-Ill.) has proven a more moderate Speaker than his predecessor, but considerable power remains centered in the party leadership in Dick Armey, House Majority Leader, and Tom DeLay, Majority Whip.

But we should not make too much of this movement toward recentralization of power. Congress has always been, to a greater or lesser extent, remarkably decentralized. This diffusion of power and expertise allows for the creation of smaller networks of interests—*issue networks* or *policy subsystems*—that, in many ways, operate to ensure the flow of benefits from the federal government to well-organized interests. Nevertheless, committees often have a narrow focus; only when issues are elevated to the full Congress—that is, moved out of the province of committees—does the legislature more actively debate the trade-offs involved in policy making.

Congress and Implications for Policy Making

What do these aspects of the legislative branch mean for policy making? Any discussion of the legislative process will inevitably reflect the difficulty in actually passing laws and policies. When a decentralized Congress and its members are more concerned with its relationships with interest groups, key bureaucracies, and citizen-clients, it is difficult to make "big" policies that require substantial legislative action, particularly since members' "clients" are often as likely to resist change as they are to support it. The founders purposefully created a system in which change was difficult to achieve, but they realized that change would be possible when a coalition of elected officials and citizens formed to promote change. But Congress's focus on politically safe casework and distributive (pork-barrel) projects may make law making less politically safe, more unpopular, and therefore may lead to greater tendencies to maintain the status quo—a situation in which less powerful, still striving interests find it difficult to press their case for sweeping policy change.

The Executive Branch

John Kingdon, in *Agendas, Alternatives, and Public Policies*, notes that when people think about the "administration" they tend to think about the president, his immediate staff, and appointees.[14] This is the sense in which I discuss the executive branch; the permanent civil service, or *bureaucracy*, is considered separately.

The president has some considerable advantages in policy making when compared with the legislature. First, the president can wield the veto against any legislation he does not like on substantive or political grounds (and these two often overlap), and it takes two-thirds of each body of Congress to override the veto. It is difficult to muster enough votes to override a veto, in part because of some level of deference to the presidency and in part because it is unlikely that any one party can control sixty-seven Senate seats and 290 House seats.

The president enjoys considerable organizational advantages as well. The presidency is a *unitary* branch of government, in that it has the president at its head and a staff (or at least, most of the staff) that works for him in pursuit of the Administration's goals. There is no such single-mindedness in Congress. Even the Speaker of the House commands only limited deference, particularly from members of the minority party, so one cannot say that Congress speaks with one voice in pursuit of an agreed-upon set of goals.

A third advantage for the president is that he gains considerable media and public attention. As head of government and chief of state, the president symbolizes America, both domestically and worldwide. Wherever he goes, he is an important focus of media attention. In his role as head of government and head of state, the president symbolizes the whole of the United States government, not simply one branch.[15] This attention often causes people to forget that the president is but one actor, whose power is still circumscribed by the Constitution and whose influence varies with his political popularity and the nature of the policy issue. We have had recent reminders of this: President Clinton's power, at least for a while, was constrained when he was being investigated and impeached for various apparent improprieties. President Nixon's power was reduced to virtually nothing when his pervasive role in the Watergate scandal became clear by mid-1974. So while the president enjoys considerable organizational, constitutional, and symbolic powers, these powers are variable based on the current winds of politics, and the president can enhance or squander his power to make him at various times relatively stronger or weaker than the other branches.

An important advantage the president enjoys is his informational advantage over the legislative branch. For decades, Congress was at a disadvantage because the executive branch had access to most information about government: what was being done, how much was actually being spent, the nature and cause of public problems. Reforms starting in the early 1970s, with the establishment of the Congressional Budget Office and the growth of committee staff, have eroded this advantage, but the president in many ways enjoys better information about policy initiatives than does Congress. This helps the president take the legislative initiative on a number of high-profile issues.

However, even with these advantages, it is important to note that the president's powers are not limitless. Indeed, many people attribute rather more power to the president than is actually apparent to the people who hold the office. In perhaps the most famous book about the presidency, *Presidential Power*, Richard Neustadt argues that the "power of the presidency is the power to persuade."[16] Through a number of anecdotes and case studies, Neustadt shows how the president uses the considerable prestige of the office to persuade people to do things; still, we learn that the president does not simply bark orders and have them obeyed. And, in his relations with Congress and the courts, the president is, constitutionally, the head of just one of three branches of government, and the executive, as Richard Nixon most notably learned in the wake of the Watergate scandal, is most assuredly subject to the checks placed on the executive by the legislature and the judiciary. While the presidency is, therefore, powerful, it is perhaps not, as Arthur Schlesinger put it, an "imperial presidency."[17]

Indeed, the Executive Office of the President—that is, the president and all the officials that work for him in such agencies as the National Security Council and the Council of Economic Advisors—is a very large organization unto itself, employing over 2,000 people. This is large enough that the president cannot supervise every initiative and action of his staff, but must rely on his key staff to ensure that the people who, in essence, work directly for him are working for his agenda and goals and are not doing anything that would detract from or embarrass his administration. A notable example was the Iran-Contra scandal, in which it appeared, at least, that President Reagan did not know that some members of his National Security Council staff were secretly and illegally selling weapons to Iran and using part of the proceeds to illegally support the Nicaraguan *contras*. While no scandal of this magnitude has arisen in the Executive Office recently, it is still a considerable challenge to manage the office, even without scandals and crises.

The presidency is particularly interesting to policy scholars because of the executive's role in policy making. In particular, Kingdon argues that the president is more involved with agenda setting than in developing policy alternatives to address the issues and problems that he raises on the agenda. This is due in large part to the president's position in the public and to his constitutional responsibilities. In the Constitution, the president is empowered to suggest legislation and to report periodically on the state of the union. Nevertheless, the president's powers go beyond mere agenda setting. During real or apparent crises and during times when his popularity is high, the president's power as the head of government is considerable.

This power is not constant over all the years of his administration. As Paul Light has noted:

> The president's main task is to narrow the stream [of people and ideas] into a manageable policy agenda. By the end of the term, the stream is reduced to a trickle and the president's major task is to pass the initial programs and get re-elected.[18]

The challenge, then, is not to come up with endless new ideas, but, rather, to define and manage the president's agenda in order to ensure some policy victories, providing a positive record to persuade voters to reelect him.

For example, after the shootings at Columbine High School in Littleton, Colorado, the president pressed for stricter gun control legislation, an issue that was relatively high on Clinton's agenda throughout his presidency.[19] Relatively little of his legislation has passed, however, illustrating the difference between elevating an issue on the agenda and actually seeing substantive change. Beyond legislative action, the president can take action, through executive orders and through his role as chief executive, to address public problems. For example, after the Littleton, school shooting, President Clinton launched a study of how the entertainment industry markets violent movies, music, and video games to children.[20] Indeed, the National Rifle Association (NRA) has pressed the president to enforce existing gun laws more stringently rather than press for new laws that create greater restrictions on gun owners. At the same time, however, the president has been castigated by the NRA for "exploiting" the Columbine tragedy. This is a very shrewd way to neutralize a focusing event by placing the onus on the president for using the event as an opportunity to advance a proposed solution to a highly visible problem.

Administrative Agencies and Bureaucrats

The prominent German sociologist Max Weber sparked the extensive use of the term "bureaucracy" in the social sciences. He used this word to describe the large organizations, both public and private, that manage the government programs that accompany modern economic and social life. Weber believed that bureaucracies were an important innovation of the modern age; indeed, the achievements of the last 100 or more years would likely not have been possible without a bureaucratic organization.

Many people use the terms "bureaucracy" and "bureaucrat" negatively. No doubt, you have said things like "I can't believe the bureaucracy at the DMV" or "I had to argue with some bureaucrat today." Weber did not mean these terms negatively; rather, he was using them simply to describe a particular kind of organization and to help us understand the features of a bureaucracy, which include the following:

- "Fixed and official jurisdictional areas," that is, a rule-based distribution of labor and of the power to give orders.
- "A firmly ordered system of super- and subordination in which there is a supervision of the lower offices by the higher ones," that is, a hierarchical organization.
- "The management of the modern office is based upon written documents ('the files')." Thus, bureaucracies retain copious documentation of their decisions, which can enhance learning about what was done and why.
- Expert training of staff. This can be seen in fields such as law, accounting, and public administration, where advanced degrees are usually required for many agency careers.
- "The full working capacity of the official," meaning that the leadership of modern bureaucracies is a full-time job, not a part-time sideline, as it was before modern forms of organization became prominent.

- "The management of the office follows general rules, which are more or less stable, more or less exhaustive, and which can be learned." In today's terms, offices are characterized by "standard operating procedures" and rules, often codified, which lay out what an agency can do and how it can do it.[21]

These features of bureaucracy are very familiar, because all of us, young and old, have lived in, worked in, or transacted business with bureaucratic organizations all our lives. Schools, universities, large private firms, government agencies, hospitals, and all manner of other institutions are hierarchically organized, with distinct division of labor, people trained to particular tasks, and a set of rules and procedures that governs operations. If you are a student, you are in daily contact with agents of a bureaucracy—your college or university. People who work at the college or university follow the rules and perform tasks that are assigned to each person, ranging from teaching classes to managing the books to serving the food in the cafeteria. In essence, everyone who works in a reasonably complex organization is a bureaucrat! This understanding of bureaucracy helps put our suspicion of bureaucrats in much sharper perspective.

One of the most persistent complaints about bureaucratic government is its sheer size. The government has grown considerably since the founders ratified the Constitution. While the federal administrative establishment in 1800 was very small, by 1999 the federal government had grown enormous: 2.8 million civilian employees and outlays of over $1.8 trillion. In 1994, over 16 million people worked for state and local governments; taken together, about 14 percent of all employed Americans work for the federal, state, or local governments.[22] Since 1980, government has shrunk somewhat in terms of spending (the technical term is "government outlays") as a fraction of the gross domestic product (Figure 3.2). The federal government has also shrunk slightly when measured by the number of people it employs (Figure 3.3), but spending continues to grow annually. Government's size, complexity, and growth in spending reflect, to a great degree, the size and complexity of society, government, and the economy, as well as the demands placed on government and all our social institutions by interest groups and citizens. In other words, the government is big because many of us want the various services provided by government. Adding up all these demands yields a large governmental establishment.

Figure 3.2   **Federal Spending, Current and Adjusted Dollars (in millions), 1980–1999**

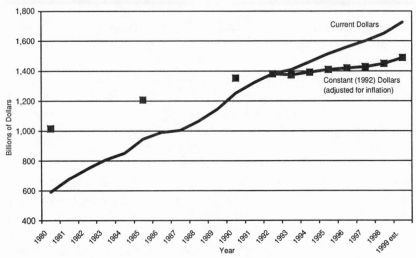

Source: U.S. Bureau of the Census, *Statistical Abstract of the United States, 1999*, Tables 542 and 546.

What Do Government Agencies Do?

In simplest terms, government agencies provide services that are uneconomical for the private sector to provide directly, or they carry out the tasks that we demand from government but that we have chosen not to ask the private sector to provide. In general, any good that carries with it major *free-rider* problems is a public good. *Public goods* are goods that are, as economists put it, indivisible and nonexclusive. Indivisible means one cannot divide a good or service among the public and let each citizen use the good or service as they see fit. Rather, the goods are provided for everyone collectively. Nonexclusivity means that just because a citizen uses the services of the fire department does not mean the citizen is the only one who can use the fire department. By contrast, private goods are divisible and exclusive: companies can make a fixed number of sports cars, and if you and I and some other people buy all the sports cars, there are none left for everyone else (exclusivity) and we get to enjoy them ourselves without any usefulness (utility) being provided to others (divisibility).

Free riding is the problem that results when a service is provided for everyone, but not everyone chooses to pay for it. Imagine a system in

Figure 3.3   Federal Civilian Employment As a Fraction of Total
              Employment, 1980–1999

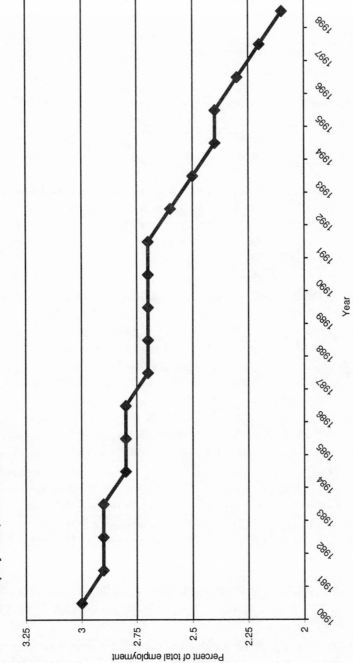

Source: U.S. Bureau of the Census, *Statistical Abstract of the United States, 1999,* Table 567.

which roads, national defense, police and fire services, and public health and sanitation were provided by private companies, and we were all sent letters asking us to contribute some money for these services. Many of us might choose to ignore the bill, because we might reason that many other people may contribute, that their contributions are sufficient to pay for the service, and therefore we can free ride on other peoples' contributions. Government provides these goods, then, to avoid the free-rider problem. This is not to say, however, that the government always has to be the ultimate provider of these goods. In some communities fire protection and prison management are contracted out to private sector firms. Still, these functions are paid for by tax dollars and are therefore not truly based on a market for these services. Thus, as Charles Cochran and Eloise Malone note, an important feature of public goods "is that they can be provided only by collective decisions,"[23] which requires that institutions—in this case, government—be created to facilitate decision making about what goods are to be provided.

Communities may choose to keep certain functions in the public sector, even though private companies often handle them. For example, in Anchorage, Alaska, where I grew up, the telephone company and the electric utility were both owned by the city (the city recently sold the phone company to a private firm) because it was believed that these functions were more responsive to the public if the public owned them. Some functions, like public transit and intercity passenger railroad service, were once viable as private firms, but, in a changing economic and social setting, became unprofitable so the public sector assumed their operation because they remain important to the users of these services.

While the complaints about bureaucracy in the United States often relate to the size of the administrative infrastructure, the complaints more often relate to our frustrations with what the bureaucracy does. These frustrations range from the extreme antigovernment position that government and its workers should have virtually no role in our lives whatsoever to the more moderate sort of complaints that what the bureaucracy does is unaccountable to the public or that the decisions it makes are erroneous or undemocratic. Most Americans probably do not know how large their government is or what its budgetary priorities are, but a broad range of the American people have direct experience with unpopular bureaucracies: the postal service, the Internal Revenue Service, the state motor vehicles offices, and so on. These bureaucracies are historically unpopular because they are perceived to be slow, inefficient, and less adept at service delivery than private sector firms are, particularly when the services provided by government agencies are also provided by the private sector. For example, the postal service has private sector counterparts such as FedEx and UPS that provide seemingly superior service.

While the perception persists, however, that these public agencies are inefficient, many governments have taken steps to make their services easier to use and friendlier to the public. The U.S. Postal Service has become remarkably efficient and competitive, and its marketing and products have been quite successful. In New York State, like many states, the Department of Motor Vehicles went from a slow, unresponsive, and customer-hostile agency to a highly customer-oriented, more responsive agency that draws far fewer citizen complaints

Bureaucracy and the Problem of Accountability

A more basic reason for our distrust of bureaucracy rests on the problem of accountability. The vast majority of civil servants at all levels are not political appointees; they serve in their positions based on their skills and expertise, not based on which party or leader is in power. Expertise is what the designers of modern civil service systems—reacting to the abuses of political patronage—had in mind when they developed systems based on merit, not political connections, in the late 1800s. Nevertheless, with this detachment from elected officials comes a belief that "faceless bureaucrats" make rules based as much on a thirst for power as on a desire to serve the public.

Before engaging this question of bureaucratic accountability, it is important to first consider whether the bureaucracy makes policy at all. After all, if it does not make policy—that is, if the bureaucracy does not decide who gets what—then there is no accountability problem, because we can simply assume that the bureaucracy carries out the will of the democratically accountable branches of the government, and in particular, the legislature's will.

Some of the most astute political thinkers of the 1800s and early 1900s believed that the bureaucracy is not a political or policymaking branch of government. Students of administration and politics simply assumed that agencies exist to carry out the will of the people, as expressed by the legislature. The bureaucracy's duties were to be carried out separate and apart from "politics," which is the proper domain of the legislature. This is how future U.S. President (and early president of the American

Political Science Association) Woodrow Wilson viewed the relationship between the Congress and the agencies. He argued in his classic article, "The Study of Administration," that the *administration* of the laws and policies of the government stood apart from *politics*, that is, the grand and broad planning that is properly the province of Congress and the president. Consider, for example, this passage:

> Most important to be observed is the truth already so much and so fortunately insisted upon by our civil-service reformers: namely, that administration lies outside the proper sphere of politics. Administrative questions are not political questions. Although politics sets the tasks for administration, it should not be suffered to manipulate its offices. . . . The broad plans of governmental action are not administrative; the detailed execution of such plans is administrative.[24]

Today, we would consider this claim to be naïve. We know that agency decisions have to engage "political" dilemmas and questions.[25] Every day agencies make decisions without explicit instruction from Congress. These decisions require that the bureaucracy exercise administrative *discretion*. This bureaucratic discretion, much like legislation, is part of the process of deciding who gets what from government. The problem, from a democratic perspective, is that unelected officials often make these decisions without popular or legislative input or oversight. Thus, those who do not get what they want from the bureaucracy—or who believe that the bureaucracy should not do what it is doing at all—often argue that the bureaucracy is unaccountable to the public and its elected officials, and its decisions are therefore suspect on democratic grounds, regardless of the substance of the decisions. (Of course, we must recognize that people and groups may make this argument when they have lost on more substantive grounds).

Bureaucratic accountability to the broader public interest is very difficult to achieve in the American system because there is no single, easily defined "public interest" that all of us can agree upon. Thus, we—citizens and legislators alike—often ask the government to do many things. The bureaucracy has grown to meet these demands. Because these demands are complex—ranging from medical research to space exploration to business regulation—the citizens, through the legislature, have sought to hire many very knowledgeable people that hold their jobs based on *merit*—that is, they serve due to their technical expertise. Many positions at the state, federal, and local level are filled by people who have taken civil service tests that demonstrate that they have the basic knowledge needed to fulfill the duties of the job. Citizens and Congress must therefore defer to the expertise of the bureaucrats on a wide range of issues.

A primary way Congress defers to administrators' expertise is by granting *discretion* to the bureaucracy. Discretion is the ability of the agencies to make decisions about how they will administer policies and programs with relatively little input or interference from Congress or other institutions. Congress will sometimes grant discretion to agencies to avoid having to make difficult political decisions; it is sometimes easier to leave legislation somewhat vague and let the competing interests fight over the details in the regulatory process. The more usual reason for the grant of discretion is the Congress's inability to deal with the myriad issues that bureaucrats are better prepared to address.

The grant of discretion by Congress to the administrative agencies is not uniform across all agencies and problems. Kenneth Meier argues:

> The amount of discretion accorded an agency is a function of its resources (expertise, cohesion, legislative authority, policy salience, and leadership) and the tolerances of other actors in the political system. Each actor has a zone of acceptance; and if agency decisions fall within that zone, no action will be taken.[26]

That comfort range is smaller in the more active subsystems because actors in the most active and contentious systems are likely to respond to nearly any action taken by an agency that the other actors feel runs contrary to their interests. Where the policy subsystem is composed of tightly connected, mutually reinforcing relationships, the agency's decisions will probably be well known to all interested parties before the decision is put into effect, but such mutually reinforcing relationships, as we will review in chapter 4, cannot be said to be open and democratic.

The next problem we must consider is to what purpose bureaucrats use this discretion. If it is exercised by bureaucrats responsive to popular pressure, voiced directly through the public's daily relationships with the agency, or indirectly through the elected branches, then we might say that the agency is broadly responsive to public demands. This situation, however, is quite rare. Rather, agency discretion is often exercised as a result of the agency's own perception, as signaled to it through legislation and relationships with Congress, of its relationship with "the public interest." Thus, the National Transportation Safety Board (NTSB) and the Federal Aviation Administration (FAA) both have different conceptions of the public interest; the NTSB sees its mandate as ensuring safety of transportation, most prominently aviation, while the FAA has historically seen its role as promoting aviation or at least protecting the interests of the industry. This debate has become open in the news media and may help elected officials and citizens to understand the competing issues.

Related to discretion is the question of private influence or even control over the activities of an agency. For many years, students of bureaucracy wrote about how agencies were "captured" by the interests they regulated. For example, the Federal Communications Commission was once said to be "captured" by broadcasters because its system of allocating frequencies and licenses served the interests of the industry at least as much as the broader public interest. More recently, it is plausible to argue that the FAA, in working harder for airline industry interests than for safety interests, was captured and doing the bidding of the airline industry.[27] Private influence became even more controversial when the House Republican leadership allowed representatives from a wide range of industries (most of which were opposed to stringent environmental regulation) remarkable access to the daily activities of subcommittee and committees after the Republicans became the majority party after the 1994 elections. This inevitably led to fears that the legislative and regulatory processes would come under the undue sway of industry representatives to the exclusion of other voices. However, these fears were not borne out in actual policy making.

These problems are more of degree than of absolutes, leading us to ask how much power do the regulated have over the regulators, and vice versa. The potential for regulatory capture varies with the type of policy and the coalitions that build to deal with these issues. In summary, there are substantial problems with bureaucratic accountability. These relate in large part to the discussion in Chapter 4 of subgovernments or issue networks.

To conclude this discussion, when we consider accountability, we must also consider the popular portrayal of government as a single-minded monolith that is completely accountable only to it and pursuing its own ends. However, bureaucratic government may be more accountable than we might at first glance think. B. Guy Peters describes how the myriad agencies may serve as a check on each other:

It is also customary to consider government as an undivided entity and to regard government organizations as monolithic. In fact, this is not the case at all. We have mentioned that American government is divided horizontally into a number of subgovernments and vertically into levels of government in a federal system. Moreover, the federal and state governments, and even single government departments, contain a number of bureaus, offices, and sections all competing for money, legislative time, and public attention. Each of these organizations has its own goals, ideas, and concepts about how to attack the public problems it is charged with administering.[28]

With so much internal competition going on, agencies seek to advance their ideas before Congress and among their allied interest groups. In so doing, the agencies compete with and check each other and, at least theoretically, gain some accountability to the congressional subcommittees and committees charged with their oversight, particularly when the agencies seek congressional support. Again, the example of how the FAA and the NTSB check and balance each other is an excellent example of the nonmonolithic and competitive nature of modern American government and offers some hope for greater accountability.

The Courts

As Alexander Hamilton argued in *Federalist* 78, "the interpretation of the laws is the proper and peculiar province of the courts" and, since the Constitution is the most fundamental of laws, the courts cannot help being responsible for ensuring that laws remain within the boundaries set by the Constitution.[29] It is an idea that the new Supreme Court was relatively quick to claim in *Marbury v. Madison*,[30] which established the courts' legal right to *judicial review* over the constitutionality of the acts of the Congress and the executive branch. Judicial review gives the courts a potential veto over every act of government that is generated by the popularly elected legislature and executive. In addition, the power of judicial review allows the courts to have the "final word" in the application of laws.

While we might assume that judicial review would make the courts the center of power in the United States, the opposite has been true since the creation of the republic. Hamilton proposed that since the judiciary lacks "either the sword or the purse," it can therefore be defined as "the weakest of the three departments of power." It cannot simply spend or tax in order to encourage the citizenry to fulfill its policy goals as the legislature can do. Nor can it simply force through military strength the acceptance of its policy goals as an executive can do. Instead, the courts have only the legitimacy accorded to the law and their ability to argue their case as the sole power accorded to them. No wonder Hamilton proposed we had little to fear from the judiciary. Historically, however, the role of the courts has fallen somewhere between the impotence claimed by Hamilton and the unfettered, undemocratic omnipotence attributed to the courts by their critics, who, not coincidentally, are often associated with the losing end of the political battles that are played out in the courts.

What role have the courts played in public policy making? In a long accepted practice, most public policy scholars have divided the courts from the other branches under the notion of separating law from politics. As noted earlier, Woodrow Wilson argued that Congress makes public policy and the bureaucracy simply carries out that policy without exercising discretion. In making this argument, Wilson implicitly embraced the notion that courts cannot be policy makers because they are engaged in the *neutral* discovery of legal principles. Where the legislature is identified with compromise and the exchange of votes in the pursuit of policy preferences, the legal system is identified with the pursuit of more abstract principles, such as justice, associated with the notion of law. Thus, the Wilsonian perspective established a distinction between law and politics in relation to policy making—politics created policy, and law ensured that such policy was implemented justly.

While the simplicity of the Wilsonian perspective has long since been rejected, subsequent public policy theories have accepted, without serious question, his implicit distinction between law and politics. For example, Easton defines the actions of political actors and institutions as structured by the constitutional order.[31] In this context, the courts determine the boundaries of policy making by the other branches, but these boundaries are claimed to have been created neutrally; that is, without the consideration or involvement of policy making. The court is assumed not to be engaged in policy making when it sets the boundaries of acceptable policy; it is simply engaged in the practice of articulating a socially accepted and predetermined set of rules. In this way, the court is simply discovering or clarifying rules that we, as a society, have previously agreed to follow, from divinely inspired law to popularly sanctioned constitutions. For example, the Supreme Court, in *Brown v. Board of Education of Topeka, Kansas*,[32] ruled that school segregation was unconstitutional because it unfairly discriminated against and stigmatized African-Americans, thereby denying them the full potential of citizenship, including political participation. Therefore, the courts stepped in to restrict the deleterious use of race in determining educational policies.

The problem with such an approach is that establishing boundaries across which "politics" may not intrude is itself a form of policy making. In the case of race, *Brown* restricted the negative use of race in state policies in a manner similar to the way in which the *Civil Rights Cases*[33] and *Plessy v. Ferguson*[34] had first allowed race to be so used. Thus, while the courts might be setting constitutional boundaries, the changing definitions of these boundaries allow the courts to make public policy.

Even the everyday act of resolving disputes requires the courts to determine the acceptable application of many policies. As Edward Levi[35] notes, the bargaining process inherent in legislatures and the uncertainty as to all possible future applications often requires elected officials to be purposely vague in the drafting of laws. This fact means that the courts are required to make choices in the application of these laws to new situations or to fine-tune laws to ensure their successful application in the real world. Thus, legislatures and executives *initiate* public policy, while courts *react* to the practical effects of such policies, such that "law was not what the *legislature* ordered but what the *courts* decided in concrete cases."[36] These choices in determining the outcome of the policies in the real world act to further draw the courts into the policy-making arena.

In 1957, Dahl claimed that "[t]o consider the Supreme Court of the United States strictly as a legal institution is to underestimate its significance in the American political system. For it is also a political institution, an institution, that is to say, for arriving at decisions on controversial questions of national policy."[37] In making this statement, Dahl was recognizing that the courts have played a significant role in policy making in a variety of areas.

Conclusion

Merely reading the federal Constitution, the state constitutions, and the relevant laws will reveal some sense of the institutional organization of the federal and state governments. Nevertheless, while the federal and state constitutions and laws specify the role and function of the official actors, the law is not fully clear on many aspects of their relationships, and the relationships between official actors and unofficial actors. Indeed, the substantial social, political, and economic changes that have occurred since the drafting of the Constitution are reflected in the changing balance of power among all the official actors. This change will continue as our needs change. Meanwhile, it is important to understand how these actors interact now, so that we can better understand the process by which some policies are enacted and others are rejected.

4

Unofficial Actors and Their Roles in Public Policy

Having reviewed the important official participants in the policy process in Chapter 3, the discussion now turns to the unofficial actors in the policy process. These actors are unofficial because their participation in the policy process is not a function of their duties under the Constitution or the law. This is not to say that these actors have no legal rights or standing to participate in the process; rather, it means that their mode of participation is not specified in law. Rather, their participation has evolved and grown as the nation has evolved and grown.

Individual Citizens

Many treatments of the policy process seem to be disconnected from the activities and preferences of individual citizens. This is for a very sound reason: Most Americans do not vote in every election, or join and participate in interest groups, or follow many issues very closely. The overall level of political participation—including voting and other activities—is remarkably low.[1] To the extent that any sort of political participation is evident in American politics, it is usually shown in voting; we can assume that the rates of participation in other forms of expression are even lower than voting turnout. During presidential election years, election turnout ranges between 50 and 60 percent; in off-year local elections, turnout can be as low as 20 percent, and after the "Super Tuesday" primaries in 2000, when the major party nominees were determined before mid-March, turnout plummeted to as low as 15 percent. In some special elections, such as for school bonds or other financing, turnout is so low that communities have instituted rules requiring that there be a certain minimum turnout *and* a majority yes vote for new bonds. These starkly low participation rates have led to widespread concern among citizens and democratic theorists that a majority of potential voters do not express their opinion on important matters of the day, thereby alienating them from the political system and the decisions made in it.

Further fueling this concern about political participation is Americans' low level of participation in other means of political expression. More Americans vote than write to elected officials, attend public meetings or hearings, circulate petitions, join groups and lobby officials, or even engage in peaceful (or sometimes violent) protest. In the end, we can say that a sizable majority of people do not participate in policy making, for whatever reason: indifference, alienation, or a belief that others—other citizens, groups, elected officials, bureaucrats—will take care of the problem. Economists would call the latter activity "free riding," because the free rider pays no price for the benefits achieved by others on his or her behalf.

Whether this low level of political participation or "free riding" is good or bad is a topic I will leave to the theorists for now. My goal here is to discuss how individuals play a role in policy making. If one believes in broad-based political participation as a key feature of democracy, it may be heartening to realize that people have been and can be *mobilized*—that is, anyone can be persuaded to care about particular issues. Nonvoters and relatively uninterested people can still be sufficiently motivated to write letters, join an interest group, or take other political action. People will often act when something threatens, or appears to threaten, their livelihood or their lifestyle, such as when new commercial development may disturb their neighborhood, or when government is unresponsive to local needs for education or public safety. While some people will mobilize to try to get the government to do something about a problem, other people will often organize to get the government *not* to do something—*not* approve a new mall, *not* teach creation (or evolution) in the schools, *not* raise taxes. The decision to not approve a program or not do something is as much policy as the decision to aggressively act to do something, and it is often true that blocking an action is more readily achieved than actually moving a policy idea forward.

Given the low level of political participation, can we postulate what individuals want from government? Political scientist Morris Fiorina suggests that we want the most benefits at the least cost, with other people paying for the benefits we receive.[2] In essence, we *individually* define efficiency as getting the most services for ourselves while paying the least taxes for that package of services. Of course, when everyone defines efficiency that way, conflict is likely to ensue because all of us cannot gain the things we want from government *and* expect that someone else will provide them. Once again, the "who gets what" question in politics is starkly illustrated.

While many people do not get routinely involved in politics or policy making, many individuals can be motivated to address issues of immediate interest to them. These people may remain mobilized until the issue is somehow resolved, whether or not it is resolved to their satisfaction. The open question in American politics is the extent to which these relatively discrete issues and mobilization episodes adds up to what we might call "public opinion" or the "public mind." It is likely that it does not, and that there is no one single public mind. As Theodore Lowi argues in *The End of Liberalism*, American government is less concerned today with vital issues of national importance than it is with the distribution of benefits to particular interests.[3] If this is true, then there is no one public interest, but sets of separate interests with separate publics and separate opinions about what should be done. Interest groups most effectively represent these interests.

Interest Groups

Interest groups have been a part of the American political scene since the founding of the republic, if not before. James Madison recognized this, and one of his reasons for supporting the creation of a *federal* union was the possibility of dispersing "faction"—that is, group-based interests —into geographically contained states and their subdivisions, in order to prevent the spread of populist ideas from overwhelming what the founders considered to be the cooler reason of the elected officials.

Since the 1960s, the number of interest groups has rapidly expanded.[4] Today, while many groups are local and deal with local issues, many interest groups and popular movements cannot be confined to small states or communities in the manner contemplated by Madison in *Federalist* 10. Clearly, our national evolution into more than a collection of states, coupled with transportation and communications capabilities unimagined by the founders, has made it possible for groups to mobilize quickly on a regional or national scale.

The American system of democracy, with its respect for freedom of association and speech, does not place great legal burdens in the path of those who wish to mobilize and form an interest group. Grassroots organizations form nearly daily to pursue myriad goals, such as halting the construction of cellular phone towers in residential areas or promoting the formation of a new charter school. While mobilization and group development are not greatly constrained in our political system, the mere existence of a group does not necessary suggest that it will have any voice in policy making. As you may have experienced directly, some groups, particularly those representing concentrated economic and business interests, have considerably more power than other groups. Groups that represent powerful or privileged interests are partly responsible for Americans' suspicion of interest groups or, as they are often called, "special interest groups." In fact, some groups call themselves "public interest groups" to signal that they view their mission as a counterweight to these "special" interests.

There are several reasons for the differences in power between some groups and others, particularly within a particular policy area. First, as Howlett and Ramesh note, "One of the most important resources of interest groups is knowledge: specifically, information that might be unavailable or less available to others."[5] Legislators and bureaucrats draw on this information to help them make decisions; groups that are the most effective at channeling that information to bureaucrats and legislators often have an advantage in ensuring that their definition of the problem, and the range of potential solutions, is taken into account. Communication with key decision makers, in turn, requires substantial resources that emergent groups may not have and that established groups often have in abundance.

Money, knowledge, and information are related to the size of the group and the resources that it and its members can bring to policy conflicts. Some interest groups have very few members, and others have millions of dues-paying members. Such large groups include the National Education Association, the Sierra Club, and the American Association of Retired Persons (AARP). "All other things being equal, larger groups can be expected to be taken more seriously by the government." Even more powerful groupings, called *peak associations*, "may be expected to be more influential than those operating individually." The National Association of Manufacturers and the various other industry groups, who combine forces within an industry to wield lobbying power, are peak associations. And, of course, money is very important for interest groups. More money "enables them to hire permanent specialized staff and make campaign contributions to parties and candidates during election."[6]

A rough calculation of the political power of an interest group (and thus of one's political influence as a group member) is derived from the size of the group. A group with 500,000 members is likely to have more clout (or at least be "louder") than a group with 500 members. But this isn't always the case, and we cannot assume that the larger group in this example is a thousand times more powerful than the smaller one. As social scientists have learned, it is very difficult to create a committed membership group unless there are some sorts of incentives for people to join.[7] Business interest groups, such as the National Association of Realtors, can be powerful because their members are vitally interested in the issues addressed by the group. If Congress were to reduce the mortgage interest tax deduction, real estate agents would take note because their livelihoods could be directly and negatively affected, because fewer houses would be sold. However, a person interested in animal conservation may be less *directly* affected by changes in the Endangered Species Act and therefore with no personal *economic* stake in endangered species, might be less motivated to join the Sierra Club; on the other hand, such a person may belong to the Sierra Club because of a belief in the importance of the environment and because of the benefits of membership, including a magazine and a sense of group identity.

Another example involves the imposition of tariffs on goods made overseas. When tariffs are imposed, the benefits are reaped by relatively few domestic suppliers of the product, who seek tariff protections to ensure that their goods remain competitive. Consumers do not benefit from tariffs, but the harms imposed on consumers may be so slight as to be almost unnoticeable. Thus, consumers are unlikely to mobilize against tariffs, but the beneficiaries of the tariff, who are more directly injured by foreign competition, will be very motivated to promote and keep tariffs in place.

When interest groups coalesce and create broader demands for change, a *social movement* is created. A social movement involves far more people—although not all at a high degree of activity—than the membership of relevant interest groups. Social movements often involve a coalition of groups with similar goals, and other people support movements without a formal group affiliation. Recent social movements include the civil rights and women's rights movements; the gay and lesbian rights movement might also be considered a social movement. A countermovement of evangelical, politically conservative Christians has also developed to oppose policies that offend their sense of morality and ethics. All these movements have waxed and waned as the political conditions and the consequences of their work have changed. When movements suffer political setbacks, they can sometimes recruit new adherents to their cause, but when goals are achieved coalitions can break up and the social movement can die out.

Types of Interest Groups

There are many ways to categorize interest groups. One can distinguish between an *institutional* interest group, whose members belong to a particular institution, and a *membership* group, whose members have chosen to join. If you are a student at a university, you are a member of an institutional interest group—university students—because you share some interests with your fellow students, such as affordable tuition and quality education. If you join the National Rifle Association or your on-campus Public Interest Research Group (PIRG), you are part of a *membership* group because you have chosen to join.

One can also categorize interest groups as *economic* or *private interest* groups versus *public interest* groups. While the difference between the two is sometimes rhetorical—after all, almost every group believes it is acting, directly or indirectly, in the broader public interest—there is also a more technical way to distinguish between the two. Public interest groups, such as environmental groups, Common Cause, and the like, seek to create broad benefits for the entire society, not simply their members. Indeed, it is difficult to allow only public interest group members to reap the benefits of, say, a cleaner environment without providing such benefits to others. While public interest groups would like more people to join their causes, they also know that nonmembers constitute a potential force of supporters, and, as mentioned earlier, when many such people are mobilized, a social movement may result.

In economic terms, we can say that nonmembers of public interest groups are free riders who benefit from the work of the group without contributing resources such as labor or money. *Economic groups*, on the other hand, seek to overcome the free-rider problem by creating benefits only for the members of their groups. For example, labor unions, particularly in "closed shop" states where all workers must pay dues to the union, work to provide wage and benefit agreements that benefit only the members of the union. By restricting benefits in this way, the union seeks to promote cohesion and to encourage others to join the union. Industry groups, such as the American Petroleum Institute, the National Association of Manufacturers, and the National Automobile Dealers Association, are clearly economic groups. These tend to be small groups in terms of the actual numbers of members, but are powerful because of what these groups are: collections of powerful economic interests that often enjoy considerable local, regional, or national political support. Finally, we can consider professional and trade associations to be economic associations. Groups such as the American Medical Association and the American Bar Association seek to promote and protect the professional and economic interests of doctors and lawyers. While they provide important benefits and services to their members, such as journals and continuing education, they also seek to protect the economic interests of their members. They play an active role in the education and licensing of doctors and lawyers, thereby seeking to keep the size of the profession relatively fixed. When their interests are threatened, they lobby elected and appointed officials; for example, the American Medical Association has been a traditional opponent of many plans for government-sponsored health care programs for those without insurance.

In both public interest and economic groups, people join because they gain some benefit. The challenge for public interest groups is to make clear what those benefits are in order to attract and keep members. As a rule, it is easier for economic groups to do so because their members have their economic security at stake, and the benefits are then more tangible. Public interest groups, on the other hand, must appeal to other motivations than economics. Most public interest groups make an appeal to people's desire to do good, augmenting it by material benefits like discounted nature tours, glossy magazines, calendars, and tote bags: these benefits seem trivial, but they help to attract new members and promote group cohesion. Still, they are not as powerful as economic inducements in promoting group unity.[8]

Finally, it is important to note that some groups do not fit neatly into the public interest/economic dichotomy. In particular, the United States contains many religious and ideological groups that come together without being based on economics or a broader public interest mission. Rather, their mission is to promote their religious, moral, and ideological values among their members and, sometimes, in the broader society. These groups range from the mainstream churches to the more "fundamentalist" churches, and from the politically moderate to the politically extreme on both ends of the ideological spectrum. Such groups can become important players in the policy process, at least briefly, during times of social upheaval and crisis or when issues of morality and values are paramount.

To make group members' voices heard, interest groups engage in a range of activities. Many groups engage in lobbying elected and appointed officials. The term "lobbying" has gained negative connotations, because it conjures up images of "smoke-filled rooms" and secret dealings between shadowy lobbyists and less-than-honest officials. This perception is reinforced by current campaign contribution practices, which have led many people to believe that campaign contributions are made to ensure friendly access to elected officials and, thereby, to the decision making process more broadly. This perception was explicitly noted by U.S. Supreme Court Justice David Souter in his decision in *Nixon v. Shrink Missouri Government PAC,*[9] in which he noted that

> the cynical assumption that large donors call the tune could jeopardize the willingness of voters to take part in democratic governance. Democracy works "only if the people have faith in those who govern, and that faith is bound to be shattered when high officials and their appointees engage in activities which arouse suspicions of malfeasance and corruption." *United States v. Mississippi Valley Generating Co.*, 364 U.S. 520, 562 (1961).

Attempts to influence government decision making are not, however, solely a function of campaign contributions, although campaign financing plays an important role in influencing decisions. After all, the First Amendment to the Constitution guarantees the right of people "to petition the Government for a redress of grievances," and there is no prohibition on people gathering together in groups to petition the government. One can therefore think of lobbying activity—that is, the organized, continuous act of communicating with the government—as one way to petition government, not only for the redress of grievances, but also to encourage government to support particular interests with various benefits. Thus, people's objection to lobbying may not be to lobbying per se, but rather to the differences in power between the well-funded and the poorer interest groups in Washington and the state capitals.

While lobbying sometimes carries with it tawdry overtones, one of the most effective forms of lobbying is merely the provision of information to elected officials. Elected officials generally have large staffs, and members of Congress have access to the work of the Congressional Research Service. Interest groups can provide further information that is unknown or unavailable to elected officials. Such information has to be reasonably good—outright distortions and fabrications are likely to be exposed, and no elected official wants to use grossly inaccurate information for fear of damaging his or her credibility. Groups consequently try to feed good information to elected officials who may already be predisposed to the group's position, hoping that their supporters can use information to make a better case for the group's preferred solutions.

Of course, not all groups have equal power and equal access to elected officials. There are many instances in American history in which elected officials were actively hostile to a particular group's goals. A prime example is found in the history of the civil rights movement. Clearly, African-Americans could not gain a fair hearing for redress of their grievances before the very state governments that passed and enforced segregationist laws in the first place. At the same time, a sufficiently large number of senators and representatives were unsympathetic to the civil rights cause, making policy change more difficult.

The groups involved in the civil rights movement turned then to three strategies: mass *mobilization*, protest, and litigation. An example of mass mobilization was the 1962 March on Washington, sponsored by several civil rights organizations and featuring Martin Luther King's "I Have a Dream" speech; the 1955–56 Montgomery (Alabama) bus boycott, occasioned by the refusal of Rosa Parks to sit in the back of a city bus, was an example of both mass mobilization and nonviolent protest. The bus boycott actually triggered the creation, in 1957, of the Southern Christian Leadership Conference, a very prominent civil rights organization.

These actions were accompanied by litigation. The NAACP Legal Defense Fund, Inc. (known as the "Inc. Fund"), under the leadership of Thurgood Marshall, had, in the 1940s and early 1950s, begun to score successes in court. The Inc. Fund won cases to desegregate law schools and graduate education, but its most prominent victory was the decision in *Brown v. Board of Education*, in which the Supreme Court ruled that "separate but equal" schools were in fact not equal.

Other groups have used litigation to some advantage; those supporting abortion rights brought the *Roe v. Wade* case as a way to cause the
states to eliminate abortion restrictions. And, while litigation has long
been considered a last-ditch strategy, and its efficacy has been questioned, the choice of litigation as a technique is an important example of
"*venue shopping,*" in which groups pick the branch or agency of government that is most likely to give their concerns a sympathetic hearing.[10]

While controversial as a method of political expression, riots and protest marches are also a form of political participation. Protest marches
are, of course, generally legal in democratic countries, and when riots
related to them break out, they are often instigated by a very small number of people, such as the protests against the World Trade Organization
in Seattle in November 1999. Such actions can reach the national consciousness, like the riots that followed the verdict in the Rodney King
case in Los Angeles in 1992 or the anti–World Trade Organization protests, or they may be confined to a community, as in Eugene, Oregon, in
June 1999, when an anti-capitalism rally turned violent and was met
with tear gas. Protests that turn violent may be labeled illegitimate, because the protest breaks the law (by looting and burning, for example),
but legal or not, such activities do constitute *inputs* to the policy process
that reflect the dissatisfaction of the protesters and rioters. The antiwar
and civil rights protests of the 1960s, for example, may have sometimes
broken the law and may not have been the ultimate reason why the Vietnam war ended or why civil rights laws were passed, but they were
certainly among the very many inputs that led to policy changes. To
make an argument that riots and direct action are important inputs into
the policy process is not to say that one necessarily condones such activities. Most violent protests (more against property than against people)
are conducted by fringe groups that feel they cannot get a hearing through
established methods of political participation.

Political Parties

Political parties serve important functions in the policy process.[11] First,
party labels provide voters with cues for voting. Voters know, in general, that Republicans tend to be more socially conservative and dis-
trustful of "big government" than Democrats are. Second, political parties
provide a rough way of transmitting political preferences from the electorate to the elected branches. The Congressional elections of 1994, for

example, in which the Republican party took control of both houses of Congress, may have reflected in some ways a shift—although, in real terms, a relatively small one—in the preferences of some of the voting public. Third, political parties help elected officials and their supporters create packages of policy ideas that can be used to appeal to voters and then to shape legislation. During the 1960s and 1970s, this was not a particularly important role of the parties, but the Republican House leadership used its "Contract with America" as the package for a set of policies, the creation of agendas, and the packaging of ideas. Finally, the political parties are crucial to organization of the legislative branch. The Congress and state legislatures elect their leaders along party lines, and committee assignments and other positions are made based on party (and seniority within the party). In this way, a rough connection is made between the ideological preferences of the electorate and policy making apparatus of the Congress. Theoretically, this enhances democratic accountability, although the organization of Congress along party lines has been controversial, particularly when very senior members in very safe districts wield disproportionate power over policy.

Think Tanks and Other Research Organizations

The development of more complex government problems and the need for greater analytic capacity than that possessed by the federal and state governments have led to the growth of independent research organizations, or what are often called *think tanks*.[12] Some of the most famous think tanks include the Brookings Institution, the Cato Institute, the Urban Institute, RAND, and the American Enterprise Institute. Employing academic scholars and policy experts, these organizations provide information that policy makers and other influential people can use to make "better" policy. Many think tanks are associated with a particular ideological position: Brookings and Urban Institute are center-left, the American Enterprise Institute is somewhat more to the right, and Cato is libertarian. Others, like RAND, are more closely associated with their methodological style; RAND uses very sophisticated techniques in its analyses of a range of public issues.

A recent trend has been the development of more clearly ideological think tanks, such as the Heritage Foundation, which is explicitly conservative in its orientation. Other think tanks seek, at least in their name, to blur their ideological orientation while obviously advocating positions with an ideological slant. One such example, used by a student in one of my public policy courses, is the National Center for Policy Analysis (NCPA). A review of NCPA's reports and of their board of directors (listed on their Web site, www.ncpa.org) reveals a conservative bent. This is not to say that this is the only group that blurs its ideological leanings or that one should be concerned with the formation of such groups. And, in fairness, the NCPA site links to other conservative and liberal think tanks and values policy discourse for its own sake. The point is that any consumer of analysis from think tanks should have a good sense of the ideological leanings of the think tank in question.

Other think tanks and research organizations are associated with universities and provide valuable input into the policy process. Such centers tend to be more scholarly and less ideological than some think tanks, and state and local governments often rely upon them for expert advice. Indeed, one of the missions of public institutions of higher learning is to provide such politically and socially relevant research to units of government. They are often good sources of information and ideas for your own research on important policy issues.

Communications Media

The news media are important actors in the policy process. Indeed, the freedom of the press—which today includes radio, television, the Internet, and other new media—was stipulated in the First Amendment to the Constitution, and similar provisions in state constitutions, to provide for a vigorous, activist press that could serve as a "watchdog" on government. Journalists and academics have reinforced the belief that the news media play an important role in informing citizens about issues and what their government is doing about them.[13] There are many historic examples of the media exposing some of the troubling activities and shortcomings of business and government. In the early 1900s, crusading journalists, called "muckrakers," aligned with progressive publishers and interests to expose the problems of child labor, tainted foods, and useless medicines. Later in the twentieth century came the revelations of wrongdoing by President Nixon and his staff, as reported in a series of stories by journalists Robert Woodward and Carl Bernstein in the *Washington Post* from June 1972 until Nixon's resignation in 1974.

Newspapers remain important to policy elites and to some mass audiences. Nearly every city of consequence in the United States has a local paper, and many papers serve a statewide or regional audience, such as the *Los Angeles Times*, the *Chicago Tribune*, the Portland *Oregonian*, or the Newark (New Jersey) *Star Ledger*. Other papers have grown from local and regional papers to nationally important newspapers, such as the *New York Times* and the *Washington Post*, both of which are widely read in policy making circles. The *Wall Street Journal* is an important and respected source of business and economic news, and its op-ed pages are a bastion of conservative thought. *USA Today* is the national paper launched by the Gannett Company in 1982 as a consciously colorful, entertaining national newspaper. *USA Today* concentrates on sports, entertainment, and lifestyle news to a greater extent than most national papers.

Television is, however, the primary source of news for those Americans who consume news. The importance of the nightly network news broadcasts has significantly diminished in the 1990s, and their audience has progressively grown smaller and older. The nightly broadcasts are less prone to cover breaking news and more prone to cover health, economic, and lifestyle issues. Still, audiences for nightly news are large, and the older viewership is more likely to vote than younger people, particularly those in college.

Younger audiences, to the extent that they consume news programming, turn to cable TV sources such as CNN, MSNBC, and Fox News. In particular, CNN has become an international news channel[14] with a remarkable ability to cover breaking news worldwide, as it demonstrated during the fall of the Berlin Wall, the Gulf War, and the Yugoslavia conflict. CNN is an important news source for policy makers worldwide—and few congressional offices are without cable TV and CNN.

Radio was once a primary source of news, but its importance as a news source has been supplanted by TV. Nevertheless, some larger cities have all-news radio stations, such as WCBS in New York, WTOP in Washington, and KCBS in San Francisco. These stations tend to rebroadcast news already covered in newspapers and TV. A notable exception is National Public Radio (NPR), which offers several hours of news every day to its listeners. NPR has aggressively covered some stories, such as the Senate's failure to confirm Robert Bork to the Supreme Court, thereby serving as an influential news source. Policy elites tend to listen to NPR. And many public radio stations carry news programs from the British Broadcasting Corporation.

Other cable TV outlets also play an important role. C-SPAN and C-SPAN-2, networks set up as a public service by the cable TV industry, devote a considerable amount of time to unedited recordings of House and Senate activity. Much of this activity seems tedious and incomprehensible to the uninitiated, but political junkies and policy entrepreneurs avidly watch these networks. Even "nonnews" cable can have an influence on policy making, such as when MTV mounts its "Rock the Vote" campaigns to encourage youth voting or when ESPN covers a sports scandal. Regular network entertainment programs can greatly influence the national agenda, as occurred when Vice President Dan Quayle criticized the fictional character Murphy Brown for her single parenthood or when *All in the Family* sparked a national discussion of racism and bigotry in the early 1970s.

The very nature and tone of entertainment programs can spark passionate debates about the nature of our national culture, with important implications for policy. In the 1980s, films like *Top Gun* and the *Rambo* series presented viewers with what some critics called a glorified, jingoistic depiction of war and American values. In the 1990s, as in every decade since the advent of movies, records, and TV, periodic debates focused on the extent to which entertainment contains a socially unhealthy degree of sex, profanity, and violence. The debate continues over whether such programming influences people to commit acts of violence and mayhem, such as the spate of school shootings that culminated in the Littleton incident in 1999. These issues became an important part of the 2000 presidential campaign.

Citizens who follow TV, movies, and music—or monitor their kids' consumption of such materials—often protest the content of these products through grassroots efforts and through support of political leaders and public figures. Congress takes note of this protest through means ranging from urging the posting of the Ten Commandments in schools to pressuring recording, TV, and movie interests to voluntarily rate their products for age-appropriateness before Congress mandates such a system in federal law. With the advent of advanced computing technology in the 1980s and 1990s, realistic video games with violent themes, such as *Doom* or *Quake*, have been singled out as examples of inappropriate violence, leading the video game industry to follow the movie example and institute a voluntary ratings system. In summary, what is in the media, and how it is presented, are important inputs to the policy process and are the subjects of policy making itself.

The particular importance of the media is in its *agenda-setting* function; that is, they help to elevate some issues to greater public attention. This function is very important, particularly in the major national news outlets used by key decision makers, such as CNN, the *New York Times*, the *Washington Post*, the *Wall Street Journal*, and the *Los Angeles Times*. More specialized magazines, such as *Reason*, *The Nation*, *Mother Jones*, and the *National Review*, appeal to certain ideological preferences. All of these sources can highlight the importance of certain issues and provide ideas and feedback to elected officials and bureaucrats. In political science terms, we can say that greater levels of news coverage are closely (but not identically) associated with greater levels of institutional attention to public problems.[15] Moreover, the media's influence goes beyond its ability to pressure policy makers to pay attention to problems. The news media can expand issues from narrow groups to broader audiences, thereby creating more pressure for change, or, in E.E. Schattschneider's term, can expand the scope of conflict.[16] Less powerful groups and interests can gain access to media attention when their stories are sufficiently compelling to attract news coverage, thereby making access to the agenda more democratic[17] and helping to open up policy subgovernments,[18] as discussed in the next section.

We should keep in mind, however, that the news media are not simply passive actors in the decisions to cover certain news stories. First, interest groups often try to "arouse" or "provoke" the news media to devote greater scrutiny to an issue or a problem.[19] Sometimes this is successful; other times it is unnecessary when dramatic, "mediagenic" events, such as airplane crashes, crimes, and natural disasters, occur. However, the decision to cover any event or issue necessarily means that other issues are unlikely to be covered, even when those issues are arguably more important. In other words, what journalists call "the newshole" is limited by various constraints. Time is the major constraint for TV and radio news; a half-hour nightly news broadcast must carefully pick its stories to maintain viewer interest. Newspapers and magazines are limited in the amount of space they can devote to news; the amount of space is often a function of the amount of advertising sold in the newspaper or magazine. And the use of the space is often determined by what editors believe will be most interesting to their readers and audiences: stories of domestic crisis, particularly with a compelling human element and a sense of conflict, are often more interesting and more extensively covered than foreign policy issues, as reflected in Figure 4.1.

Figure 4.1   **Who Chooses What's "News"?**

Aside from these constraints, the news media are profit-driven businesses, and the decisions over what stories to cover can have economic consequences for the media outlet publishing the story. An extreme example of this occurred recently at the *Los Angeles Times*, where news reporting and business were commingled in a newspaper supplement on the new Staples Center, which replaced the Great Western Forum in Los Angeles. In this case, it was revealed that the *Times* and the promoters of the arena had shared the advertising profits from a special magazine, written by *Times* reporters, marking the opening of the arena. The *Times* subsequently investigated its practices in this case and took steps to keep journalism and business separate.[20] In general, however, the connection between journalism and business is subtler. While many in this age of media consolidation, such as the Time Warner-America Online or the Capital Cities/ABC-Disney mergers, worry that the corporate owners of these media outlets will unduly influence news content,[21] the evidence of such influence is still unclear at best. After all, journalists are professionals who often believe that their first duty is to inform the public, not to ensure the profitability of their corporate owners. The next decade is likely to see this conflict between journalistic norms and profitability become more intense and more public.

A subtler and yet more pressing problem for our purposes is the biases that are introduced in news coverage based on the competitive and economic needs of news outlets, particularly in the electronic media. Students of the news media[22] have long known that the selection of stories for coverage is often influenced more by the dramatic and narrative features of the "story" than by the substantive importance of the story. Thus, the old saying "if it bleeds, it leads" is played out in hundreds of newspapers and even more so on hundreds of local TV news programs across the nation. Stories involving murder, crime, fires, grisly car accidents, and the like are presented because they are dramatic and novel and therefore easily told as a story with good guys, bad guys, winners, losers, and even a moral (crime doesn't pay, don't drink and drive).

Such stories tend to distort people's perceptions of the relative risks they confront every day. A steady diet of crime reporting on TV will lead viewers to believe that the crime rate is higher than it is, because the news is often taken out of its context. Because of the time and space constraints facing news outlets, they often fail to place events in context, such as by explaining during a murder story what the actual murder rate in a city is and how it compares to the rate in other places. In international reporting, news outlets tend to focus on the immediate conflict, such as between Serbs and Kosovars, rather than explaining the historical roots of this conflict. In policy debates, the media focus on the conflicting positions and, in particular, the people that represent the positions; this is called *personalizing* the news and is used by journalists to make the news more interesting and comprehensible to readers and viewers. Personalization reduces conflict to sometimes absurd depictions: the media, for example, often depicted the Gulf War as a confrontation between George Bush and Saddam Hussein, rather than as a war between one nation and a coalition of other nations.

A common argument against these critiques of the media is what I call the "diversity" argument: there are thousands of different news outlets, so people can choose (particularly via cable TV and the Internet) what news sources they want to use. But diversity is much less evident than one might suppose, considering that several journalists often cover the same events in packs, such as political campaign events, and file remarkably similar reports with their outlets. Indeed, a journalist for a mainstream publication who deviates too far from the consensus line of the story is likely to be asked why.[23] Nor is it clear that most people take advantage of alternative sources of information, such as the more consciously ideological media discussed earlier.

Like many social scientists, I tend to be critical of the media because of their shortcomings in providing information that citizens can use to make political and policy choices. The news media are not the only way, and may not be the major way, in which policy makers (as opposed to citizens) get their information, and we are therefore at a disadvantage compared with the "insiders." John Kingdon, in his interviews with key decision makers in transportation and health care, found that relatively few of them cited the media as an important source of information and ideas.[24] And Howlett and Ramesh note that

> policy-makers are for the most part intelligent and resourceful individuals who understand their own interest and have their own ideas about appropriate or feasible policy options and are not easily swayed by media or the mere fact of media attention. Indeed they often use the media to their own advantage. It is not uncommon for public officials and successful interest groups to provide selective information to the media to bolster their case.[25]

Note that Howlett and Ramesh are saying two things here: that *ideas* do not necessarily come from media attention or coverage pressure, but that groups still recognize the value of the media in helping them make their case. In this realization, groups and officials know what students of the media have suspected for years: that the media do not tell us what to think, but help shape the things we think *about*. And, as Baumgartner and Jones note, when the news media cover an issue intensively and "negatively" (from the perspective of the groups under scrutiny), the more likely that public pressure for some sort of solution will ensue.[26]

Subgovernments, Issue Networks, and Domains

If this chapter were to end here, you might be left with the impression that there are no patterns in the relationships between the actors in the policy process and that the process is characterized by chaos or a lack of interaction between groups. You know intuitively that this is not true: the actors in the policy process can and *must* interact with each other to advance policy proposals. Without this interaction, nothing would happen, and policy making would come to a standstill. Fortunately, we need not worry that Congress, bureaucrats, the president, the courts, the people, the media, interest groups, and all the other actors will suddenly stop making policy. Rather, our task is to make some sense of these very complex interactions between the actors. The Constitution and statute law structure many of these interactions, such as the relationships among the three branches of government. Others are informally structured but equally important to policy making.

To understand how these interactions work, we start with the idea of a *policy domain*. A policy domain is the substantive area of policy over which participants in policy making compete and compromise,[27] such as the environmental policy domain or the health policy domain. Of course, some of these domains are so vast that they contain other domains, such as the air pollution domain, the water pollution domain, or the mental health domain. The activities that take place within these domains are influenced by other domains, and issues and ideas often spill over from one domain to others.[28]

The political culture of the nation and the existing legal environment and doctrine in which the policy is made influence the overall environment in which policy is made in these domains. These environmental features are fairly stable in the short run but often do change in the long run; our political culture and legal doctrines treat women and minorities considerably differently than they did fifty years ago, for example. The domain is also influenced by how people conceive of the nature of a problem, what causes the problem, and the range of potential solutions to the problem.

Contained within the policy domain is the *policy community*, which consists of those actors who are actively involved in policy making in a particular domain. This is a small subset of people that could possibly be involved in an issue; the policy community consists of those who are most expert in studying, understanding, negotiating, or explaining an issue. The nature and composition of the policy community is not, however, permanently fixed. There is variation in how easily one can join a policy community. Some are open to participation by a variety of interests and actors. Others tend to be closed and operate in relative obscurity.

A considerable amount of effort has been expended by political scientists in trying to explain how policy communities organize themselves into something less than a political free-for-all in which every possible

Figure 4.2 **The Iron Triangle Subgovernment**

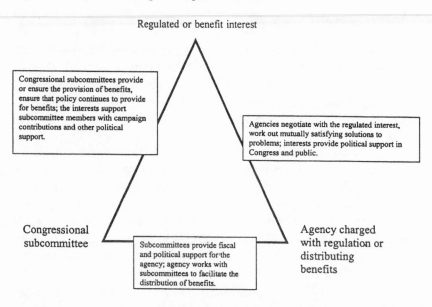

Regulated or benefit interest

Congressional subcommittees provide or ensure the provision of benefits, ensure that policy continues to provide for benefits; the interests support subcommittee members with campaign contributions and other political support.

Agencies negotiate with the regulated interest, work out mutually satisfying solutions to problems; interests provide political support in Congress and public.

Congressional subcommittee

Subcommittees provide fiscal and political support for the agency; agency works with subcommittees to facilitate the distribution of benefits.

Agency charged with regulation or distributing benefits

interest fights with all comers. Rather, we know intuitively that these interests and groups are likely to form connections, alliances, and coalitions. One way these participants organize is in an "iron triangle" of mutually reinforcing relationships between regulated interests, the congressional committee or subcommittee charged with lawmaking on the particular issue, and the agency charged with regulating the interests in question (Figure 4.2).

The most striking feature of the iron triangle is the mutually reinforcing nature of this relationship. The regulated interest, the agency, and the congressional subcommittee make policy based on their common perception of the issues and goals. The regulators tend to negotiate with the regulated, rather than imposing their ideas. Because there are benefits to all parties, this relationship has the potential for long-term stability. Baumgartner and Jones call such tightly knit relationships "policy monopolies."[29]

For example, farm policy is largely controlled by the appropriate bureau in the United States Department of Agriculture, by its parallel subcommittee (for example, the Subcommittee on Livestock, Dairy, and Poultry), and by the interest being regulated or supported (in this case, livestock, dairy, and poultry interests). Other areas in which iron triangles are found include public works projects and big water projects, particularly in the West, where subcommittees in the Department of the Interior committee are committed to *logrolling* (that is, trading commitments to vote on each other's bills) and promoting member interests, usually related to helping local constituents, in their districts.

The iron triangle continues to have a significant influence over the way in which authors of American politics texts depict the relationships involved in policy making. Given that so much policy is made outside of popular or media scrutiny, this seems sensible. But the problem with this depiction of policy making is that, as Hugh Heclo writes, the "iron triangle concept was not so much wrong as it is disastrously incomplete."[30]

The examples of the types of policies that iron triangles address are largely *distributive* policies in which costs are dispersed and benefits are concentrated. (I discuss these policy types in detail in Chapter 6.) In such policies, few "outside" interests meddle in decision making: bureaus, subcommittees, and regulated interests dominate; and the relationship between organizations remains stable. But if we look at the other policy types, we see greater conflict, more *peak organization* involvement, and greater involvement on the part of committees and whole houses of Congress, rather than individual subcommittees. Given that we know that some policies are very controversial, we know that something less closed and secretive than iron triangle styles of subgovernments must exist and that the iron triangle concept covers only a small part of policy making.

Even the policies that were characterized by iron triangle politics have become more complex and conflictual as new actors and new voices enter and others exit the debate. Congress's assertion of its power in the early 1970s, combined with the decentralization of power in the Congress itself, created more intercommittee conflict and created opportunities for greater points of entry to the political and policy processes. Baumgartner and Jones argue that these multiple points of access allow interest groups to go "*venue shopping*" in a search for a committee or subcommittee to serve as the most likely forum for their claims.[31] Additional access to the policy process has been afforded through greater government openness, such as through sunshine laws and the Freedom of Information Act, and through greater sophistication of interest groups in exploiting points of access, such as committee hearings and public comment opportunities for regulations. This is not to say that policy is generally made out in the open; rather, social scientists now believe that policy making is not as closed as the old iron triangle model would lead us to believe.

Heclo also notes that the federal budget and the volume of rule making activity have substantially increased since 1950. With very large amounts of money and power at stake, politics and policy have become more contentious; the opening of government to greater citizen participation has allowed more groups to weigh in on policy, with an associated increase in conflict, number of veto points, and the like. Heclo notes that, with greater funding being passed to state and local units of government, and greater regulation accompanying these transfers of funds, more of these units of government are operating as lobbyists and serve as interest groups in their own right.[32] All state governments, many city governments, and the key associations that represent governors, legislators, state judges, and local governments have offices in Washington and participate in federal policy making at every stage of the process. At the same time, the devolution of power to local and state governments creates new venues for interest groups to participate in policy making, because state and local governments are again very important decision-making bodies.

How, then, do we describe policy making relationships without reverting to the old iron triangle formulation? The term *subgovernment* came into use in the late 1960s to describe a *policy network* or *policy subsystem* that was most involved in making policy in a particular policy domain. As Ripley and Franklin define them, "subgovernments are clusters of individuals that effectively make most of the routine decisions in a given substantive area of policy."[33]

Heclo proposes the "issue network" as a superior way of depicting subgovernment politics. The issue network consists of the various government agencies, committees, groups, and interests that are interested in an issue. Subgovernments that are more open than iron-triangle, or small issue networks are called "policy communities." In large and contentious issues like health care reform, the policy community is vast, with hundreds of interest groups plying every member of Congress (not solely key committee members) with ideas to promote their interests.

While these depictions of issue networks and policy communities have proved useful to students of public policy, they do not help us to understand the ebb and flow of policy making over time. Baumgartner and Jones argue that policy making still involves relatively long periods of stasis punctuated by changes in the political equilibrium. Paul Sabatier provides a framework for policy making called the *advocacy coalition framework* (ACF), which helps us to make some sense of what often look like chaotic issue networks.[33] We return to the ACF in Chapter 9, in which we examine current models of public policy.

Prying Open Policy Networks

While policy scholars now think more in terms of communities and coalitions than issue networks, access to policy making is clearly not wide open. In environmental policy, as in many other policy domains, major corporate interests often dominate smaller groups with limited resources. This is particularly true when an issue is local or when the big national environmental groups, such as the Sierra Club, choose not to engage an issue.

But policy change is possible, as we have seen during the New Deal, the civil rights movement, and the Great Society programs, all periods in which government took on more tasks and protected more groups and interests. Policy changed in the other direction during the Carter, Reagan, and Bush administrations, when more conservative preferences led to attempts to make government smaller. These changes happened because policy networks were forced to open up to other voices and participants. As a result, the nature and composition of advocacy coalitions changed, and new coalitions were created or significantly altered.

Nor are big, sweeping changes, involving great matters of state and ideology, the only sorts of policy changes. There are many examples of relatively small, focused movements grabbing attention and adherents nationwide. Civil rights and environmental groups started as relatively small groups in the early twentieth century. These groups grew as concerns with equality and with environmental damage became more important to more people. In the past twenty years, groups such as Mothers Against Drunk Driving (MADD) have spawned policy changes. MADD not only advanced the issue of drunk driving to the national agenda, but also actually succeeded in inducing states to stiffen their penalties for driving while intoxicated (DWI). In a sense, a small social movement was created calling for greater individual responsibility and stricter sanctions against those who do not exercise responsibility.

There are many ways that new and established groups can follow in the footsteps of these historic examples, all of which have one thing in common: creating opportunities for participation in policy making where such opportunities were inaccessible. There are at least four ways to gain this access.

Creating and Exploiting Focusing Events

A *focusing event* is a sudden event that can generate attention to public problems or issues.[35] Focusing events often trigger new social movements, but more often they provide opportunities for existing groups to exploit the greater attention to an issue and press for change. Environmentalists and fishers in Alaska had mobilized and were apprehensive about the threat of an oil spill in Prince William Sound long before the *Exxon Valdez* oil spill, yet their interests were never given much attention after the Trans-Alaska Pipeline was built—until the spill occurred, thereby giving these groups new energy and legitimacy in policy debates. Suddenly, after the spill, fishing and environmental interests had new venues in which to press their claims, particularly in the news media and in congressional hearings, whereas before the spill these hearings were dominated by industry interests. Other focusing events include well-publicized incidents like the Rodney King beating[36] or the beatings of African-Americans during civil rights marches in the 1960s, or events that are staged by groups to great effect, such as large rallies and protests. An example is the 1963 March on Washington, a milestone of the civil rights movement, at which Martin Luther King gave his now-famous "I Have a Dream" speech.

Social Movements and Mobilization

Even without large, widely publicized focusing events, interest groups can come together to create major social movements that can influence policy. In the 1960s and 1970s, and continuing today, women's groups promoted policies to create equal pay in the workplace, access to abortion, more stringent laws governing sexual harassment, improved laws that reduce, to some extent, the stigma attached to rape victims, and so on. These actions are the result of citizens coming together and pressing for change, both within and outside official institutions.

The civil rights movement is a classic example of a movement that lobbied or pleaded its case to government institutions—Congress, the president, and the courts—as well as appealing to the "court of public opinion." Indeed, the imagery of the civil rights movement—the police dogs in Alabama, and kids being escorted to school by federal troops, for example—appealed directly to Americans' sense of justice and fairness, and, while not all Americans supported the enforcement of civil

rights for minorities, there were certainly enough Americans to constitute an important social movement to press for policy and social change.

The examples given here are of liberal social movements, which are
historically more common given the conservative tendencies of the political system.[37] However, in recent years, politically conservative groups
have also mobilized, often to counter perceived liberal gains. Conservatives (and religious groups, often with a conservative outlook) have
mobilized against abortion, in favor of restoring school prayer, and against
textbooks and teaching that contradict their political or religious values.
Conservatives have formed groups, much as have liberals, to advance
their views on welfare, economic regulation, and environmental protection. Clearly, there is no reason why conservatives or liberals cannot
mobilize and press for change. Those that are successful will be those
that touch a chord with the current sentiments of the American people;
the truly successful among them will be led by people who know, intuitively or otherwise, how to work within their issue domains to gain
political advantage and policy gains.

Exploiting the Decentralization of American Government

By definition, grassroots groups are unlikely to tackle vast federal-level
problems. Indeed, James Madison, one of the founders of our Constitution, argued that the constitutional structure was designed to prevent or
compartmentalize national movements. In MADD's case, drunken driving was to a large extent a state and local issue, involving establishing
and enforcing DWI laws. Tackling the problem at the local level—in
this case, California—made the most sense in terms of the early MADD's
limited resources and because the founder of the group, whose child
was killed by a drunk driver, lived in California.[38] Modern communications media, however, make it easier for new and grassroots groups like
MADD to mobilize, expand issues, and grow in both membership and
geographic reach.

Going Public

If government institutions such as congressional committees are closed
off to groups promoting change, such groups are likely to appeal to others besides these institutions. Given that, at least theoretically, political
power is derived from *our* consent, it is reasonable for groups to appeal

to us directly in conjunction with trying to gain status within a policy network or community.

There are many ways groups can "go public." Traditionally, groups have run direct mail campaigns and phone solicitations and have placed ads in major newspapers. If you subscribe to magazines with an identifiable ideological label, you will often get mailings from groups associated with that ideology: those who subscribe to *The Nation*, for example, are more likely to get mail from the American Civil Liberties Union (ACLU) than are readers of the more conservative *National Review*. Large full-page ads run in the *New York Times* and other important journals of news and opinion, both to mobilize people to join a cause such as protesting the World Trade Organization or questioning the importance of global warming, and to influence the key policy makers who read these publications.

An emerging method of going public is the increasing use of the Internet and its possibilities for very low cost communication among group members and potential members. Kevin Hill and John Hughes argue that the Internet allows groups to communicate at considerably lower "transaction costs" than more traditional means of communication: after all, once a group sets up a Web site, it costs no more for one person or one thousand or one hundred thousand to see the Web site. An e-mail message to one member of a group can just as easily be sent to several thousand simultaneously.[39] It may be too early to tell what the importance of the Internet will be for politics and group mobilization, but it is likely that it will add to the tools available to groups as they seek to advance their policy ideas.

Conclusion

Many people find it very hard to understand what the government does and how they can play a role in it. As many public opinion polls have learned, people think that the government is distant, uncaring, hard to understand, and unable to be influenced by individual action. This feeling is understandable—governments *are* large, complicated, and sometimes frustrating institutions. However, to give up on trying to understand government and to fail to participate in its decisions is to abdicate one's rights and, indeed, one's duties as a citizen. Because our government rules us, in John Locke's words, "with the consent of the governed"—that is, with *our* consent—we have a role as citizens in overseeing the government. This argument is clearly rooted in a sense of civic obligation, induces some people to vote, keep up with the news (and not just by watching the TV), and to be aware of community concerns. But do-ing one's civic duty is often less compelling than the desire to do a good job, be a good parent/friend/neighbor/partner, or just relax and avoid the stress that sometimes accompanies current affairs.

A more compelling reason for getting involved in making public policy is that if you and your friends fail to get involved, other people, who may very likely be working contrary to what you perceive to be your interests, may be more effective with your and your friends' opposition. For example, you may find a book in the library that you believe con-tains racist, sexist, obscene, or antisocial material that is suitable for adult use only. You believe that minors' access to the book should be prohibited. If you and your friends (or political allies) do nothing, it is likely that the book will remain on the shelf. If, however, you and your political allies mobilize to restrict access to the book to adults only, it is likely that this restriction will be imposed. Conversely, if you believe strongly in freedom of thought and information, you might mobilize to counter the actions of those who would restrict access to books.

A cynic would argue that the inequities in power and resources make it impossible to take on interests that would block policy change, and that any effort to promote change would be a waste of time. Policy mak-ing is indeed a slow and challenging process, and sometimes groups are disadvantaged and unable to do much to cause change. It is not easy to achieve social change. Indeed, the constitutional structure of the United States is in many ways explicitly designed to promote stability and hin-ders change.[40] I am *not* suggesting here that policy change is easy, that you or a group that you form or join will see results immediately, or even that your policy preferences will be translated into actual govern-mental policy. But if a goal is worth achieving, it is worth both hard work and patience to achieve the goal.

American policy history is full of examples in which people decided not to remain on the sidelines. The women's suffrage movement, the civil rights movement, the women's equality movement, and the crack-down on drunk driving are examples of social movements that relied upon the involvement of citizens, not big interest groups with an army of expensive lobbyists.

In recent years, citizens and their attorneys have sued tobacco compa-nies for damages caused by smoking. This success in turn emboldened states to sue the tobacco companies to recover state Medicaid costs in-curred by sick smokers. In pursuit of tougher drunk-driving laws, MADD stood its ground against the restaurant, bar, tavern, and beverage interests. Labor unions have fought and won political battles with management. In addition, in perhaps the most important social change in our nation's history, people coalesced to fight institutionalized racism and to secure the rights of African-Americans to vote, buy property, and seek and hold employment. Lest you think that all these movements are "liberal" in the popular sense, there are current social movements to press for abortion restrictions or prohibitions, to reduce taxes, to ensure the right to own and legally use firearms, to introduce moral education and values in the school.

All these struggles are difficult, none have been fully resolved to everyone's satisfaction, and we may not agree on what they are trying to accomplish, but they do yield important changes in policy and in public attitudes. And regardless of whether you agree with the ideologies behind these struggles, these issues are important and worth debating and discussing, if for no other reason than to ensure the continued vitality of our political process. Unfortunately, many people do not participate in these debates, leading to atrophy in our political institutions. This trend will continue at great peril to our social, political, and economic well-being.

Why, if the odds are stacked, as they often seem to be, against the "little people," do people get involved in policy making? Perhaps a main reason is that people sense that they can influence policy, particularly at the local level, by taking a clear and public position on an issue that affects them. Often people have an intense interest in the substance of issues. Many people who care deeply about the environment, for example, feel they have a responsibility to future generations to address these problems to make life better for those future generations. Other people get involved simply because they like to participate in politics and enjoy it the same way other people enjoy sports or hobbies. Most people get involved in the policy process when something happens in their local community that mobilizes them and induces them to care deeply about a particular issue.

Those of us who are intensely interested in politics and policy should not condemn those who fail to meet our standards of passion and fascination with the process. While most people do not follow day-to-day politics, many people can be mobilized to address a particular issue when it is of interest and concern to them. Sometimes their mobilization will dismay you—if you are a liberal, you would rather not see conservatives mobilize to exclude certain books from libraries—but keep in mind that there are plenty of people who will work with your side to attempt to advance your preferred style of policy change.

5

Agenda Setting, Power, and Interest Groups

In *The Semisovereign People*, E.E. Schattschneider asserts, "the definition of the alternatives is the supreme instrument of power."[1] The definition of alternative issues, problems, and solutions is crucial, because it
establishes which issues, problems, and solutions will gain the attention
of the public and decision makers and which, in turn, are most likely to
gain broader attention. This chapter considers the processes by which
groups work to elevate their issues on the agenda while denying other
issues a place on the agenda. The discussion begins with a discussion of
the agenda setting process and then turns to a review of current thinking
about political power in the context of public policy making.

Readers who value broad-based participation in politics and policy making—that is, those with a *pluralist* bent—may find this discussion of political power dispiriting, as much of the current literature on political power
and interest groups adopts the elite theory perspective. Elite theory suggests that relatively few people in key positions in government, industry,
academe, the media, and other institutions control a disproportionate share
of the nation's economic and political resources. In the discussion that follows, you will see distinct echoes of this way of thinking. But I hope you do
not read this chapter and believe that all is hopeless. As discussed in earlier
chapters and as noted here, while the American system of government and
politics often favors more powerful and more focused economic interests
over less powerful, more diffuse interests, often the less powerful interests—or, as I sometimes call them, disadvantaged interests—can coalesce
and, when the time is right, find avenues for the promotion of their ideas.

Before we turn to this discussion, let us consider how issues reach public attention in the first place: that is, how they reach the *agenda*.

Agenda Setting

Agenda setting is the process by which problems and alternative solutions gain or lose public and elite attention. Group competition to set the agenda is fierce because no society or political system has the institutional capacity to address all possible alternatives to all possible problems that arise at any one time.[2] Groups must therefore fight to earn their issues' places among all the other issues sharing the limited space on the agenda or to prepare for the time when a crisis makes their issue more likely to occupy a more prominent space on the agenda. Even when an issue gains attention, groups must fight to ensure that their depiction of the issue remains in the forefront and that their preferred approaches to the problem are those that are most actively considered. They do so for the very reasons cited by Schattschneider: The group that successfully describes a problem will also be the one that defines the solutions to it, thereby prevailing in policy debate. At the same time, groups fight to keep issues off the agenda.

To understand groups, power, and agenda setting, I begin with a brief discussion of the idea of political power, since one of the main uses of political power is to keep ideas and issues on or off the public agenda. I then describe how the debate over issues begins with a debate over whether something is a *problem* about which something can be done or a *condition* about which little can be done. I then turn to a discussion of the levels of the agenda and how groups will use their power to influence what reaches the agenda by advancing alternative social constructions of problems.

Central to understanding agenda setting is the meaning of the term *agenda*. An agenda is a collection of problems, understandings of causes, symbols, solutions, and other elements of public problems that come to the attention of members of the public and their governmental officials. An agenda can be as concrete as a list of bills that are before a legislature, but also includes a series of beliefs about the existence and magnitude of problems and how they should be addressed by government, the private sector, nonprofit organizations, or through joint action by some or all of these institutions.

Agendas exist at all levels of government. Every community and every body of government—Congress, a state legislature, a county commission—has a collection of issues that are available for discussion and disposition. All these issues can be categorized based on the extent to which an institution is prepared to make an ultimate decision to enact and implement or to reject particular policies. Furthest from *enactment* are issues and ideas contained in the systemic agenda, in which is contained any idea that could possibly be considered by participants in the policy process. Some ideas fail to reach this agenda because they are politically far beyond the pale in a particular society; large-scale state ownership of the means of production, for example, is generally off the systemic agenda in the United States because it is contrary to existing ideological commitments.

Because the agenda is actually quite vast, it is useful to think of several levels of the agenda, as shown in Figure 5.1. The "largest" level of the agenda is the *agenda universe*, which contains all ideas that could possibly be brought up and discussed in a society or a political system. In a democracy, we can think of all the possible ideas as being quite unconstrained, although, even in democracies, the expression of some ideas is officially or unofficially constrained. In the United States, aggressively racist and sexist language is usually not tolerated socially in public discourse. In Germany, it is illegal to write in praise of Nazism or to deny that the Holocaust happened, and Canada has laws prohibiting hate speech and expression that would probably conflict with the First Amendment of the United States Constitution. Ideas like the establishment of aggressively racist, fascist, or communist policies are so far out of bounds of politically appropriate discourse that they rarely are expressed beyond a fringe group of adherents. The vast numbers of ideas in the agenda universe, however, are more or less "acceptable" in a political sense, and appear on the *systemic agenda*.

Cobb and Elder say that "the systemic agenda consists of all issues that are commonly perceived by members of the political community as meriting public attention and as involving matters within the legitimate jurisdiction of existing governmental authority." The boundary between the systemic agenda and the agenda universe represents the limit of "legitimate jurisdiction of existing governmental authority."[3] That boundary can move in or out to accommodate more or fewer ideas over time. For example, ideas to establish programs to alleviate economic suffering have waxed and waned on the agenda so often as to become a recurrent feature of the systemic agenda when the national mood is more expansive toward the poor.

Figure 5.1   **Levels of the Agenda**

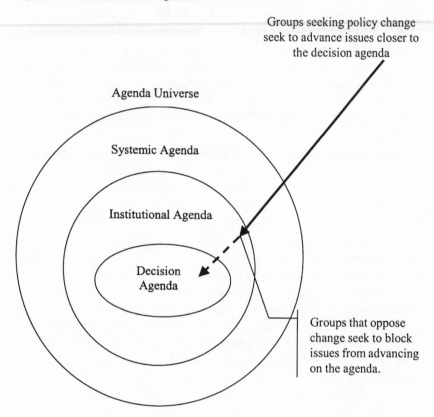

Groups seeking policy change
seek to advance issues closer to
the decision agenda

Agenda Universe

Systemic Agenda

Institutional Agenda

Decision
Agenda

Groups that oppose
change seek to block
issues from advancing
on the agenda.

If a problem or idea is successfully elevated from the systemic agenda, it moves to the *institutional agenda*, a subset of the broader systemic agenda. The institutional agenda is "that list of items explicitly up for the active and serious consideration of authoritative decision makers."[4] The limited amount of time or resources available to any institution or society means that only a limited number of issues is likely to reach the institutional agenda.[5] Even fewer issues will reach the *decision agenda*, which contains items that are about to be acted upon by a governmental body. Bills, once they are introduced and heard in committee, are relatively low on the decision agenda until they are reported to the whole body for a vote. Notices of proposed rule making in the *Federal Register* are evidence of an issue or problem's elevation to the decision agenda in the executive branch. Conflict may be greatest at this stage, because when a decision is reached at a particular level of government, it may trigger conflict that expands to another or higher level of government. Conflict continues and may expand; this expansion of conflict is often a key goal of many interest groups. The goal of most contending parties in the policy process is to move policies from the systemic agenda to the institutional agenda, or to prevent issues from reaching the institutional agenda.

Figure 5.1 implies that, except for the agenda universe, the agenda, and each level within it, is finite, and no society or political system can address all possible alternatives to all possible problems that arise at any time. This is very important: because the agenda is finite, interests must compete with each other to get their issues, and their preferred alternative policies, on the agenda. They must also compete with each other to keep their issues off the agenda, using the power resources at their disposal.

The Idea of Political Power

The ability of groups—acting singly or, more often, in coalition with other groups—to influence policy is not simply a function of who makes the most technically or rhetorically persuasive argument. We know intuitively that some groups are more powerful than others, in the sense that they are better able to influence the outcomes of policy debates. This argument suggests an elite model of policy making, in which relatively few people make the important decisions affecting public policy. But power is more than this, as we will explore. Social scientists have developed more sophisticated ways of thinking about the sources and uses of power; an overview of some of this thinking is provided here.

When we think of power, we might initially think about how people, governments, and powerful groups in society can compel people to do things, often against their will. In a classic article in the *American Political Science Review*, Peter Bachrach and Morton Baratz argue that this sort of power—the coercion of one person by another—is one of two faces of power. The other face is the ability to keep a person from doing what he or she wants to do; instead of a coercive power, the second face is a blocking power.

> Of course power is exercised when A participates in the making of decisions that affect B. But power is also exercised when A devotes his energies to creating or reinforcing social and political values and institutional

practices that limit the scope of the political process to public consideration of only those issues which are comparatively innocuous to A. To the extent that A succeeds in doing this, B is prevented, for all practical purposes, from bringing to the fore any issues that might in their resolution be seriously detrimental to A's set of preferences.[6]

In the first face of power, "A participates in the making of decisions that affect B," even if B does not like the decisions or their consequences. This is the classic sort of power that we see in authoritarian regimes, in which the government (and its supporters, of which there are many, even in authoritarian regimes) imposes policies on its citizens without their input or even approval. In the United States and other democracies, this sort of power exists because there are many groups that have very little power to influence decisions made on their behalf or even against their interests. Consider, for example, how groups of people and the policies applied to them are depicted in debates over policy. Prisoners, for example, have little power to influence the conditions of their sentencing and incarceration, because they are social "deviants" and therefore find it difficult to mobilize in defense of their very real but socially marginal interests.[7] This is not to say that other people and groups do not speak for prisoners. There are several prison rights organizations in the nation, and concerns about the rate of incarceration of young black men and those who commit nonviolent drug offenses are growing. But the people who speak for people in prison are speaking for this socially deviant population that carries with it a severely negative construction.

In the second face of power, A *prevents* B's issues and interests from getting on the agenda or becoming policy, even when actor B really *wants* these issues raised. Again, criminals or potential criminals provide an extreme but vivid example of a group that may want change, but whose interests are denied a hearing. But even issues with some public support find it difficult to gain a place on the agenda. Environmentalism, for example, was, until the late 1960s and early 1970s, not a particularly powerful interest, and groups that promote environmental protection found that their issues rarely made the agenda because these issues in no way were those of the major economic and political forces that dominated decision making. Not until crises such as the environmental damage done by DDT, coupled with the writing of authors like Rachel Carson's book, *Silent Spring*, was the issue elevated to the point where some attention was paid to it.[8] Even then, one can argue that actor A, representing the business and industrial sector, bent but did not break on environmental issues and is still able to prevent B, the environmental movement, from advancing the comprehensive (some might say radical) ideas that could have a profound effect on the environment.

The blocking moves of the more powerful interests are not simply a function of A having superior resources to B, although this does play a substantial role. In essence, we should not think of the competition between actor A and actor B as a sporting event on an field, with even rules, between two teams, one vastly more powerful than the other. Rather, the teams' power imbalance is as much a function of the nature and rules of the game as it is a function of the particular attributes of the groups or interests themselves.

E.E. Schattschneider explains why this is the case:

> All forms of political organization have a bias in favor of the exploitation of some kinds of conflict and the suppression of others because *organization is the mobilization of bias*. Some issues are organized into politics while others are organized out.[9]

In other words, some issues are political because the bias of the political system allows them to be raised. Other issues do not come up because they are not, according to the bias of the system, fit for political consideration. There is no political right in America for people to have decent housing, or health care, or a job, because the bias of the American political system is heavily influenced by cultural values of self-reliance; this has led to the United States lagging behind other nations in the state provision of these goods. This bias is not static or God-given, but is continually reinforced by interests that, for whatever reason, oppose broader access to these things *as a matter of right*.

Other scholars of political power have conceived of a third face of power, which differs substantially from the second face of power in that large groups of people who objectively have a claim that they are disadvantaged remain *quiescent*—that is, passive—and fail to *attempt* to exert their influence, however small, on policy making and politics. This is the story John Gaventa tells in his book *Power and Powerlessness*.[10] In this book, Gaventa explains why a community of Appalachian coal miners remained under the repressive power of a British coal mining company and the local business and social elite. As Harry G. Reid notes in his review of the book,[11] Gaventa takes on the traditional idea that political participation in Appalachia is low because of the people's own shortcomings, such as low educational attainment and poverty. Rather, in the third face of power, social relationships and political ideology are structured over the long term in such a way that A, the mining company, remains dominant and B, the miners, cannot conceive of a situation in which they can begin to participate in the decisions that directly affect their lives. When B does begin to "rebel" against the unfair system, the dominant interests can employ their ability to make nondecisions: in essence, they ignore the pressure for change because they can withstand such pressures. In the long run, people may stop fighting as they become and remain alienated from politics; quiescence is the result.

This necessarily brief discussion of the idea of power is merely an overview of what is a very complex and important field of study in political science in general. It is important to us here because an understanding of power helps us understand how groups compete to gain access to the agenda *and* to deny access to groups and interests that would damage their interests.

Groups and Power in Public Policy

Social constructionist understandings of agenda setting complement E.E. Schattschneider's theories of group mobilization and participation, which rest on his oft-cited contention that issues are more likely to be elevated to agenda status if the scope of conflict is broadened. There are two key ways in which traditionally disadvantaged (losing) groups expand the scope of conflict. First, groups go public with a problem by using symbols and images to induce greater media and public sympathy for their cause. Environmental groups dramatize their causes by pointing to symbols and images of allegedly willful or negligent humanly caused environmental damage (for example, the *Exxon Valdez* spill).

Second, groups that lose in the first stage of a political conflict can appeal to a higher decision-making level, such as when losing parties appeal to state and then federal institutions for an opportunity to be heard, hoping that in the process they will attract others who agree with them to their cause. Conversely, dominant groups work to contain conflict to ensure that it does not spread out of control. The underlying theory of these tendencies dates to Madison's defense, in *Federalist* 10, of the federal system as a mechanism to contain political conflict.

Schattschneider's theories of issue expansion explain how in-groups retain control over problem definition and the way such problems are suppressed by dominant actors in policy making. These actors form what Baumgartner and Jones term *policy monopolies*,[12] which attempt to keep problems and underlying policy issues low on the agenda. Policy communities use agreed-upon symbols to construct their visions of problems, causation, and solution. As long as these images and symbols are maintained throughout society, or remain largely invisible and unquestioned, agenda access for groups that do not share these images is likely to be difficult; change is less likely until the less powerful group's construction of the problem becomes more prevalent. If alternative selection is key to the projection of political power, an important corollary is that powerful groups retain power by working to keep the public and out-groups unaware of underlying problems, alternative constructions of problems, or alternatives to their resolution.[13] If this argument sounds similar to elite theory, it is: many of the arguments made by proponents of group power such as C. Wright Mills and E.E. Schattschneider acknowledge the shortcomings of the pluralist approach. As Schattschneider famously put it, "The flaw in the pluralist heaven is that the heavenly chorus sings with a strong upper-class accent."[14] While an accent is not the same thing as perpetual upper-class or elite domination, it does suggest that the upper classes—the social, political, and economic elites—have power disproportionate to their numbers in society.

Overcoming the Power Deficit—Ways to Induce Policy Change

Baumgartner and Jones argue that when powerful groups lose their control of the agenda, less powerful groups can enter policy debates and gain attention to their issues. This greater attention to the problem area tends to increase negative public attitudes toward the status quo, which can then produce lasting institutional and agenda changes that break up policy monopolies.

There are several ways in which groups can pursue strategies to gain attention to issues, thereby advancing issues on the agenda. The first set of ways for less advantaged interest groups to influence policy making relates to Kingdon's streams metaphor of agenda change.[15] "Windows of opportunity" for change open when two or more streams—the political, problem, or policy streams—are coupled. In the political stream, electoral change can lead to reform movements that give previously less powerful groups an opportunity to air their concerns. Examples include the Lyndon Johnson administration, which promoted legislation collectively known as the Great Society. These programs sought to attack poverty, poor health, racial discrimination, and urban decline, among other problems. This package of programs was made possible by an aggressively activist president and a large Democratic majority in the Congress, the result of the Democratic landslide of 1964. Second, changes in our perception of problems will also influence the opening of a window of opportunity for policy change. In the 1930s, people began to perceive unemployment and economic privation not simply as a failure of individual initiative, but as a collective economic problem that required governmental solutions under the rubric of the New Deal. In the 1960s and 1970s, people began to perceive environmental problems, such as dirty air and water and the destruction of wildlife, not as the function of natural processes but as the result of negative human influences on the ecosystem. And, third, changes in the policy stream can influence the opening of the window of opportunity. In the 1960s, poverty and racism were seen as problems, but were also coupled with what were suggested as new and more effective policies to solve these problems, such as the Civil Rights Acts, the Voting Rights Act, and the "War on Poverty."

Lest we think that all this change is in the liberal direction, it is worth noting that other periods of change, notably the Reagan administration, were also characterized by the joining of these streams. These include changes in the political stream (more conservative legislators, growing Republican strength in the South, the advent of the Christian right as a political force), the problem stream (government regulation as cause, not the solution, of economic problems, American weakness in foreign affairs), and the policy stream (ideas for deregulation and smaller government, increased military spending and readiness) that came together during the first two years of the Reagan administration. These factors help explain policies favoring increased military spending, an increase in attention to moral issues, and a decrease in spending on social programs.

In each of these instances, it took group action to press for change. Groups worked to shine the spotlight on issues because, as Baumgartner and Jones argue, increased attention is usually negative attention to a problem, leading to calls for policy change to address the problems being highlighted.[16] But the simple desire to mobilize is not enough. Groups sometimes need a little help to push issues on the agenda; this help can come from changes in indicators of a problem or focusing events that create rapid attention. And groups often need to join forces to create a more powerful movement than they could create if they all acted as individuals.

Indicators, Focusing Events, and Agenda Change

John Kingdon discusses changes in indicators and focusing events as two ways in which groups and society as a whole learn of problems in the world. Changes in indicators are usually changes in statistics about a *problem*; if the data various agencies and interests collect indicate that things are getting worse, the issue will gain considerable attention.[17] Examples include changes in unemployment rates, inflation rates, the gross domestic product, wage levels and their growth, pollution levels, crime, student achievement on standardized tests, birth and death rates, and myriad other things that sophisticated societies count every year.

These numbers by themselves do not have an influence over which issues gain greater attention and which fall by the wayside. Rather, the changes in indicators need to be publicized by interest groups, government agencies, and policy entrepreneurs, who use these numbers to advance their preferred policy ideas. This is not to say that people necessarily play fast and loose with statistics; while statistics cited to drive home political points are often distorted to make a political point, groups can also cite official numbers to suggest that problems exist. The most familiar indicators, such as those reflecting the health of the economy, almost need no interpretation by interest groups or policy entrepreneurs—when unemployment is up and wages lag behind inflation, the argument is less about whether there is an economic problem but, rather, what to do about it.

An example of indicators used by less advantaged groups is the growing gap between rich and poor in the United States. In 1970, those households making $75,000 or more per year, in constant (1997) dollars, comprised 9 percent of all American households; by 1997, this group had doubled its share to 18.4 percent of all households. Where did the other groups shrink to make up this difference? The middle categories, those earning between $25,000 and $49,999, saw their share decrease from 37.2 percent of households in 1970 to 29.6 percent. This evidence is used to argue that the rich are getting richer, while the middle class and, to some extent, the lowest economic classes are worse off in terms of their share of the wealth.[18] While these numbers are not in great dispute, the *meaning* of the numbers is in dispute, and the numbers have not had much of an impact on public policy to date. On the other hand, indicators of educational attainment do have an impact on the agenda, causing periodic reform movements in public education. This is due, in large part, to the activism of the very influential teachers' unions, parent-teacher associations, and other groups that use these indicators to press for greater resources for schools. In the end, the numbers have to be interpreted by groups and advanced on the agenda in order to induce mass and policy maker attention.

Focusing events are somewhat different. Focusing events are sudden, relatively rare events that spark intense media and public attention because of their sheer magnitude or, sometimes, because of the harm they reveal. Focusing events thus attract attention to issues that may have been relatively dormant. Examples of focusing events include airplane accidents, industrial accidents such as factory fires or oil spills, large protest rallies or marches, scandals in government such as Iran-Contra, Watergate, and, to a lesser extent, the Clinton administration scandals, and events that are inherently unusual or that may be usual but have some feature that makes them noteworthy. Two examples of the latter are the alleged beating of motorist Rodney King by the Los Angeles Police Department in the early 1990s and O.J. Simpson's murder trial in 1995; the Rodney King incident was noteworthy because, unlike most such incidents, the event was caught on videotape, while the Simpson trial was noteworthy because of the fame of the defendant.

Focusing events can lead groups, government leaders, policy entrepreneurs, the news media, or members of the public to pay attention to new problems or pay greater attention to existing but dormant (in terms of their standing on the agenda) problems, and, potentially, can lead to a search for solutions in the wake of perceived policy failure.

The fact that focusing events occur with little or no warning makes such events important mobilization opportunities for groups that find their issues hard to advance on the agenda. Problems characterized by indicators of a problem will more gradually wax and wane on the agenda, and their movement on or off the agenda may be promoted or resisted by constant group competition. Sudden events, on the other hand, are associated with "spikes" of intense interest and agenda activity. Interest groups—often relatively powerful groups that seek to keep issues off the agenda—often find it difficult to keep major events off the news and institutional agendas. Groups that seek to advance an issue on the agenda can take advantage of such events to attract greater attention to the problem.

In many cases, the public and the most informed members of the policy community learn of a potential focusing event virtually simultaneously. These events can very rapidly alter mass and elite consciousness of a social problem. I say "virtually" because the most active members of a policy community may learn of an event some hours before the general public. A classic example is the grounding of the *Exxon Valdez* in Alaska in March 1989. This ship ran aground just after midnight in Alaska, or just after 4:00 A.M. on the East Coast. Most people were asleep when the spill occurred, but learned of it through the morning radio or TV news or late morning newspapers. Certain members of the policy community, however, such as key employees of the Exxon Corporation, the local Coast Guard contingent, fishers in southcentral Alaska, and others with a direct interest in the event, learned of the spill within minutes or hours. Still, the span of time that passed between local and national knowledge—or between elite and mass knowledge—of the spill was far too short for Exxon and its allies to contain news of the spill, which, therefore, suddenly became a very prominent issue on the agenda.

Group Coalescence and Strategies for Change

A major shortcoming of the elite theory, and of power theories, is that some interests simply accept their fate and give elite groups relatively little trouble. Related to this is the assumption that the elite is somehow a monolith, single-mindedly marching toward the same class-related goals. Neither of these assumptions is true. Less advantaged interests in the United States, and indeed the world, often fight against power, often against long odds and at considerable personal risk to the individuals involved. In the United States, fortunately most policy disputes can be entered without inviting the wrath of the state. Of course, it hardly need be said that powerful economic interests often conflict with each other, such as when producers of raw materials, such as oil and steel, want to raise prices and producers of goods that use these inputs seek to keep raw material costs low. Within industries, vicious battles over markets and public policy can result, as in the ongoing legal and economic battles between Microsoft and its rivals such as Netscape. We must also keep in mind that many movements that seek policy change are led by people whose socioeconomic condition and background are not vastly different from that of their political opponents. In this section, we will review how less advantaged interests, led by bright and persistent leaders, can and sometimes do overcome some of their power deficits.

The first thing to recognize about pro-change groups is that they, like more powerful interests, will often coalesce into advocacy coalitions. An advocacy coalition, as noted in Chapter 4, is a coalition of groups that come together based on a shared set of beliefs about a particular issue or problem. These are not necessarily these groups' core belief systems; rather, Paul Sabatier, the originator of the advocacy coalition framework, argues that groups will coalesce based not only on their core beliefs, but often on their more peripheral beliefs, provided that the coalition will advance their goals in the debate at hand. For example, after the *Exxon Valdez* oil spill in 1989, fishing and environmental interests coalesced to keep the oil spill on the agenda and to seek stringent new laws regulating oil transportation and the construction of tankers. Often, fishing and environmental interests are at odds with each other: fishers, understandably, want to be able to catch as many fish as possible and may have different ideas about the sustainability of a fishery than would environmentalists, who may value the fish as much for their aesthetic or spiritual value as for their value as a food commodity. Indeed, fishing interests are in disputes with environmentalists over the protection of seals and sea lions, which fishers believe eat too much of the fish in some regions, thereby reducing fish stocks. In these cases, the core beliefs of environmental and fishing interests are in conflict. But in the *Exxon Valdez* case, the fishing and environmental interests coalesced on their shared interest in maintaining a clean environment so that fish and other creatures could survive. Because of this shared interest, fishers and environmental groups could pool their resources and gain attention to their issues.

This is one way in which the dynamics of groups and coalitions can work to break down the power of dominant interests. Changes in indicators and focusing events may bring the issue to greater mass and policy maker attention and at the same time may induce groups to form coalitions to promote their common interests. This strength in numbers results in greater attention from policy makers and greater access to the policy making process, thereby forming what social scientists call *countervailing power* against the most powerful elites. But where should a group begin to seek to influence policy once it has formed a coalition and mobilized its allies and members? This question is addressed by Baumgartner and Jones in their discussion of "venue shopping."[19]

Venue shopping describes the efforts groups undertake to gain a hearing for their ideas and grievances against existing policy. By *venue* we mean a level of government or institution in which the group is likely to gain the most favorable hearing. We can think of venues in institutional terms—legislative, executive, or judicial—or in vertical terms—federal, state, local government. The news media are also a venue, and even within a branch of government, there are multiple venues.

Groups can seek to be witnesses before congressional committees and subcommittees where the chair is known to be sympathetic to their position or at least open-minded enough to hear their case. This strategy requires the cooperation of the leadership of the committee or subcommittee, and unsympathetic leaders will often block efforts to include some interests on witness lists. But the large number of committees and subcommittees in Congress, and their relative autonomy, allow groups to do some venue shopping within Congress itself, thereby increasing the likelihood that an issue can be heard. After a major focusing event, it is particularly hard to exclude aggrieved parties from a congressional hearing, and members whose support was formerly lukewarm may be more enthusiastic supporters when the magnitude of a problem becomes clearer. In the months after the *Exxon Valdez* oil spill, the number of witnesses representing fishing and environmental interests grew significantly, and oil company representatives were less prominent than they were in the policy process before the spill. Of course, as interest in the spill faded, the balance of forces returned somewhat to normal, but not to where it had been before the spill.

Groups that cannot gain a hearing in the legislative branch can appeal to executive branch officials. Environmentalists who cannot get a hearing in the House Resources Committee may turn to the Environmental Protection Agency, the Fish and Wildlife Service, the various agencies that compose the Department of the Interior, and other agencies that may be more sympathetic and might be able to use existing legal and regulatory means to advance environmental goals. While an appeal to these agencies may raise some conflict with the legislative branch, this tactic can at least open doors for participation by otherwise excluded groups.

Groups often engage in litigation as a way to get their issues on the agenda, particularly when other access points are closed to the group. A classic example of the litigation strategy involves the civil rights movement, in which black lawyers sued and desegregated law schools, graduate schools, universities, and, ultimately, all schools for blacks. While

Gerald Rosenberg argues that this litigation strategy was not entirely successful, requiring legislation to fully implement policy change, others argue that the legal strategy served as a catalyst for the civil rights movement and that landmark cases such as *Brown v. Board of Education* sparked a movement that resulted in more effective demands for change. Had the civil rights proponents not taken their fight to court, this argument holds, it is less likely that Congress and the president would have taken their claims seriously.[20]

Groups may appeal to local or state government before taking an issue to the federal government, because the issue may be easier to advance at the local level or because a grass-roots group may find it can fight on an equal footing with a more powerful group. This often happens in NIMBY (not in my back yard) cases, such as decisions on where to put group homes, cell phone towers, expanded shopping centers, power plants, and the like.

On the other hand, groups may expand conflict to a broader level (from local to state or state to federal) when they lose at the local level. E.E. Schattschneider calls this "expanding the scope of conflict." This strategy sometimes works because expanding the scope of conflict often engages the attention of other actors who may step in on the side of the less powerful group. An example of the expanding scope of conflict is the civil rights movement, which in many ways was largely confined to the South until images of violent crackdowns on civil rights protesters became more prominent on the evening news, thereby expanding the issue to a broader and somewhat more sympathetic public. Indeed, groups often seek media coverage as a way of expanding the scope of conflict. Media activities can range from holding news conferences to mobilizing thousands of people in protest rallies. Sometimes an issue is elevated to greater attention by the inherent newsworthiness of the event, without preplanning by the protest groups, such as the just-cited example of media coverage of civil rights protests.

Finally, gaining a place on the agenda often relies on coalescing with other groups, as was discussed earlier. Many of the great social movements of our time required that less powerful interests coalesce. Even the civil rights movement involved a coalition, at various times, with antiwar protestors, labor unions, women's groups, antipoverty workers, and other groups who shared an interest in racial equality. By coalescing in this way, the voices of all these interests were multiplied. Indeed, the proliferation of interest groups since the 1950s has resulted in greater opportunities for coalition building and has created far greater resources for countervailing power.

Before concluding this discussion, we must recognize that elevating issues on the agenda in hopes of gaining policy change is not always resisted by political elites. Cobb and Elder[21] argue that, when political elites seek change, they also try to mobilize publics to generate mass support for an issue, which supports elite efforts to move issues further up the agenda. Such efforts can constitute either attempts to broaden the ambit of existing policy monopolies or attempts by some political elites (such as the president and his staff) to circumvent the policy monopoly established by interest groups, the bureaucracy, and subcommittees (the classic iron triangle model). The president or other key political actors may be able to enhance the focusing power of an event by visiting a disaster or accident scene, thereby affording the event even greater symbolic weight.

The Social Construction of Problems and Issues

Humans and their governments are problem solvers. Many of the social and technological advances made throughout human history are solutions to problems: Vaccination is a solution to disease, the electrical light is a superior solution to the desire for illumination at night, and the wheel, the railroad, the telephone, and the airplane are solutions of the problems posed by distance.

At the same time, there remain many social problems that people believe should be "solved" or, at least, made better. Poverty, illiteracy, racism, immorality, disease, disaster, crime, and any number of other ills will lead people and groups to press for solutions. Often, these social problems require that governmental action be taken because services required to alleviate public problems that are not or cannot be addressed by private actors are *public goods* that can primarily be provided by government actors. While in the popular mind, and often in reality, economic and social conservatives believe in limited government activity, these conservatives also believe there are public goods, such as regulation of securities markets, road building, national defense, and public safety, that are most properly addressed by government. In the end, though, it is probably best to think about problems by thinking first about a clear definition of the problem itself, before concerning ourselves with whether public or private actors must remedy the problem. Beyond this, whether a problem really is a problem at all is an important part of political and policy debate.

The Social Construction of Problems

Problems can be defined and depicted in many different ways, depending on the goals of the proponent of the particular depiction of a problem and the nature of the problem and the political debate. The process of defining problems and of selling a broad population on this definition, is called *social construction*. Social construction refers to the ways in which we as a society and the various contending interests within it structure and tell the stories about how problems come to be the way they are. A group that can create and promote the most effective depiction of an issue has an advantage in the battle over what, if anything, will be done about a problem.

Deborah Stone, in *Policy Paradox*, considers how people tell the stories about how problems come to be by using *symbols*, *numbers*, and stories about *causes*.[22] Rather than summarize or paraphrase her argument, I will raise some issues highlighted by Stone and others, but particularly urge you to read Stone's book yourself to get a better sense of these important issues.

Before discussing symbols, problems, and stories, it is useful to consider the idea of a *problem* itself. The *American Heritage Dictionary* defines a problem as "a question or situation that presents uncertainty, perplexity, or difficulty" or "the source of trouble or annoyance." In politics and public policy, it is not hard to think of many problems that create all these feelings. Economic problems, the uneven distribution of resources, the forces of nature, the spread of diseases, social disorder, rapid technological change, fetters on business success caused by regulation, and many other features of modern life create considerable annoyance and uncertainty to some or many people. Indeed, we can think of public policy as being intended to solve problems so that some measure of uncertainty can be reduced. Social welfare programs can relieve the anxiety of worrying about what we will do if we lose our jobs; regulating content on television or the Internet can reduce our uncertainty over whether our children are seeing inappropriate sexual or violent images.

However, many policies that reduce one group's or person's uncertainty create a burden or greater uncertainty or "annoyance" for others. And for some people a pressing problem about which immediate action is required is for others merely a fact—sometimes unpleasant—about which nothing can be done, or a *condition*. People and groups will work very hard to prove that a problem *is* a problem about which something can and should be done. But merely stating a problem is not enough: one must persuade others that the problem is real or that the problem being cited is the *real* problem.

The way a problem is defined is an important part of this persuasive process and is important in the choice of solutions. Joseph Gusfield argues that one can look at the drunk driving problem in a number of ways.[23] Most of us tend to look at the drunk driving problem as one of individual responsibility: this presumes that stiffer penalties to punish the responsible are needed to address the problem. But what if we looked at the problem as one of inadequate transportation? If the United States had better systems of mass transit, it is likely that fewer people would need to drink and drive; they could drink and ride a bus or a train. Or what if the problem is deeply embedded in our culture, one that prizes recreation, relaxation, and even glamour and links these benefits to relatively easy access to alcohol by adults?

The social construction of a problem is linked to the existing social, political, and ideological structures at the time. The United States still values individual initiative and responsibility and therefore makes drinking and driving a matter of personal, not societal, responsibility. The same values of self-reliance and individual initiative are behind many of our public policies, dealing with free enterprise, welfare, and other economic policies. These values differentiate our culture from other nations' cultures, where the community or the state takes a more important role. In those countries, problems are likely to be constructed differently, and different policies are the result.

Conditions and Problems

Conditions can develop over time into problems as people develop ways to address conditions. Until Dr. Jonas Salk developed the polio vaccine, millions of children and their parents lived in fear of this crippling disease. Without the polio vaccine, this disease was simply a dreaded condition that could perhaps be avoided (people kept their kids away from swimming pools, for example, to avoid contracting polio) but certainly not treated or prevented without very high social costs. However, as medical technology progressed, polio became a *problem* about which something more effective than quarantining children could be done. In this case, governments—in particular, public health officials—have responded by encouraging or directly providing polio vaccine to children. Today, the polio rate is vastly lower than it was just sixty years ago, and one can plausibly argue that the polio problem is largely solved. Today, the discussion of polio revolves more around the safest method (oral or via injection) of vaccination than around the disease itself: in other words, the solution became a problem in its own right, although not as big a problem as the disease itself.[24]

When people become dependent on solutions to previously addressed problems, then the interruption of the solution will often constitute a major problem, resulting in efforts to prevent any such interruptions. Have you ever had the power fail while working at a computer or watching a favorite show on television? One year, when I was in high school, the power failed while nearly everyone in my hometown was watching the Super Bowl, leading to howls of anger from most people in the city. One hundred and fifty years ago, this would not have constituted a major problem, because electricity or television as a solution to a problem—cold, dark, social isolation, or boredom—did not exist.

Today, an interruption in the supply of electricity and other utilities is a problem that we believe can be ameliorated—indeed, we believe it should never happen at all! And lest we believe a power outage is a minor inconvenience with few political repercussions, consider the power outage that struck Auckland, New Zealand, in February 1998.[25] The outage lasted for over ten days, closing businesses, forcing evacuations of apartments due to water and sewer failures, and ending up costing New Zealanders millions of dollars. The cause of the outage was the failure of overtaxed power cables; regardless of its cause, people do not expect, nor lightly tolerate, the loss of something taken for granted for so long.

Many problems are not as obvious and dramatic as the Auckland power outage. After all, it did not take a lot of argument to persuade those evacuated from their apartments that there was some sort of problem! But other problems are more subtle, and people have to be persuaded that something needs to be done; still more persuasion may be necessary to induce a belief that government needs to do something about a problem.

Symbols

Because policy making is usually a process of political argument and persuasion, groups and individuals promoting particular policy options will work to gain whatever rhetorical advantage they can in these debates. Because a hallmark of successful policy advocacy is the ability to tell a good story, groups will use time-tested rhetorical devices, such as the use of symbols, to advance their arguments.

A *symbol* is "anything that stands for something else. Its meaning depends on how people interpret it, use it, or respond to it."[26] Politics is full of symbols, some perceived as good, others as bad, and still others as controversial. Some symbols are fairly obvious: the American flag, for example, is generally respected in the United States, while flying a swastika flag is considered in very bad taste.

Deborah Stone outlines four elements of the use of symbols. First, she discusses *narrative stories*, which are stories told about how things happen, good or bad. They are usually highly simplified and offer the hope that complex problems can be solved with relatively easy solutions. Such stories are staples of the political circuit, where candidates tell stories about wasteful bureaucrats or evil businessmen or lazy welfare cheats to rouse the electorate to elect the candidate, who will impose a straightforward solution to these problems. Stories are told about how things are getting worse or *declining*, in Stone's term, or how things were getting better until something bad happened to stop progress, or how "change-is-only-an-illusion" (p. 142). An example of this last is the stories told on the campaign trail and on the floor of the legislature in which positive economic indicators are acknowledged but are said not to reflect the real problems that real people are having.

Helplessness and control is another common story of how something once could not be done but now something can be done about an issue or problem. This story is closely related to the condition/problem tension.

Often used in these stories is a rhetorical device called *synecdoche* (sin-ECK'-do-key), "a figure of speech in which the whole is represented by one of its parts" (p. 145). Phrases such as "a million eyes are on the Capitol today" represent great attention to Congress's actions on a particular issue. In other cases, people telling stories about policy use anecdotes or prototypical cases to explain an entire phenomenon. Thus, as Stone notes, the idea of the cheating "welfare queen" took hold in the 1980s, even though such people represented a small and atypical portion of the welfare population. Related to such stories are "horror stories" of government regulation run amok. Such stories are usually distorted: Stone cites the example of how those opposed to industry regulation claimed that the Occupational Safety and Health Administration (OSHA) "abolished the tooth fairy" by requiring that dentists discard any baby teeth they pulled; the actual regulation merely required that appropriate steps be taken to protect health workers from any diseases that may be transmitted in handling the teeth. Recently, the media stirred up a small controversy by reporting that OSHA was advising companies with home workers that companies are responsible for the health and safety of these home workers in their own offices. The media, elected officials, and business interests raised the specter of OSHA invading every home worker's privacy to inspect their work space; this horror story, coupled with long-standing industry dislike for OSHA and the prior propagation of horror stories, made this a very compelling and disturbing prospect. The truth of the matter was more subtle: OSHA had simply sent a letter to an employer that interpreted its existing rules on workplace safety, stating that the employer does bear some responsibility for home workers' safety in home offices. Regardless of this important distinction, OSHA backed away from the letter in the face of media ridicule and political pressure.[27]

You probably have heard or even told these and other horror stories about policies. Television news shows like *20/20, 60 Minutes*, and *Dateline* have made an industry out of telling these horror stories, often failing to place them in their proper context. In the same way, interest groups are not often interested in placing stories in their proper perspective; rather, groups are most interested in advancing their policy preferences. Interest groups will therefore tell stories that stretch the truth to the breaking point, to gain attention from other members of the policy community and to mobilize support or opposition for a particular policy direction.

Causal Stories

An important part of story telling in public policy is the telling of *causal stories*.[28] These stories attempt to explain what caused a problem or an outcome. These stories are particularly important in public policy making, because the depiction of the cause of a problem strongly suggests a solution to the problem. In general, Stone divides causal stories into four categories: mechanical causes, accidental causes, intentional causes, and inadvertent causes. These examples are shown in Table 5.1.

Contestants in policy disputes will fight for the depiction of the cause of a problem that is most consistent with their goals. A particularly apt example of disputes over causal stories is the story about the causes of

Table 5.1

Types of Causal Theories with Examples

Actions	Consequences	
	Intended	Unintended
Unguided	MECHANICAL CAUSE	ACCIDENTAL CAUSE
	intervening agents	nature
	brainwashed people	weather
	machines that perform as	earthquakes
	designed, but cause harm	machines that run amok
Purposeful	INTENTIONAL CAUSE	INADVERTENT CAUSE
	oppression	intervening conditions
	conspiracies that work	unforeseen side effects
	programs that work as intended,	avoidable ignorance
	but cause harm	carelessness
		omission

Source: From *Policy Paradox and Political Reason* by Deborah A. Stone. Copyright © 1997, 1998 by Deborah A. Stone. Used by permission of W.W. Norton & Company, Inc.

the *Exxon Valdez* oil spill in 1989. The *Exxon Valdez* ran aground in Prince William Sound, spilling about 11 million gallons of oil into what was often depicted as "pristine wilderness." Immediately, the search began for someone to blame for the spill: who caused the spill of the *Exxon Valdez*? Exxon and the captain of the *Exxon Valdez*, Joseph Hazelwood, argued that the spill was an accident or an "act of God," because the tanker was trying to avoid icebergs that had broken from nearby Columbia Glacier. This explanation was widely dismissed, because the captain was discovered to have been legally drunk and because of his apparently poor seamanship. Exxon's opponents argued that Exxon assumed the blame for staffing cuts on tankers leading to tired and stressed crews, and blamed the oil companies for failing to keep the promises they made when the pipeline was originally built. In these stories, the cause moved from the realm of accident to the realm of inadvertent causes: the spill was caused by the captain's "carelessness" or even Exxon's "avoidable ignorance" of the likelihood of a spill and its consequences.[27]

Many environmental groups, however, moved the causal theory to the "intended" side of Stone's typology. They argued that lax government regulation and continued pressures for profit led Exxon to take shortcuts in the hiring, training, and supervision of its tanker crews. Crews did not get enough rest for the grueling voyage from Alaska to California, and ships were understaffed compared with previous years. Meanwhile, the oil industry had failed to meet its obligations to be ready to respond to an *Exxon Valdez*–sized oil spill.

These three stories—the act of God, drunken captain, and willfully negligent company stories—all competed for public attention and sympathy. In the end, Exxon suffered a severe public relations blow because its preferred stories were not well accepted. Federal law passed in the wake of the spill accepted the story that the government and industry had been lax in addressing the potential of a large spill and created a new regulatory scheme, initially opposed by industry, that would make such spills much more expensive, from a clean-up and liability perspective, than they had been before the spill. In the end, the policy reflected the causal story that was most broadly accepted, thereby illustrating the importance of telling plausible and persuasive stories. This is why interest groups and companies hire public relations firms and spend millions a year burnishing their images and the stories of their companies' work.

Numbers As Indicators of Problems

Debates and controversies often involve the use of numerical information to make their points. Such numbers include the number of people living in poverty, the average amount of taxes people pay to the government, the number of people killed or hurt by various hazards, and so on. The use of numbers in policy debates is very attractive because numbers appear to have accuracy that anecdotal evidence lacks, particularly when the numbers provide a description of *aggregate data*—that is, when the data reflect a broader phenomenon. Such aggregate data include the unemployment rate, average school test scores, median family income, and the like.

The use of numbers is particularly interesting, as Stone points out, because deciding to count a phenomenon is a policy decision itself. We collect data about phenomena because we want to know something more about them. We count unemployment, crime, health, education, and other statistics. Once we begin to start counting, there is considerable pressure to continue counting to see how problems are behaving: we want *indicators* of good things to go up (the gross domestic product (GDP), wages, educational achievement) and bad things to go down (diseases and death, crime, welfare rolls). For each of these things, there is political pressure to make the problem better.

But numbers are not entirely objective measures of a phenomenon. Indeed, they are *indicators* of a problem; that is, they measure the underlying problem, but they are not the same as the underlying problem itself. Some of these indicators are problematic, for several reasons.

First, the numbers themselves are of questionable accuracy. Numbers on the GDP, unemployment, inflation, test scores, and so on have often been challenged. The census, which the Constitution requires be taken every ten years, is notorious for undercounting immigrants and minorities, placing cities at a disadvantage in the allocation of federal funds dispersed on the basis of population. Educational tests, such as the Scholastic Assessment Test, are often accused of being racially and ethnically biased, such that the scores do not accurately reflect the academic potential of all the people who are taking the tests. Perhaps the most notoriously questionable statistics come from the Uniform Crime Reports (UCR), collected by the United States Department of Justice. The UCR compiles reports of crime from police departments nationwide; but they include only those crimes about which the police have information. They do not include unreported crimes; what is more, some police departments may have an incentive to inflate or underreport crimes. In some cases, when police place special emphasis on particular crimes such as domestic violence, the apparent rate of crime goes up because more crime is reported and known to the police.[30]

Second, even if some measures are reasonably accurate, an important question remains: whether the indicator in question is the best measure of a phenomenon or of progress toward a goal. For example, the GDP is a measure of all the goods and services produced in the nation; when it is growing from quarter to quarter or year to year, this is said to be a good thing; the financial press concentrates a great deal of attention on this figure. Yet the GDP may not be the best measure of *overall well-being.* Does the GDP, for example, deduct from the value of some goods the pollution and subsequent environmental damage they cause? Indeed, if there is an environmental disaster, such as an oil spill, the money spent to clean up the spill is included in the GDP. Other things that perhaps we would not want to spend money on, such as lawyers' fees, cancer treatment, and fixing car wrecks, are all counted in the GDP. Thus, economic growth may not equate with the good life, but rather reflects all the things that we spend money on, including the things we might not really want to buy.[31]

Third, the choice of the statistic being reported has a big influence on how one is supposed to interpret the underlying idea being conveyed. For example, let us take King County, Washington, the county that includes Seattle and, quite important, Redmond, the home of Microsoft and of Bill Gates. There are at least three major billionaires in the Seattle area: Bill Gates, who as of this writing is worth over $100 billion; Paul Allen, a cofounder of Microsoft, worth about $50 billion; and Jeff Bezos, founder of Amazon.com, worth about $5 billion.

There are 2 million people in King County, but let us assume that there are only 100 people in the county: the three mentioned and ninety-seven other people, each with a net worth of $1 million, which is not poverty level, but is *a hundred thousand times* less wealthy than Bill Gates. If we were to simply average all 100 people's net worth, we would say that these 100 people were very, very wealthy indeed, with an average net worth of a little more than $1.5 billion! But what if we choose to represent this community's wealth by showing the *median* net worth: the median is the middle value in a set of values. In our example, the middle value is $1 million; that is, over one thousand times less than the average. Or we could represent the wealth of the category by showing the modal value, which is the most often occurring value in the series, which is also $1 million.

This example is less an expression of the prosperity of King County than it is an extreme example of how the choice of statistics can influence the conclusion we reach about information. In statistical terms, Bill Gates, Paul Allen, and Jeff Bezos are called *outliers*—they fall outside the range of the bulk of the data points. This example shows why we sometimes talk in terms of median figures, such as median family income or median home prices: because if we used the mean or average of these figures, the few outliers, such as the really expensive houses or the really well-paid people, would distort the story we are trying to tell with the numbers.[32]

Many of you have taken (or are required to take) a statistics class or two in your studies as social science, science, or other majors. Many of us approach such classes with trepidation. But the example just shown shows how useful some background in statistics can be for your own political self-defense. Being able to find and explain statistical fallacies is a very important skill in our number-driven world.

Finally, two things you should know about numbers and their depiction in policy debates. First, advocates for policy positions will always choose numbers that put their arguments in the best light. This means that the use of numbers is likely to be significantly skewed or distorted for rhetorical advantage. This distortion is most often seen in charts and graphs, which citizens and policy makers must use with extreme caution. Many charts and graphs are deliberately or accidentally misleading, and it is an unfortunate byproduct of modern printing and publishing technology that allows newspapers and magazines (*USA Today* being notorious for this) to print remarkably misleading and distorted statistical graphs. Indeed, with the advent of desktop publishing and the ease of creating graphics for the World Wide Web, nearly anyone with a personal computer and a spreadsheet program can create charts and graphs that range from hard to read to purposefully misleading. Edward Tufte's three-volume series on graphic design discusses these problems and will arm you with considerable defenses against what he calls "chartjunk."[33]

Second, and summarizing this discussion, there is a difference between a number (that is, a data point) and the interpretation of that data. There is an old saying in information management that there is a big difference between data and information: data are just the raw numbers, while information is what we get when we interpret the numbers—and as you know, that information is very much subject to the interpretation of those with a stake in the meaning of that information.

Conclusion

The study of agenda setting is a particularly fruitful way to begin to understand how groups, power, and the agenda interact to set the boundaries of political policy debate. But agenda setting, like all other stages of the policy process, does not occur in a vacuum. The likelihood that an issue will rise on the agenda is a function of the issue itself, the actors that get involved, institutional relationships, and, often, random social and political factors that can be explained but cannot be replicated or predicted.

6

Policies and Policy Types

This chapter discusses the nature and substance of policies themselves. Because a definition of *policy* has not yet been outlined in this book, the chapter begins with a broad definition of policy. The bulk of the chapter then turns to a discussion of the different ways to categorize policies into different policy types. The effort to place policies into types has consumed a considerable amount of time and effort among political scientists, for good reason. Most political scientists seek to create policy typologies because we suspect, based on intuition and experience, that some policies will involve more groups, lead to more conflict, and will be more visible than other types of policies. There is no final word on how best to categorize policies, so when reading this chapter, it is important not to simply learn how to pigeonhole policies into different categories, but to consider the strengths and weaknesses of each typology in telling us something meaningful about the way policy is made and what its results likely will be.

What Is a "Policy"?

As we discussed in Chapter 1, public policy is, in general, what the government, acting on our behalf, chooses to do or not to do. This suggests a working definition of policy that may seem obvious, but that is a bit more complex than the simplest definition.

I define a *policy* as a statement by government of what it intends to do or not to do, such as a law, regulation, ruling, decision, or order, or a combination of these. For example, a law that says that those caught driving while intoxicated will go to jail for up to one year is a statement of governmental policy to punish drunk drivers. The National Environmental Policy Act (NEPA) is a statement of government policy toward the environment. Judicial decisions are also statements of policy: the Supreme Court's decision in *Brown v. Board of Education* is a statement of policy that the government cannot and will not support racially segregated schools.

Forms of Policies

Imagine if presidents made policy by decree. In such a world, the president's word would likely compel compliance, since the president would be the only actor to whom all policy implementers would be accountable. If the president signed a law stating that the rivers will be fishable and swimmable in five years, then all agencies would work toward this one goal. This would be a simple, effective way of declaring policy and seeing that it is carried out.

Clearly, the American political system is not this simple. A major theme of any book on policy studies is the division of powers, both among the three branches of government and among the various levels of government. In addition, policies are often not implemented the way the designers intended, as discussed in Chapter 7.

Because the American system of government consists of three branches of the federal government, plus fifty states each with three branches, plus 80,000 local governments, many of which are themselves organized along the three branches, there is obviously considerable complexity in designing and delivering a policy. Thus, a public policy is not simply one document. It is a collection of documents, statements, decisions, and other elements.

Let us return to an example used earlier in this book, the Turtle Exclusion Device (TED). A TED is part of a shrimp trawling net that is designed to catch shrimp while allowing sea turtles to escape. The sea turtle is an endangered species under the Endangered Species Act, which was enacted as Public Law (PL) 93–205 codified as 16 U.S.C. (United States Code) 742a *et seq.*, 1361a *et seq.*, and 1531–1544. This law is known as the *authority* for *regulations* to be passed by the implementing agency to enforce the meaning of the Endangered Species Act.

Under the *Administrative Procedures Act* (5 U.S.C. 500 et seq.), the federal government is required to follow particular procedures in its drafting and publishing of regulations. One way that the government meets these obligations is by publishing notices of proposed rules (which people sometimes call regulations), final rules, and other material in the *Federal Register*. The *Federal Register* is the daily publication of federal regulatory activity and can be accessed on line and in most university libraries.

Once a federal law has passed, the implementing agency—in this case, the National Marine Fisheries Service, a unit of the National Oceanic and Atmospheric Administration—must implement the law by issuing regulations, which consist of more detailed guidelines and rules for putting the intent of the law into effect. The regulatory process requires that proposed rules be published in the *Federal Register*, and when the rules go into effect they are codified in the *Code of Federal Regulations*.

Why doesn't the Congress just draft and apply the rules? First, Congress delegates the drafting of rules to others, in this case the National Marine Fisheries Service, because laws are not intended to specify every element of their implementation. Lawmaking would be difficult, if not impossible, if we asked the Congress to specify every aspect of the implementation of every program or policy. In this example, there are many endangered species, and many different agencies have to pick the best way to protect these species. For example, you may remember that, in the early and mid-1990s, the United States Forest Service, a unit of the United States Department of Agriculture, was embroiled in a serious controversy involving protection of the northern spotted owl, a species that lives in the forests of the Pacific Northwest. This is considerably different from the turtle issue, and it is difficult, if not impossible, for Congress to draft highly technical laws for species as diverse as turtles and spotted owls. Even if Congress wanted to draft the detailed rules for every aspect of legislation, the public would demand opportunities for comment and input into the rule making process, such that Congress would find itself bogged down simply in the process of making rules.

A second reason for having agencies draft rules is that the implementing agencies have considerably greater expertise than does Congress and considerably greater resources for designing rules and managing the process.

A third reason is that the bureaucracy is depicted by many as being more "neutral" than the more "political" Congress. Congress can draw the broad parameters of policy and leave the bureaucracy to fill in the gaps, using neutral expertise rather than political judgment. Of course, the degree to which the bureaucracy is truly neutral is open to question.

Policy Types

An important element of the public policy process is an understanding of how various interests are organized and how various interests react to different kinds of policies. We consider these two issues in one section because the two concepts are inextricably linked—one cannot profitably discuss policy types without understanding their apparent influence on politics, including group organization, mobilization, and reaction.

Like many elements of policy studies, work on creating typologies of public policies started with a great deal of enthusiasm, but quickly bogged down into some major problems. We will discuss these problems, but we wish to stress that the value of at least thinking about policy typologies is still great; such typologies are useful in understanding how and why some policies are made the way they are, and why some groups do better than others in policy debates and actual enactment. Again, as we stress throughout the book, the application of these theories is often more important than the internal consistency of the theories themselves.

The earliest policy typologies generally separated policy into topical categories: education policy, health policy, or transportation policy, for example. This system was useful for sorting different kinds of policy domains, but it did not help us draw general conclusions about the *politics* that underlie these policies. The particular problem is that, by failing to tell us something more *generalizable* across the policy domains, these simple typologies made it difficult to learn from other types of policies and their underlying politics: by lumping together all policy types in one category, we were no closer to understanding similarities and differences among and between policies in all *domains* and were therefore no closer to a useful science of public policy.

Distributive, Redistributive, and Regulatory Policies

One of the most persistent efforts among policy scholars is the work intended to develop categories of public policies, or what we call *typologies*. The modern era of developing policy typologies began in 1964 when Theodore Lowi laid out the classic policy types often taught in undergraduate and many graduate courses today.[1] In simplest terms, Lowi divides policies into three categories: distributive, redistributive, and regulatory policy. Later, Ripley and Franklin updated the typologies by dividing regulatory policy into two categories, protective regulatory and competitive regulatory.[2] The updated Ripley and Franklin formulation is shown in Table 6.1.

Table 6.1

Actors, Stability, and Visibility of Various Policy Types

Policy type	Primary actors	Relationship among actors	Stability of relationship	Visibility of decision
Distributive	Congressional subcommittees and committees; executive bureaus; small interest groups	Logrolling (everyone gains)	Stable	Low
Protective regulatory	Congressional subcommittees and committees; full House and Senate; executive agencies; trade associations	Bargaining; compromise	Unstable	Moderate
Competitive regulatory	Subcommittees; executive bureaus and commissions; small interest groups	Logrolling among favored actors	Stable	Very low; very little full congressional involvement
Redistributive	President and his appointees; committees and/or Congress; largest interest groups (peak associations); "liberals/conservatives"	Ideological and class conflict	Stable	High

Influence of

Policy type	President, presidency, and centralized bureaucracy	Bureaus	Congress as a whole	Congressional subcommittees	Private sector
Distributive	Low	High	Low (supports subcommittees)	High	High (subsidized groups)
Protective regulatory	Moderately high	Moderate	Moderately high	Moderate	Moderately high (regulated interests)
Competitive regulatory	Low	High (regulatory agencies)	Low	Moderate to low	High (regulated interests)
Redistributive	High	High	High	Moderately low	High ("peak associations" representing clusters of interest groups)

Source: Table adapted from *Congress, the Bureaucracy, and Public Policy,* by Randal B. Ripley and Grace A. Franklin. Copyright © 1991 by Harcourt, Inc. Reprinted by permission of the publisher.

Distributive Policies

Distributive policies involve the granting of some sort of benefit to a particular interest group or other well-defined, relatively small group of beneficiaries. Examples of distributive policy include farm subsidies and federal spending on local infrastructure projects like dams, flood control systems, aviation, highways, and schools. These benefits are usually distributed in the process of developing authorization and appropriations bills as part of the budgeting process.[3]

Distributive policy allows for a considerable amount of negotiation and distribution of benefits to members of Congress, because they cite their effectiveness in bringing home money from Washington in their reelection campaigns. Because all members benefit equally from this "pork-barrel" spending, there is a powerful incentive to engage in what political scientists call *logrolling*, in which members pledge to vote for each other's funding bills. For example, a member of an urban congressional district may pledge to support a rural member's farm subsidy bill in exchange for support for a mass transportation bill. This "horse trading" is probably necessary for the expeditious passage of federal spending bills, but Congress's procedures and norms also encourage this sort of negotiation, leading to more "pork-barrel" spending, which serves to allow members to "bring home the bacon" to their districts.

Distributive policy making is made even easier by the inability, in this style of policy making, to easily identify particular groups of people that are benefiting from the policy, while the costs of the policy are more broadly spread across society. Local officials and congressional representatives depict these policies as good for the local community, but as being paid for by the entire nation through general federal funds. Indeed, local spending programs are often justified as a way of gaining a community's "fair share" of federal taxes paid by the district or state's taxpayers. Because of the actual or assumed benefits to particular people without any countergroups seeking to stop spending, there is little conflict over distributive policy. It is usually made fairly quickly, easily, and with a minimum amount of scrutiny of individual spending decisions. When the news media or other members do scrutinize such spending, there may sometimes be a call for reform of this system, but the benefits of the current system of pork are so clear that the system of distributive policy endures.

This type of policy making is problematic in a democracy, as Theodore Lowi notes in *The End of Liberalism*.[4] Because government programs

often create beneficiaries and create groups to represent these beneficiaries, the United States is now characterized by what Lowi calls *inter-*
est group liberalism, in which all claims to federal support and funding
are assumed to be legitimate, and few, if any, decisions are made to
separate the most compelling claims from the most minor. In such a
system, the elected branches of government are more interested in servicing particular interests than in servicing the public interest—or at
least something approximating it—as a whole.

Regulatory Policies

Regulatory policies are, in general terms, policies that are intended to
govern the conduct of business. There are two broad types of regulatory
policies. *Competitive regulatory policy* involves policies designed to
"limit the provision of goods and services to one or a few designated
deliverers, who are chosen from a larger number of competing potential
deliverers."[5] Ripley and Franklin cite the allocation of radio and television frequencies and the awarding of cable television franchises as examples. Another example is policies intended to regulate trades or
professions, such as law, medicine, engineering, electrical and plumb-
ing contractors, or hairstyling. States generally assign the power to li-
cense professions to members of that particular profession: lawyers,
through the state bar associations, and physicians, through their state
medical associations, are licensed and regulated by their peers. This system assures professional oversight over the activities of professionals,
who must be trained and regulated to assure competent service to their
clients. These policies, on the other hand, also create barriers to enter a
profession, thereby limiting the number of professionals who provide a
service and, possibly, maintaining high fees.

For the most part, competitive regulatory policy is made without much
public scrutiny. Much of this policy is made at the state level, further ensuring its low visibility, and the most active participants in such policies tend to
be at the legislative committee and trade group levels. Much of this type of
policy is relatively arcane and stimulates little public notice.

Protective regulatory policy, on the other hand, is intended to protect
the public at large from the negative effects of private activity, such as
tainted food, air pollution, unsafe consumer products, or fraudulent business transactions. While most businesses and their leaders are responsible citizens who do not wish to hurt or alienate their customers,

businesses are also motivated by profit. Businesses often resist regulation on cost grounds, saying that it would reduce or eliminate profit margins, make products uncompetitive on the market, place firms at competitive disadvantages vis-à-vis their foreign competitors (or competitors in other states, if the policy is made at the state level), and so on.

Because businesses resist regulation while regulatory agencies insist that they are acting in the public interest, protective regulatory policy tends to be highly contentious. Congressional committees and the full body of Congress get involved, along with major trade organizations (such as the National Association of Manufacturers or the American Banking Association). Decisions are reached based on negotiation and compromise, because, in most cases, neither business nor the regulators can entirely dominate policy making; Congress and its committees are often put in the position of broker, mediating between the goals of the regulatory agency and business interests.

Redistributive Policy

Redistributive policy is highly controversial, involving the highest levels of government and the leaders of what are called *peak associations* in policy making characterized by a high level of conflict and difficulty in changing policy.

Redistributive policy is characterized by actions "intended to manipulate the allocation of wealth, property, personal or civil rights, or some other valued item among social classes or racial groups."[6] Based on this definition, obvious examples include welfare, civil rights for racial or social minorities, aid to poor cities or schools, and the like. While there has been considerable redistributive policy making in the United States since the Roosevelt administration, these policies are difficult to pass because passage requires that the less powerful prevail over the more powerful interests or at least persuade more powerful groups that it is right and just to approve the redistribution of some resource to the less powerful.

It is worth noting, however, that redistributive policy can involve the transfer of resources from the less well off to the better off. During the Reagan administration, the recipients of federal redistributive benefits—the poor, urban areas, economically depressed areas—were depicted as unworthy recipients, and the policies intended to help them were severely criticized. The growing dismay with relatively expensive federal social programs, coupled with the disdain felt by many people for these programs' recipients, created a political atmosphere in which it became easier—and even politically acceptable—to propose policies such as tax cuts that shifted benefits from the poor to the wealthy.[7]

Still, some people do speak for the less powerful, and any redistribution of resources—money or rights—is expected to engender considerable controversy. Such policies include the classic welfare policies and also civil rights and liberties policies. The civil rights example is a good illustration of this notion of at least the *perception* of the redistribution of rights. When blacks began to demand the rights and resources guaranteed them under the Constitution—rights such as equal educational, housing, and job opportunities, the right to vote, and the right to due process in criminal proceedings)—many people resisted these policies because they believed that they would somehow be losers if blacks were "winners" of these rights. Civil rights legislation was passed in the mid-1960s, but only with high-level governmental participation and after intense and rancorous debate that suffused political and social life from Washington to Main Street.

Lowi's ideas continue to be quite influential, and for good reason. As Daniel McCool argues, Lowi is a leading theorist of policy types because he approaches policies not merely as outputs of government but as something that shapes and is shaped by political conflict. Thus, in the typology described in Table 6.1, the nature and visibility of political conflict will differ considerably with the type of policy in question.

You can apply these ideas to your own policy interests to understand how the politics of your issues of greatest interest will play out. For example, if you deeply appreciate the natural world, you may be very interested in environmental policy. As you know, however, environmental policies have been historically contentious, and the politics of environmental policy often involves the highest levels of government in a particular area. Environmental policy shares many of the characteristics of protective regulatory policy: high levels of trade association, executive, and legislative involvement, high visibility, considerable conflict, but also a propensity to be addressed via compromise. You might conclude that your participation in environmental policy making would be most effective if you joined with an existing environmental group, such as the Natural Resources Defense Council or Sierra Club, to contribute your voice to the debate. This is because your lone voice would be drowned out by the thousands of other voices in this policy domain.

James Q. Wilson: Concentrated and Diffuse Costs and Benefits

A persistent criticism of Lowi's typology of policies is that it is difficult to assign policies to just one category. Some policies have redistributive and regulatory attributes, such as the regulation of consumer product safety that redistributes the responsibility for risk away from consumers and to the companies that manufacture products. This also has a strong regulatory component. James Q. Wilson, in response to these problems with Lowi's conception of policy types, developed a policy typology that rejects the use of ambiguous policy types and considers instead a way of arranging policies in terms of the extent to which their costs and benefits are focused on one particular party or diffused, is spread across numerous people or interests. This typology is depicted in Table 6.2.

What might be the easiest policies to advocate and enact? In this typology, a policy that provides an obvious benefit to one group would motivate that group to press for enactment of the policy; its task would be made even easier if the costs of the policy are hard to assign to a particular group, that is, if the costs are distributed broadly throughout some larger group. Wilson cites as examples the Civil Aeronautics Board (CAB) and the Federal Communications Commission (FCC) as two agencies that administer this kind of clientele-oriented policy. In the aviation example, before the major airlines were deregulated in 1978, the CAB regulated airline routes and fares, and airlines had to apply to and gain approval from the CAB to gain permission to fly a new route or to change fares. This system meant that the airlines enjoyed a substantial benefit (protection against cut-rate competition) while the burden of this policy, in the form of higher fares, fell on the flying public. In a similar way, the FCC's policies for licensing broadcasters ensure that the number of radio and TV stations in a market remains relatively fixed, thereby creating some stability at the expense of the general public, which may favor a greater number of broadcast voices.

On the other hand, if the costs are easily pinned to a particular group or interest, it is likely that the cost-bearing group will take steps to oppose the policy. There are two examples of this in Wilson's typology. If the costs are concentrated and the benefits are concentrated, a style of policy making involving interest group conflict becomes prominent. Wilson's example is the battle between labor and business interests in the field of occupational safety. In particular, both the enactment and

Table 6.2

Wilson's Cost-Benefit Policy Typology

		Benefits	
		Concentrated among very few people	Distributed among many people
	Concentrated among very few people	Interest group politics: conflict between groups that would benefit and those that would bear the costs. Treated as a zero-sum game.	Entrepreneurial politics: groups and their leaders seek to persuade policy makers to regulate in the public interest, in the face of opposition from the groups that would bear the cost.
Costs	Distributed among many people	Clientele oriented politics: close "clientele" relationships between policy makers, regulators, and the regulated interest.	Majoritarian politics: relatively loose groups of people, or those acting on their behalf, who seek a substantive or symbolic statement of policy. Often leads to weak, ambiguous policies.

Source: Derived from James Q. Wilson, *Political Organizations* (Princeton: Princeton University Press, 1995).

implementation of the Occupational Safety and Health Act, and its administration by the Occupational Safety and Health Administration (OSHA), have led to fierce battles between labor unions and business, because the participants in this debate believe that the benefits of this policy flow to a relatively small number of interests (labor) and are paid for by a relatively small number of interests (business).

Another example involving concentrated costs involves regulation of business in the interest of public safety. Wilson uses highway safety policy, as administered by the National Highway Traffic Safety Administration (NHTSA), as an example of a policy that distributes benefits (safer cars) very broadly across the driving public, but that places the more immediate burdens on the automobile manufacturers. In this case, NHTSA is confronted with a hostile target of regulation, and politics are likely to remain fairly contentious. This policy type is called entrepreneurial policy because policy entrepreneurs and interest groups, such as Ralph Nader and his public interest organizations, seek openings to advance these policies in the name of a diffuse but still real public interest. The auto safety example may not be the most apt today, however, as public demands for safety, as expressed in consumer choices for antilock brakes and airbags, have made safety a mainstream feature of cars, and manufacturers tout the safety of their vehicles in their advertising. It is not difficult, however, to find contemporary examples of policies that seek to regulate industry and that are promoted by entrepreneurial groups and their leaders, such as environmental policy.

What results, however, if both the costs and benefits of a policy are diffuse? Wilson uses as an example the Sherman Antitrust act. This law prohibits firms from creating anticompetitive "trusts." Since so few firms are at any one time prepared to create a trust, there are very few firms that feel the cost of this policy; at the same time, the benefits of promoting competition are often diffuse, affecting lots of people a little bit rather than having a major influence on our individual economic decision making. This sort of policy is therefore called majoritarian policy making because majorities of the public want antitrust legislation as a way of curbing big business power or at least as a means of symbolically reining in business. This sentiment was translated to policy without much heated opposition, in large part because the language of the law was so ambiguous—prohibiting "combinations in restraint of trade"—that "it was not exactly clear what *was* aimed at."[8]

The value of Wilson's typology is not in the names of the policy types. Indeed, we should think of the concentration of benefits and costs as tendencies or as ends of two continua rather than as two dichotomies adding up to a four-cell matrix. This said, we can see some relationships between Wilson's and Lowi's ways of thinking about policy types and their connections to issue networks or subgovernments. For example, clientelism is closely associated with Lowi's distributive policy type, in which interest groups gain benefits that are "paid for" (financially or otherwise) by the bulk of society. This in turn is associated with the subgovernment or "iron triangle" model of interest relationships, in which interest groups, bureaucracies, and congressional subcommittees work together in a mutually reinforcing relationship.[9] On the other hand, policies that seek to redistribute costs and benefits—redistributive policy—are highly contentious because they are often perceived as zero-sum situations, in which any gain for one interest is accompanied by an equal and opposite loss by the other.

But it is important to understand that this distribution of costs and benefits may be as much a social construction as the result of a real calculation of costs and benefits. If a group believes or is *convinced* that it will bear the costs of a policy, it is likely to act against the policy. Thus, a policy that seeks to reduce youth crime by providing after-school services may be resisted by a large number of citizens because they believe that they are paying a high cost for a less-than-obvious benefit to themselves. This illustration shows the difficulty of linking policies to actual benefits, but also illustrates how benefits and costs seem to be as much in the eye of the beholder as a carefully calculated accounting exercise.

If these attributes of policy (cost/benefit, distribution/redistribution) are so prone to perception, then what good is any exercise in assigning policy types? Lowi noted in 1964 that "it is not the actual outcomes but the expectations as to what the outcomes can be that shape the issues and determine their politics."[10] Peter Steinberger also addresses this issue by "conceptualizing some of the ways in which participants tend to define policies."[11] In other words, policies may not have inherent meanings in terms of any policy typology, but may gain their meanings only when groups discern meanings and propagate them among friendly and hostile audiences. For example, many safety innovations in automobiles and other consumer products cost relatively little per item produced, but manufacturers and their allies *believe* that the additional cost will make their products unprofitable. This argument will help persuade groups to mobilize in a particular way based on a perception of policy.

Other Policy Typologies

The Lowi and Wilson typologies are not the only ways to categorize public policies. Following are four additional and not mutually exclusive ways we can categorize policies. Of course, as in any typology, policies may not fit into perfectly delineated boxes or cells, but thinking about policies in these different ways may help you gain insight into the features of policy that are most important from an analytic perspective.

Substantive and Procedural Policies

James Anderson reminds us of the very important difference between policies that set the rules for policy making and the more familiar policies that actually provide the goods and services we expect from government. He defines the difference between substantive and procedural polices as what government does versus how it does it. Nevertheless, procedural policies are very important and actually have, in the end, a substantive effect on politics.[12]

Anderson cites the federal Administrative Procedures Act (APA) of 1946 as a particularly important procedural policy; the states also have similar laws. The APA establishes the procedure by which government agencies make, issue, and enforce rules and regulations as they implement the laws passed by Congress. If a regulation (or a "rule," in the language of the act) is established by an agency following the processes laid out by the APA, then it is assumed to have the force of law (like *statute* or *case law*). The APA governs how federal agencies let citizens know that they are going to make a rule and how the public can comment on the rule and offer suggestions or express their opposition to the rules.

While the details of federal rule making sound pretty dry, overall we can say that the APA is a very important policy. How would American government be different if there was no one way for the federal government to make rules in the open, accessible to public comment and opposition? Could certain interests be benefited and others harmed if the regulatory process were kept a secret? It would seem so, which is why, in future enactments, Congress amended the APA to make government even more open through the Freedom of Information Act of 1974, the Government in the Sunshine Act, and the Privacy Act of 1974. The overall goal, while procedural, is to ensure fairness in governmental dealing with citizens, which is substantively important as well.[13]

Material and Symbolic Policies

Another way to categorize policies is to examine whether the policy is material or symbolic. While the distinction between these two is not absolute, one can distinguish between material policies, which provide a material (that is, tangible and obvious) benefit to people, and symbolic policies, which simply appeal to people's values without any resources or actual effort behind them. A material policy, for example, may be a federal grant that provides money to local communities to hire police officers, as was implemented in the Clinton administration. Examples of symbolic policies include antidrug efforts such as the "just say no" and DARE campaigns and legislation and proposed constitutional amendments that would prohibit burning the flag (such laws were held unconstitutional by the Supreme Court in *Texas v. Johnson*[14]). As Anderson notes, these policies appeal to our values and our sense of idealism, but do not really deliver any particular benefit, whether they claim to or not. Sometimes symbolic policies claim to have an impact, but this is often based on faulty causal reasoning. For example, the system of TV show ratings was developed in response to a widespread belief that various social ills, particularly among children, result from violent or sexually expressive TV shows. There is little research to substantiate this, but the TV industry implemented a voluntary ratings scheme to preempt federal legislation. In this case, TV ratings systems are the symbolic policies intended to address the perceived problem.

Public Versus Private Goods

One of the main ways we distinguish between what should be provided by government and what is better provided by the private sector is by analyzing whether a good is a public good versus a private good. Again, public goods are goods that, once provided for one user, are available to all in a society and that cannot be exclusively consumed by a single person or group of people. Private goods are goods that can be used by only the immediate consumer and whose enjoyment is then denied to others.

Laws that provide for clean air and water are classic examples of public goods: a decision to clean up the air or water for one person requires that everyone be provided with a better environment. Similarly, it would be difficult to set up a system of police protection in which only those who subscribe to police services receive protection against crime.

The public-private goods distinction, like most typologies, is not a fine distinction. There are other factors to take into account besides the consumption of a particular good. For example, the United States Postal Service (USPS) is a quasi-governmental corporation that provides document and package delivery services. FedEx, United Parcel Service, Airborne, and other firms are also in the same business. Why, then, should the USPS continue in business if private firms can do the job? After all, mail and parcel delivery has all the hallmarks of a private good: the service is consumed individually, when a person decides to send a letter or package.

But the USPS exists because of a goal that the private sector firms do not pursue: universal service. A person can send a letter from Key West, Florida, to either Miami (about 150 miles away) or to Kotzebue, Alaska (thousands of miles away), for the same thirty-three cents. Many private firms would not serve Kotzebue, a remote village on the shores of the Bering Sea, because it is not profitable. Federal law therefore requires that certain kinds of mail can be carried only by the USPS, because the profits made on easily delivered mail, such as from Manhattan to Queens, covers the costs of delivering remote mail. When categorizing a good as public or private, the system of providing that good may be as important as the good itself.

Liberal and Conservative Policies

This is perhaps the most commonly employed typology in everyday discussion of politics. In fact, to many people, the terms themselves are terms of pride or derision. During the 1980s, the term "liberal" was used by President Reagan and his allies as a term of scorn for the failed social policies of the 1930s and 1960s, while self-described liberals use the term to identify themselves as believing in the power of government to better the lives of everyone, rich or poor. In today's usage, a conservative is one who believes in the primacy of individual initiative and effort over government action. Conservatives are likely to believe that government is too big, that it tends to be as much or more an instrument of mischief as of progress. Liberals, on the other hand, believe that government can and should work to equalize differences between the wealthy powerful and the poor and less powerful.

Of course, this description is written in remarkably broad strokes. Not all conservatives think that government is evil, just as no liberals believe that government is always a force for good. Indeed, when we analyze the sorts of policies that people who self-style themselves as liberal or conservative propose, it becomes clear that these distinctions become very blurry. Conservatives prize individual liberty, yet often propose more stringent anticrime measures than liberals. Liberals pursue governmental initiative to solve problems, yet are often the most concerned with government incursions on privacy and liberty. In the end, it is quite hard to characterize a policy as merely liberal or conservative.

Conclusion

There are many ways to think about how decisions are made on what to do about a policy problem. These theories of how decisions are made lead explicitly to theories of how decisions *should* be made. As you study and participate in public policy, it is worthwhile to ask yourself whether the decisions that are being made could be made better. When you do so, however, remember to think carefully about what you mean by "better." The theorists really do not have an opinion about what a better policy is; a rationalist would argue that the best policy is the policy that is most likely to solve a problem; you might have different goals and values that would make defining the "best" policy as much a political as it is an analytical problem.

7

Policy Design and Policy Tools

Once a problem has been identified and decision makers place the issue on the agenda for active consideration, there is still more to do to move an idea from a successful contestant on the agenda to a fleshed-out policy. This chapter reviews two more aspects of the policy process. The first is what policy scholars call *policy design*, which is the process by which policies are designed, both through technical analysis and the political process, to achieve a particular goal. After the policy is designed, it is enacted and then implemented, at which point the administrative agencies translate the will of the executive and legislative branches into actual policy outcomes.

Like many treatments of the policy process, this description is greatly simplified. I discuss policy design first, but it is impossible to separate the process of designing policies from their implementation—much as all the stages of the policy process are hard to separate. Design and implementation are very closely related to each other because the choices made in the design of a policy will profoundly influence the way a policy is implemented, which then influences the outcomes of these policies. In fact, policy designers often base their policy designs on experience with similar policies that have already been implemented.

Another reason why design and implementation are hard to separate from the rest of the policy process is that the policy process continues during design and implementation. As the Turtle Excluder Device case illustrates, Congress's enactment of law does not result in a simple translation from Congress's will to agency action. Rather, the administering agencies must take what Congress has passed and figure out what it

requires or allows them to do. The process of translating vague legislative commands into rules and regulations can be among the most contentious and difficult activities in the entire policy process.

While policies are being implemented, experience with the policy
and with similar policies will often change the policy design, even when
the policy and goals are supposedly in place and operating. For example,
federal targeted spending on particular urban problems was often granted
based on very focused federal goals and programmatic interests; this
was changed because, to a considerable extent, implementation was not
as successful as was hoped. This more targeted policy was replaced by
block grants, in which states and local governments are freer go make
choices about how the money is spent, provided that relatively broad
federal goals are met.

Some General Concepts

Systems models of the policy process call laws, decisions, regulations,
and the like *outputs* of the policy system. We can also think of outputs of
government: the goods and services produced by government. One can
think about outputs in two ways, one of which is easy to measure and
the other of which is quite difficult to measure.

The first way is to consider outputs as the effort that government
expends to address problems. The harder way is to try to measure the
outcomes of all this effort. Both of these things are important to measure, but for different reasons. A good example is found in a state transportation department. (This is a good example because I used to work in
such a department!) Many transportation departments today claim that
their mission is to facilitate the safe and efficient movement of people
and goods to, through, and from the state. This mission gives us a clue
as to the outcomes we are seeking in transportation policy. We would
need to find information on safety (say, number of accidents per 100,000
miles driven) and efficiency (hours spent waiting in gridlock, perhaps).

These numbers are sometimes hard to come by and, even when they
are accessible, may be politically embarrassing to an agency that is not
meeting its stated goals. In either case, many agencies measure their
effort by simply measuring their outputs—that is, they measure what
they *do*, not what its impact is on a system. For example, transportation
departments might measure how many miles of road were paved and
had stripes painted on them or how many potholes were filled. These

are important activities that are necessary for achieving the stated goals, but measuring them is simply a measure of the *effort* expended by the agency. There is nothing in these measures that suggests that these activities somehow result in an *outcome* that is consistent with the agency's mission; that is, it is hard to make the connection between paving, striping, pothole filling, and the safe and efficient movement of goods and people.[1]

But it is possible, with some care, to link actual outcomes to results. This requires a good *causal model*, that is, a model of how the effort expended *causes* there to be a particular outcome. Let's say that paving and striping is reserved for the roads in the worst condition, judged by some objective measures, including the roughness of the road (potholes, ruts, etc.) and how badly worn the stripes are. Rough roads can promote accidents, vehicle damage, and slower traffic; worn stripes can lead to accidents by not providing lane information to motorists who might cross the center line or run off the road. Thus, we might measure the average speed, safety, and other factors of a series of road segments and see if the roads are more efficient and safer after new pavement and stripes than they were before the work crews paved and painted. If so, we can say that this improved safety and efficiency are *outcomes* related to the paving and painting.

This discussion reflects the difficulties inherent in designing policies that work to achieve their goals. Without good causal theory, it is unlikely that a policy design will be able to deliver the desired outcomes. Rather, performance measurement will remain focused on effort, because implementers and researchers will find the connection between effort and outcome so difficult to make.

With the difficulties of sound policy design firmly in mind, the next section describes factors to consider in the design of successful policies.

Preparing to Design Policies

At some point (preferably early) in the policy design process, decision makers must explicitly consider five elements of policy design, as listed in Table 7.1.

Goals

Policies are made because someone has persuaded enough of us—citizens, elected officials, or both—that something needs to be done

Table 7.1

Elements of Policy Design

Element	Questions to ask
The goals of the policy	What are the goals of the policy? To eliminate a problem? To alleviate a problem but not entirely eliminate it? To keep a problem from getting worse?
The causal model	What is the causal model? Do we know that, if we do X, Y will result? How do we know this? If we do not know, how can we find out?
The tools of the policy	What tools or instruments will be used to put the policy into effect? Will they be more or less coercive? Will they rely on incentives, persuasion, or information? Capacity building?
The targets of the policy	Whose behavior is supposed to change? Are there direct and indirect targets? Are design choices predicated on our social construction of the target population?
The implementation of the policy	How will the program be implemented? Who will lay out the implementation system? Will a top-down or bottom-up design be selected? Why?

about a problem. Think of all the problems of the twentieth century — disease, racial and ethnic discrimination, poverty, economic downturns— and you can think of goals: to prevent polio, to create racial equality, to reduce poverty, or to ease the burden of recessions, particularly on the working poor and others unable to absorb economic shocks. Policies are created to meet or at least to make progress toward these goals: policies to fund research on vaccines and to mandate their use by children; policies meant to desegregate schools, public facilities, and workplaces; policies to provide a "social safety net" for the poor and others hit by economic downturns; and policies to create jobs. All of these policies are linked to perceived problems and goals.

There are many ways to think about and categorize goals, but my favorite way of thinking about goals is presented by Deborah Stone in *Policy Paradox*. Stone lists four major categories of goals: equity, efficiency, security, and liberty. In many cases, Stone argues, these goals clash: most prominently, security often conflicts with liberty, and some political systems have tended to favor various forms of security while curtailing liberty. And efficiency can conflict with all these other goals.

Indeed, these conflicts are intensified by the many different ways that goals can be defined. Stone helps us to understand this by listing at least *eight* different ways of defining equality itself. She uses the example of how to divide a large chocolate cake among the members of a class. One might argue that the most equitable division is to simply count the number of people in the room and divide the cake into that number of pieces. But Stone argues that one can divide the cake very differently—by the rank of the people in the room (professor, graduate students, undergraduates, for example), by athletic or physical prowess —and still justify the decision for dividing resources as "equal."[2]

If this seems fanciful to you, consider traditional American notions of equality, in which we claim that we believe that everyone should have equal *opportunity* for success but no guarantee of equal *outcomes*— particularly when the opportunities themselves are not equal. Other nations, such as the Scandinavian countries, are more serious about coming closer to equality of outcome.

Defining Efficiency

Deborah Stone argues that *efficiency* is more of a means to a goal rather than a goal itself, but she treats efficiency as a goal category because many policy advocates tout their ideas on purported improvements in efficiency. Efficiency is a particularly important aspect of policy making in the United States, given our emphasis on limited government and individual initiative and in the context of calls for the government to "run more like a business." An economist might define efficiency as "gaining the most output for a given level of input," which means, in nontechnical language, "more bang for the buck." It also means "the same bang for fewer bucks," meaning that if we could improve the efficiency of a program by 10 percent, one could choose to reduce spending by 10 percent and still derive the same benefits from a program.

This sort of thinking is commonplace, particularly among those who support smaller government or who wish to shift resources to other programs. Spending cuts or budget reallocations are often justified by the belief that one can gain considerable resources by simply cutting the "waste, fraud, and abuse" from programs. This thinking in government tends to overlook important issues. First, the public sector may not be any more or less efficient in some ways than large private sector firms, like IBM or General Motors. The private sector tends to have fewer formal controls over such waste than the public sector, although accounting practices in the private sector will certainly reveal decreasing profitability or diminishing assets.

It is of course highly desirable to reduce or eliminate waste, fraud, or abuse in both the public and private sectors. However, there may not be as much waste, fraud, and abuse in government as there are decisions to provide benefits to narrower interests at the expense of the majority, as we learned in Chapter 6. People who oppose certain programs will often do so because they disagree with the substance of the policy, but find the waste, fraud, and abuse argument more successful than arguing the program on the merits, particularly because no one, including most proponents of policy, favors waste.

There are many different ways of understanding efficiency, depending on how we describe inputs and outputs. Stone argues that governmental activities provide both inputs and outputs. In her example of how we might define efficiency in a public library system, we might see the salaries paid to librarians as inputs, but their earnings have a small but discernible impact on the community, thus serving as an output.

Beyond this simplistic example, Stone uses a theme that extends our thinking about policy beyond the mere economic. She starts by contrasting two ways to think about society, as a *market* or as the *polis*, the latter meaning the "essential political society," or what I take to mean the community as a whole. The decisions we make to address our common problems are usually political (cooperation, negotiation, common or public interests) rather than market-based (voluntary exchanges between just two parties intended to increase both parties' welfare). Clearly, if more people and interests are taken into account in the polis than in the market, we could reasonably argue that the "polis model" is more complex than a simple market model. If this is true, then efficiency in political terms is quite complex, as hard to define in just one way as equity is.

For example, it is traditional to think about governmental administrative costs as merely wasted or "overhead" expenses that take resources away from more useful activity. As Stone argues, however, "merely calling something 'administrative' as opposed to 'productive' is a way of prejudicing the argument."[3] The question to ask is "what is meant by administrative?" Stone cites the example of a New Jersey plan to cut administrative costs by imposing penalties on schools with excessive "administrative" costs; the plan would categorize "school librarians, nurses, and guidance counselors as 'administrative.' " By categorizing these positions as "administrative," New Jersey was sending a signal that the responsibilities of these positions do not contribute to the goals of a school.

What might the librarians, school nurses, and counselors think of this argument? Perhaps they would mobilize to show how their activities contribute to the goals of the school *or* simply make schools better places in which to spend the better part of the day. In any case, classifying these activities as "administrative" in order to achieve some level of "efficiency" is more a political decision than an economic one, and it means that one uses political arguments to attack the proposal. This is not to say that one cannot or should not use economic or accounting data to make a case for or against moves to create efficiency. Rather, such arguments are likely to be part, but only part, of a broader political argument regarding the desirability of programs. Such evidence is thus part of the advocacy process, not the be-all and end-all of the argument.

Conflicting Goals: Security and Liberty

Two other goals that seem most obviously to conflict are security and liberty. Clearly, there are significant conflicts between these two goals: the more security one desires from the government, the more liberty one must be willing to surrender. This dilemma and the solutions to it go back at least as far as Thomas Hobbes's famous work of political theory, *Leviathan* (1651). Hobbes argues that people are naturally aggressive and that they naturally want to acquire things for themselves: they will, therefore, in the "state of nature" (that is, the state of humankind without civil government), seek to deny those things or take them from other people. Thus, people in the "state of nature" will fight with each other for wealth and power, and this constant striving will yield constant "war of man against man," resulting in a society in which life is "solitary, nasty, brutish, and short." To prevent this conflict, Hobbes argues, all of us in civil society have surrendered a considerable number of our liberties to the state, which holds the most coercive power in our name to prevent us from engaging in this war against all.

If we take Hobbes at his word, we might create an authoritarian or totalitarian system to protect ourselves from each other. Instead, the United States followed a path laid out by John Locke and extended by the founders of our Constitution, who believed that political power comes from our consent—thus, we surrender to the government or "leviathan" only those things that we believe government should manage so as to create and maintain a civil society. Under such a system, citizens retain considerable rights and privileges of citizenship until they have breached the laws of civil society, in which case individual liberties can be taken from the individual in order to make all of us more secure. The obvious example is criminals, who are largely free to act until they commit a crime, which is an affront to civil society, whereupon we restrict the liberties of criminals by imprisoning them, or, in the extreme cases, by denying them life itself.

The problem with this tradeoff is that greater security for some or all of us comes at the expense of a loss of liberty to some or all of us. Consider some contemporary examples.

First, let us imagine that the police search a house without a warrant. Such a search is a violation of the Fourth Amendment's guarantee against warrantless searches. But what if the search yields evidence that the person living in the house committed a crime? Then the evidence is what lawyers call "probative" in that it shows that the individual is a criminal. In such a case, should the evidence be admitted at trial because it is proof of guilt? Or should it be excluded, because it was seized in violation of the Constitution? What if excluding the evidence allows the clearly guilty suspect to go free?

Next, consider this question: Would you be willing to surrender some of your rights—your Fifth Amendment right not to be forced to incriminate yourself or your Fourth Amendment right to "be secure in secure in [your] persons, houses, papers, and effects, against unreasonable searches and seizures"—in exchange for more aggressive law enforcement against vandals, murderers, and drug dealers? Your decision may presume that the constitutional protections against unfair criminal procedure apply only to actual criminals, not suspects and certainly not private citizens. However, the founders believed that the protections contained in the first eight amendments protect all of us against a heavy-handed central government. Nearly every protection provided under the Bill of Rights has its historical roots in the colonial experience, when the British government routinely violated what we now call "due process of law."

At the same time, many people argue that criminals have too many "rights" and that the victims of crimes have no rights of their own in the Constitution. While one can reply that the Bill of Rights is at least as valuable as a set of restraints against government as it is a set of protections of "criminals" (actually, suspects), the niceties of political theory and constitutional law are not always observed in policy debates.

As you can see, these questions are not easily and definitely answered, because these are important political questions that both influence and reflect the nature of the political community involved and the nature of the information available to people when they make these decisions about liberty. At the time of this writing, early in the year 2000, the economy is sound, unemployment is at historic lows, inflation is low compared with the high rates in the 1970s and early 1980s, and people are freely spending money on houses, cars, computers, and other accoutrements of the good life, twenty-first-century style. At the same time, crime is also at a historic low, and drug-related crime in particular has been substantially reduced as the crack cocaine trade declines in volume.

In such an environment, people may be more willing to take risks and to seek greater liberty because they feel more secure. At other times, when the economy is poor, crime is rampant, and the future prosperity and quality of life are in doubt, people may find that their interests shift to greater security. Thus, there is no one answer to what the appropriate balance of these goals should be; rather, what is important to examine is the extent to which conflicts exist and how they are resolved.

Ambiguity and Goal Conflict

Beyond the different ways of thinking about goals, policy design can also reveal conflict over policy goals. Because policies and their goals are often vague when they are originally established, it is sometimes difficult for the agencies charged with implementation to satisfy the demands of everyone involved in formulating and approving the broad policy. For example, Congress could mandate that the Secretary of the Department of Health and Human Services create a program to reduce the teen pregnancy rate. The goal, and how attainment is measured, are clear: reduce the pregnancy rate. There may be other goals, such as reducing welfare dependency, increasing educational attainment, promoting morality, and other benefits that derive from this, but the main goal is to reduce the teen pregnancy rate.

There are multiple ways to reduce teen pregnancies. Two commonly cited methods are to provide family planning services, particularly birth control, to teens, particularly teen girls, and to stress abstinence to teens through schools, public education campaigns, and the like. Clearly, the choice of one or the other of these methods to reach the goal is going to raise controversy. Some will argue that providing family planning services will encourage rather than discourage promiscuity, with more pregnancy and moral decay the result. Others may argue that abstinence relies too heavily on mistaken causal theory; in particular, they would argue that appeals for abstinence would be ignored or even mocked by teens rather than thoughtfully and respectfully heeded.

We might call this conflict an agreement on ends, but not on means. The reason for the agreement on the ends in the first place is due to contending groups' interests in attaining their own goals. Socially conservative groups may see the reduction of teen pregnancies as meeting a moral goal, while liberal groups may view the same result as a step toward particular social goals. The hook to teen pregnancy is used because it can be agreed to by both groups, who can feel that their interests are thereby promoted. The disagreement comes later, when the decision is implemented, that is, when an agency takes specific steps to lower teen pregnancy rates, such as distributing contraception or promoting abstinence.

When the goals themselves are in dispute, or when Congress or other legislatures have specified the method for implementing a program, these post-enactment goal conflicts are less likely, because they would have been explicitly stated in the legislation or at least strongly embedded in the policy design. Nevertheless, because legislation is usually the product of compromise, sometimes the means are unspecified and the ends are fuzzy until the policy takes shape during the design phase.

Goals conflict with other goals in other policy areas, as well. Helen Ingram and Dean Mann argue that one can claim that, because the United States has so many illegal aliens living within its borders, its immigration policies have failed. This is true if the goal is to control the number of immigrants entering the United States. What about other, perhaps more important goals? One example, Ingram and Mann argue, is the desire to maintain friendly relations with Mexico, the source of most of our illegal aliens. A crackdown on illegal immigration may create social, economic, and political problems in a nation whose cooperation we hope to cultivate. Another goal is to keep food prices down; many argue that illegal immigrants, because they accept lower wages for farm work that legal citizens choose not to do, help keep food prices low.[4]

Whether one agrees that these are important goals is less important than a realization that a policy can conflict *externally* with other policies. For example, sociologists Edward Laumann and David Knoke tell the story of an oil exploration executive who read in the *Federal Register* that the Federal Aviation Administration (FAA) was proposing to require pilots of small airplanes to file flight plans for nearly all flights, regardless of the flight's length or whether the pilot planned to fly visually or on instruments. While the goal here was to promote and improve aviation safety, the oil executive opposed the new rule because it could reveal where aircraft owned by oil companies fly when they do aerial surveys of potentially oil- and gas-rich areas. Thus, the goal of encouraging the development of our energy resources was hindered by an entirely unrelated program and goal.[5]

The point of this review of goals is not to lead you to believe that all policy is hopelessly complex or that goals are never set and attempted. Rather, my goal is to simply highlight how difficult it is to set and reach goals in a complex policy environment. Often, once conflicts are resolved and the means for achieving goals are developed, one is able, through a review of the record surrounding the enactment of a policy, to isolate the important goal or goals and assess the extent to which they are met or believed to have been met. This is sometimes difficult to do when many other activities are taking place simultaneously.

Adding to the complexity of goals is the fact that there are different types of goals. One must ask a series of questions about goals to fully understand what the policy is intended to achieve. First, one must ask whether the goal is to eliminate a problem, hold steady in the face of a growing problem, or reduce a problem to some better level. For example, the Clean Water Act's goal that the nation's waters be "drinkable, swimmable and fishable by 1985" seeks not to eliminate all pollution, but rather that level of pollution that renders our waters unusable for these purposes. Similarly, national economic policy makers tend not to believe they can get rid of unemployment entirely, but they do work to bring down the level of unemployment to 4 percent, the goal specified in the Full Employment and Balanced Growth Act of 1978, also known as the Humphrey-Hawkins Act after its sponsors.[6] On the other hand, in 1995 the FAA and the NTSB announced their goal of zero fatal accidents in American commercial aviation; this is an absolute goal to eliminate deaths from air disasters.[7] The type of goal may reveal a great deal about what the policy designers believe is possible to do given current techniques for solving or alleviating problems.

Proper Causal Theory

If the participants in policy making can at least approximate goal consensus, then the next thing that policy makers must do is understand the *causal theory* that underlies the policy to be implemented. A *causal theory* is a theory about what causes the problem and what *intervention*—that is, what policy response to the problem—would alleviate that problem. If the laws made by the legislature are sufficiently vague or are drafted simply to rely on the expertise of agency officials (as in our Turtle Excluder Device example), then developing the best causal theory and then settling on the policy design are the responsibility of the agency staff. But if Congress specifies a particular solution or set of solutions to a problem, then the causal theory is implicit in the legislation. For example, after the *Exxon Valdez* oil spill, Congress passed the Oil Pollution Act of 1990, which contained, among others, two key provisions: a requirement that oil tankers have double hulls by a certain date and an increase in the monetary liability limit for shipowners whose tankers spill oil. The explicit theories here are, first, that single-hull tankers leak more oil than double-hull tankers and, second, that an increase in liability will deter companies from recklessly moving oil in United States waters.

Because social problems are very complex, it is not surprising that developing causal theories about how the social world works is very difficult. If one develops the wrong causal theory, no policy, no matter how well crafted, is likely to have a positive impact on the problem under consideration.

Deborah Stone has found the issue of causes so important that she devotes an entire chapter of *Policy Paradox* and an article to this element of policy making.[8] You may have correctly guessed that Stone finds that isolating the causes of problems is much more complex than opposing camps might believe at first glance. After all, as Stone argues, we can distinguish between cause and effect in the natural world and in the social world: "The natural world is the realm of fate and accident, and we believe we have an adequate understanding of causation when we can describe the sequence of events by which one thing leads to another."[9] On the other hand, "in the social world we understand events to be the result of will, usually human but perhaps animal. The social world is the realm of control and intent. We usually think we have an adequate understanding of causation when we can identify the purposes or motives of a person or group and link those purposes to their actions" (p. 189). Because of these different ways of understanding causation, Stone argues, we can do things to change the outcomes of human, purposive action, while few interventions will change natural phenomena such as the weather, tides, or earthquakes.

Thus, an important way of understanding how people argue about causes is to look at whether people attribute a problem to an act of God or to acts of human causation, either purposive or negligent. For example, one can argue that when a hurricane damages a city, it is an act of God that we cannot avoid and that we should simply feel compassion for victims, give aid to recover from the disaster, and move on. Another view is that hurricanes (or earthquakes, or floods, or other disasters, for that matter) do not *cause* anything but high winds, heavy rains, too much water, or shaking ground. It is the presence of human activity and the consequence of human activities that cause the damages, such as building houses too close to rivers or beaches or in such a way that they do not stand up to shaking ground or high winds. The choice to build in such places and in such ways is a *human* decision that can be altered by changing policy to induce "better" decisions that help reduce the damages from such events.

Stone argues that we can take this analysis further and, considering actions and consequences, identify four types of causal theories, as discussed in Chapter 5 and as shown in Table 5.1. This chart helps us to understand how groups compete in telling causal stories about policy problems. These stories include depictions of intended and unintended consequences. For example, environmental groups often portray environmental disasters—chemical leaks, oil spills, or leaking toxic waste dumps—as the result of carelessness (corner cutting, perhaps) or omission (failure to perform a task that would prevent an accident). The owner of the industrial facility in question will attempt to move the discussion from the realm of inadvertence, which implies liability and carelessness, to a causal theory implying chance that the accident was caused by weather or a completely unforeseeable event that Stone calls "machines that run amok."

This move between explanations is important because the causal theory strongly implies the appropriate actions that government and society might take and that may be codified in public policy. A causal theory that a problem is caused by carelessness and omission means that policies are likely to be adopted that more strictly regulate the activities in question, to prevent or at least penalize these actions. But a causal theory that undesirable effects are caused by accidents implies a much different set of policies, which may emphasize self-regulation over governmental action, particularly if one can make the claim that accidents are random, without any pattern that is somehow caused or worsened by the actions or nonactions of industry.

In these ways and others, debates over policy are debates over causes and effects, with each side trying to tell a story that leads to its own most desired result. These causal theories also imply what sorts of policy tools will be used to address the problems.

Policy Tools

Closely related to the causal theory is the choice of *policy tools* or *policy instruments* that can be used to create a desired outcome. Anne Schneider and Helen Ingram define policy tools as "elements in policy design that cause agents or targets to do something they would not do otherwise or with the intention of modifying behavior to solve public problems or attain policy goals."[10] James Anderson calls policy instruments or tools "techniques of control" that are "by one means or another, overtly or subtly, . . . designed to cause people to do things, refrain from doing things, or continue doing things that they would otherwise not do."[11] Lester Salamon and Michael Lund provide a particularly simple and useful definition of a policy tool as "a method through which government seeks a policy objective."[12]

Types of Policy Tools

Much as students of policy have developed typologies of policies, many social scientists have developed categories of policy tools. We create categories of tools because while there are many different government policies, there should be relatively few different types of tools used to achieve the goals set out in policy.[13] We can then learn more about how government works to achieve its goals by carefully thinking about the broad types of tools and how government uses them to achieve certain ends.

Thinking about tools is particularly useful because, as Salamon and Lund argue, there are "central characteristics" of tools that distinguish some tools from others. The key would then be to find the central characteristic of the various tools. One can do so by looking at four dimensions of tools. The first of these dimensions is "the nature of the activity in which government is engaged." Examining this dimension gives us a general sense of what it is that the government is doing to achieve a goal. There are, say Salamon and Lund, four broad categories of such activities: "outright money payments . . . provision of goods and services, including information . . . legal protections, such as monopolies or guarantees . . . [and] restrictions/penalties," such as regulation or criminal laws.

The next dimension to examine is the "structure of the delivery system." The delivery system reflects the extent to which implementation is likely to be more or less complex. Salamon and Lund broadly categorize delivery systems as "direct" and "indirect." Direct service delivery involves systems in which the federal government is the sole actor in the delivery of a service. Salamon and Lund cite Social Security as one such example; others would be air traffic control, provided by the Federal Aviation Administration, and regulation of broadcasting through the Federal Communications Commission. Indirect service provision involves the provision of service through an intermediary, such as another level of government or a private actor, such as a business or nonprofit agency. Examples of these types of programs include Community Development Block Grants, which go to local governments, loan guarantees, which are given to banks to encourage lending at lower rates or to riskier borrowers, and research grants, which are given to nonprofit universities or research institutes.

Related to but not exactly the same as the structure of the delivery system is the "the degree of centralization." In general, we can be fairly certain that the more direct the service to be provided, the more the administration of the program is centralized. The management of Social Security is centralized in Washington because it is directly administered by the federal government, without the assistance or participation of intermediaries. However, some federally provided services are also relatively decentralized. For example, the activities of the Park Service (a unit of the Agriculture Department) and the Forest Service (a unit of the Interior Department) are managed both by central offices in Washington and by expert staff in the field, who have some managerial and programmatic latitude because they need to respond effectively to different local conditions.

Finally, Salamon and Lund describe the "degree of automaticity" of a policy tool, or, in other words, "the degree to which [programs] require detailed administrative action." Tax incentives, they argue, are largely self-executing because individuals will seek them out, thereby promoting the goals of the policy. The mortgage tax deduction is a virtually effortless way for the government to promote home ownership, because homeowners know that they can take the deduction and actively wish to do so. On the other hand, welfare programs that rely on a determination of eligibility "require almost case-by-case administrative decision making" that requires a substantial degree of management effort.

Other Categories of Policy Tools

Salamon and Lund provide a particularly well-developed system of thinking about policy tools, but many other scholars have also sought useful tool typologies. Howlett and Ramesh provide two broad categories of policy tools: "economic models" and "political models."[14] Economic models of policy tools focus on individual freedom, initiative, and choice, therefore tending to value noncoercive tools over ones that are more coercive. Howlett and Ramesh do note, however, that welfare economists, whose focus is on overall societal well-being rather than the aggregation of individual well-being (the focus of neoclassical economists), do acknowledge the need for more coercive tools (such as an income tax) to correct some of the flaws of laissez-faire *economics*. In both cases, however, economists look at the selection of a policy tool as a positive, technical question in which the problem to be solved, the agent to solve it (government, private sector, or some combination), and the nature of the tools themselves are matched with each other to find the best possible solution to a problem.

By contrast, those who look at policy tool choice from a more political perspective tend to follow this precept: "Any instrument [or tool] can theoretically accomplish any chosen aim, but governments prefer less coercive instruments unless forced by either recalcitrance on the part of the subject and/or continued social pressure for change to utilize more coercive instruments."[15] Clearly this is not merely a technical matter: If the selection of how to deal with a problem is at least partially a function of societal pressures to favor one policy tool or another, then "politics" is involved in not only the understanding of the problem but also in the ways we choose to solve it. For example, the decision to treat as adults young people who commit violent crimes, thereby leading to much more stringent sentences, is not a technical decision based on an economic and criminological analysis of these crimes and their perpetrators. Rather, it is a response to a society that seeks to "get tough on crime."

Still, there are important shortcomings to thinking politically about instruments. First, as Howlett and Ramesh note explicitly, the matter of substitutability of one tool for another is not so simple, because political systems are constrained in their choice of tools, both ideologically and legally. On the legal side, for example, federal policy making on any number of issues, most notably civil rights, is predicated on the notion that government could regulate a wide range of activities under the commerce clause of the Constitution. These efforts have historically been successful, so successful, in fact, that Congress, in passing federal legislation making it a federal offense to have a gun within 1,000 yards of a school, justified its action in terms of the commerce clause, saying that school violence hinders interstate commerce. The Supreme Court, however, disagreed, noting that the connection between the goal and the commerce clause was so tenuous that the law was unconstitutional on federalism grounds.[16]

A potential problem with the economic way of thinking is that economics often makes too many assumptions about what is possible in policy making, on two levels. First, it assumes we really know what the problem *is*. In the give-and-take of policy making, an agreement to do *something* about a problem is often easier to achieve than an agreement on what precisely to do about it. This is the challenge faced by those who write regulations and seek to implement government policies, who seek to implement a policy without creating controversy and disagreement over the means to the ends specified by the policy makers. Second, the economic perspective assumes that we have reasonably reliable information on how policy tools *work*. As with much of politics and policy making, it is very hard to know the causal connections in any policy system. While we may start with a causal theory, these theories are often flawed.

Given these two ways of thinking about tools, let us turn to a discussion of some of the current ways policy scholars categorize tools, as summarized in Table 7.2. In the table I have sought to show where the names and concepts overlap, but, as you can see, there are many different terms, from the more general to the more specific, that we can use to arrange policy tools.

Perhaps the most useful way to think about tools is the extent to which they are coercive or noncoercive. The more coercive a policy, the more likely compliance with the policy can be achieved, but the more likely it is that considerable resources will have to be devoted to providing the coercion needed to create compliance. Noncoercive policies, like incentives and hortatory policies, are much easier to administer by virtue of their design and of the assumptions we make about how people will behave, but the likelihood of success is highly variable.

In the end, while the categories of tools are useful descriptors of the types of tools that one can use to achieve a set of goals, they do not tell us much about the relative strength and weaknesses of these techniques. Levine, Peters, and Thompson[17] provide a scheme for assessing the strengths and weaknesses of each tool. They acknowledge the tentative nature of these criteria, given what we know and do not know about how government works, but these are helpful ways of thinking about what tools might be best for particular goals. Their scheme is adapted and shown in Table 7.3.

Tools and Choices in Policy Design

Policy designers must consider a number of elements when selecting a policy tool. One of these elements is political feasibility. Because policy making is at least as much a political process as it is a technical process, even technically superior policy tools may not be adopted because they are politically unpopular. For example, the United States has an all-volunteer military and relies heavily on the military reserves for personnel when crises such as the Gulf War arise. This is a more politically feasible way of meeting personnel needs than the draft, which was very controversial during the Vietnam war and which would likely be very controversial today, given Americans' historic opposition to peacetime drafts. Other countries with different needs and political cultures, such as Israel, require compulsory military service; clearly, the political dynamics in Israel are different than in the United States.

A second factor in the policy tool choice is the resources available to implement policy. For example, there may be two ways to battle the problem of forest fires: post thousands of lookouts in the forests or employ a public education program to tell people that "only *you* can prevent forest fires," making a bear cub the symbol of that campaign. The United States Forest Service chose the latter hortatory tool because it is much less expensive than more aggressive efforts to detect and prevent fires caused by carelessness. Of course, the public education campaign may not be fully effective in addressing the forest fire risk, and many fires are still started by carelessness, but the campaign—and others, like encouraging people to stop smoking and wear seat belts—was successful in inducing behavioral change among a large enough proportion of the population to justify its costs.

Table 7.2

Types of Policy Tools or Instruments

Peters	Levine, Peters, Thompson	Schneider and Ingram	Anderson	Description	Examples
Law	Law and regulation	Authority tools	Directive power	Pronouncements of policy that carry the force of law; that is, they compel particular behaviors and compliance.	Criminal law, environmental regulations, antitrust law.
Services	Direct provision of services or goods		Services	Services provided directly by the government to users.	Postal services, air traffic control, weather forecasting.
Money	Transfer payments		Benefits	"Transfer" of money from government to various interests.	Social Security, food stamps, veterans' benefits.
	Intergovernmental grants				
	Contracting out		Contracts	Contracts with private firms to provide goods or services.	Contracts to run prisons, hospitals; contracts to supply complex goods to government, such as military equipment, computers, space vehicles.

General expenditures	General spending done by the government every day on the people, goods, and services it needs to function.	Personnel costs, supplies, utilities, etc. (Government spending on these items has a substantial national and local economic effect.)
Market and proprietary operations	Government activities that have private counterparts and that have economic and policy consequences.	Public corporations such as Tennessee Valley Authority (electrical power generation), market activities of the Federal Reserve Bank (interest rate setting, buying and selling securities to influence the market).

(continued)

Table 7.2 *(continued)*

Peters	Levine, Peters, Thompson	Schneider and Ingram	Anderson	Description	Examples
Taxes	The tax system (tax expenditures)		Taxes	Policies intended to alter behavior by making some activities more or less economically desirable.	Tax credits (such as for student loan interest), tax deductions (mortgage tax deduction, medical expenses), taxes on tobacco and alcohol, called "sin taxes," to raise revenue and discourage consumption. Tax policies to encourage economic development in particular areas, such as Urban Enterprise Zones.
Other economic instruments	Loans and loan guarantees		Loans	Loans to induce economic activity or other desirable activity.	Small Business Administration (SBA) loans, student loans.

Insurance	Subsidies	Payments to ensure the economic viability of an activity, particularly when that activity addresses some broader goals.	Farm subsidies; subsidies to sports franchises; subsidies to business to locate in particular communities.
	Insurance	Provision of insurance where it is not generally available in the private insurance market.	Flood insurance, federal deposit insurance.
Suasion	Horatory Tools	Attempts to persuade people to engage in desirable behaviors or to avoid engaging in undesirable behaviors.	Public campaigns to discourage smoking or drinking, antidrug campaigns, pro-exercise campaigns.
	Inducements and sanctions	Sanctions	Tools that induce "quasi-voluntary or quasi-coerced" actions based on tangible payoffs (Schneider and Ingram).	Fines for violating regulations; bonus payments for timely completion of contracts.

(continued)

Table 7.2 (continued)

Peters	Levine, Peters, Thompson	Schneider and Ingram	Anderson	Description	Examples
		Capacity-building tools		"Training, technical assistance, education, and information needed to take policy relevant actions" (Peters) and empower other agencies.	Technology transfer, training, the provision of information products to local government; cash transfers to hire more staff.
		Learning tools		Tools to help understand the relevant aspects of policy problems.	Focus groups, opinion polls, censuses, basic and applied research [for example, National Institutes of Health (NIH), National Science Foundation (NSF)].

Inspection		
Licensing	Government authority to engage in an activity that is prohibited without such a license.	Driver's licenses, professional licensing (physicians, lawyers, engineers, and the like). Licensing of hospitals, permits, corporate charters (Anderson).
Informal procedures	Procedures not specified in law or regulation to resolve problems.	Exchange of correspondence between taxpayers and IRS to resolve disputes; plea-bargaining in criminal process.

Sources: B. Guy Peters, *American Public Policy: Promise and Performance* (Chappaqua, NY: Chatham House/Seven Rivers, 1999), pp. 6–13; Charles H. Levine, B. Guy Peters, and Frank J. Thompson, *Public Administration: Challenges, Choices, Consequences* (Glenview, Ill.: Scott, Foresman/Little Brown, 1990), pp. 64–73; Anne Larason Schneider and Helen Ingram, *Policy Design for Democracy* (Lawrence: University Press of Kansas, 1997), pp. 93–97; James E. Anderson, *Public Policymaking*, 4th ed. (Boston: Houghton Mifflin, 2000), pp. 233–244.

Table 7.3

Probable Characteristics of Policy Instruments

	Certainty	Timeliness	Less Cost	Efficiency	Effectiveness	Flexibility	Visibility	Accountability	Choice
Explanation	Certainty of the administrative process and the compliance of targets.	Extent to which the tool works quickly.	Expense of the tool.	Extent to which the tool creates maximum outputs for a given input.	Extent to which the tool is likely to achieve its goals.	Ease with which the tool can be altered to changing needs and circumstances.	The extent to which the program is well known or less well known (sometimes invisibility is an important goal).	Extent to which implementers are accountable for their actions.	Degree of citizen choice afforded by the policy.
Direct service provision	+							+	
Transfers	+					–	+	+	–
Grants	–					–	+	–	+
Tax expenditures	–			+		–		–	+

Regula-tions	+					+	+	
Loans	−	−				−	−	−
Insurance	+	−				+	−	+
Contracts	−	−	−			−	−	+
Licensing	−	−				+	−	+
Informal proced-ures	−			−	−			
Capacity building	−	−	+			+	−	
Induce-ments	−	+	+			+		
Sanctions	+	−	−					
Hortatory tools	−		+			+		+

Source: From *Public Administration: Challenges, Choices, Consequences* by Charles H. Levine, B. Guy Peters, and Frank J. Thompson. Copyright © 1990 by Charles H. Levine, B. Guy Peters, and Frank J. Thompson. Reprinted by permission of Addison-Wesley Educational Publishers, Inc.

Note: Plus signs indicate the presence of an attribute; minus signs indicate the absence of that attribute.

The resource question actually falls within a broader category Salamon and Lund call administrative feasibility, or "the degree of ease or difficulty involved in establishing and operating a program."[18] Clearly, operating any public program is likely to be much more difficult if adequate resources are not provided.

A third element of policy tool choice is based on the behavioral assumptions about the target populations. Policy targets are the entities—people or organizations—whose behavior the policy seeks to alter. The choice of the policy tool is a function of the assumed behavior of the policy target. The choice of a coercive tool reveals something about the assumed behavior of the targets that the choice of a set of incentives would not. This link between the policy target and the policy tool falls under a broader category that Salamon and Lund call "effectiveness," which can be assessed on two levels: the "supply effectiveness" of the program in providing a necessary level of output to induce changes in the target population, and the "targeting effectiveness" of the program in altering policy targets' behaviors.

Conclusion

This chapter started with a discussion of the things policy makers must consider when designing policies. As has become a recurring theme in this book, this process is much more complex than it might initially appear. Goals conflict or are ambiguous, and policies are often designed without a sound causal theory to help policy makers know whether a particular kind of policy will work. All these aspects of design are important because policy design will have a considerable influence on the choice of tools employed to achieve the stated goals of a policy.

Policy tools and implementation are considered together because they are inextricably linked to each other. The choice of policy tools both influences implementation and is influenced by implementation. Furthermore, the choices of tools and implementation design reinforce each other throughout the implementation process. As more is learned about the success or failure of various tools and their implementation, policy makers and the various advocacy groups involved in a policy domain will continue to debate not only the underlying rationale for a policy, but the methods by which the policy is put into effect.

An important part of policy competition is the claim that policy has failed; an important part of the adjustment of policies is the learning that results from real or purported policy failure. This is the subject of the next chapter.

8

Policy Implementation
and Policy Failure

The Implementation of Public Policies

Once the designers of policies have settled upon a policy design and one or more tools to carry out the goals of the policy design, the various actors in the policy process turn their attention to the *implementation* of public policy. Until the late 1960s, there were few studies of policy *implementation*: that is, few scholars had sought to systematically study what happens *after* legislation or some other statement of policy is enacted and then put into effect. Thus, the study of "program implementation is concerned with what happens to a policy or program after it has been formulated."[1]

It is important to understand policy implementation because it is a key feature of the policy process, and learning from implementation problems can foster learning about better ways to structure policies to ensure that they have the effects that designers of these policies seek. In addition, perhaps to a greater extent than other elements of the policy process, implementation studies have emphasized advice to policy makers as to how to structure programs to increase the likelihood of implementation success. Thus, when students of policy implementation talk about "top-down" or "bottom-up" implementation designs, they are talking about both ways of studying policy design and ways of structuring policy implementation so as to enhance the likelihood of implementation success.

Before studies of implementation, the explicit assumption among students of policy and politics was that implementation largely proceeded after enactment with little or no controversy and that policies, once stated by the elected branches, were implemented precisely as the legislature wanted. This is similar to Woodrow Wilson's claim that the bureaucracy is a neutral implementer of policy that simply carries out the will of the legislature. As you know, however, the assumption of bureaucratic neutrality is not supported by actual experience. If the bureaucracy was a strictly neutral institution, then all the problems people have cited about bureaucracy—in particular, the problems of discretion and accountability—would never enter into the discussion of implementation. Because bureaucracies do have discretion in how they implement policies, this section reviews some ways of looking at policy implementation that see bureaucratic discretion as either a problem to be overcome by sound choices in policy design.

Approaches to the Study of Implementation

There are three main eras of policy implementation research. The first era, which began in the late 1960s and early 1970s, is characterized by works such as *Implementation* and *New Towns in Town*.[2] Their authors undertook these studies to understand why particular policies, such as the Economic Development Administration's efforts to relieve poverty in Oakland or the Johnson administration's "New Towns in Town" efforts, seemed to fall short of their goals. These studies focused on individual case studies and did not create more generalizable theory that could be applied to and tested with other cases.

A second era of implementation studies, which began in the mid-1970s, sought to create systematic theories of the policy process that were generalizable to many cases, rather than focused on one or a few cases. As this research progressed, one could discern two separate research approaches. The first of these approaches emphasizes a "top-down" perspective on policy implementation. Its proponents claim that one can understand policy implementation by looking at the goals and strategies adopted in the statute or other policy, as structured by the implementers of policy. These studies focus on the gaps between the goals set by a policy's drafters and the actual implementation and outcomes of the policy. The second approach emphasizes a "bottom-up" perspective, which suggests that implementation is best studied by starting at the lowest levels of the implementation system or "chain" and moving upward to see where implementation is more successful or less so.

Top-Down Approaches to Implementation

Some representative studies in the top-down research tradition include research by Carl Van Horn and Donald Van Meter, as well as Daniel Mazmanian and Paul Sabatier's studies of the factors that condition successful implementation.[3] The top-down approach is based on a set of important assumptions:

- Policies contain clearly defined goals against which performance can be measured. As Neal Ryan puts it, "Top-down implementation strategies greatly depend on the capacity of policy objectives to be clearly and consistently defined."[4]
- Policies contain clearly defined policy tools for the accomplishment of goals.
- The policy is characterized by the existence of a single statute or other authoritative statement of policy.
- There is an "implementation chain" that "starts with a policy message at the top and sees implementation as occurring in a chain."[5]
- Policy designers have good knowledge of the capacity and commitment of the implementers. Capacity encompasses the availability of resources for an implementing organization to carry out its tasks, including monetary and human resources, legal authority and autonomy, and the knowledge needed to effectively implement policy. Commitment includes the desire of the implementers to carry out the goals of the top-level policy designers; a high level of commitment means that the values and goals of the policy designers are shared by the lower-level implementers, particularly those at the "street level," such as teachers, police officers, or social workers.

In a top-down model of policy design, the implementer assumes that these features are present or that any problems suggested by these assumptions can be overcome. The focus then is on creating the proper structures and controls to encourage or compel compliance with the goals set at the top. But there are some substantial weaknesses with this approach that you may recognize from earlier chapters in this book.

Perhaps the most problematic feature of top-down models is the emphasis on clear objectives or goals. Without a consensus on what program goals *are*, it is hard to set a benchmark for program success and failure. For example, in 1973 Congress established the 55-mile-per-hour speed limit on the nation's freeways as a method for promoting energy conservation, because, in most cases, driving one's car at 55 mph is more fuel efficient than driving 70 mph. Yet most gains in fuel economy between 1973 and the early 1990s were a result of federal policies requiring that a manufacturer's vehicles achieve an average fuel economy of 27.5 miles per gallon for cars and 20.7 miles per gallon for light trucks. Most manufacturers comply with this standard. However, the 55-mph speed limit had a side benefit—it substantially reduced highway fatalities in the early years of its enforcement.

On what accomplishment, then, should the 55-mph limit be assessed? In terms of motorists' compliance and state enforcement, the 55-mph speed limit was generally unsuccessful, and its widespread unpopularity led to its repeal. In terms of fuel economy, the results were inconclusive, but the safety benefits were substantial, so highway safety advocates fought hard to keep the 55-mph limit in place and were successful in this fight until the late 1980s. This is an example of how advocates for a policy will redefine policy goals to justify the continuance of a program and how new groups can enter the debate to highlight new goals and benefits of programs.

Another example of multiple objectives is found in the management of the nation's forests by the U.S. Forest Service (USFS), which must administer the forests to serve "multiple uses," ranging from recreation to logging. By what goals should the Forest Service's efforts be measured? This is a constant source of conflict for the agency, as environmentalists and recreational users battle logging interests and their local allies over which aspect of forest policy—timber supply or resource conservation and recreation—should be emphasized by the USFS. When policy makers fail to provide one goal or a coherent, mutually compatible set of goals, implementation is likely to be difficult as agencies and people charged with putting policies into effect pursue different goals.

Another problem with top-down models is the assumption that there is a single national government that structures policy implementation and provides for direct delivery of services. The United States has a substantial national government, but it also has fifty state governments that have constitutionally protected rights and responsibilities, so that they are often loath to surrender their power and prerogatives to distant agencies headquartered in Washington. Most policies made by the federal government require considerable state and, in many cases, local governmental cooperation. One cannot say, then, that the federal government is strong

enough to mandate any policy it sees fit, without having to induce cooperation from and minimize conflict with the states. This assumption of a
strong central government also assumes a unitary method of decision
making that ignores competing or overlapping agencies and their staffs,
interest groups, and the disparate interests of the fifty state governments
and over 80,000 local units of government. Indeed, James Anderson notes
that legislators, bureaucrats, the courts, pressure groups, and community
organizations are all involved in policy implementation.[6] Thus, while the
focus of implementation may be in one agency, several other actors will
have an influence on implementation success or failure. One might assume that the federal government—the "top"—cannot structure implementation at all. However, Sabatier notes that the top can set bounds for
implementation, if not hard and fast rules.[7]

   This is related to a crucial critique of the top-down approach: the ability of local actors to ignore messages from the top that policies need to be
implemented in a particular way. Malcolm Goggin and his colleagues
have cited instances of "strategic delay" at the state level, where states
seek to slow implementation in order to develop ways to adapt the program to local needs.[8] However, not all delay is strategic—some delay or
outright refusal to implement policy is a reaction to local and state desires
to not implement a policy at all. This is sometimes due to local political
pressures, such as when some states failed to aggressively enforce the 55-
mph speed limit or when local governments resist implementing programs
such as the Brady Bill, which requires background checks for gun buyers.
At other times, rank-and-file implementers may refuse to implement a
policy that comes from the top: the police, for example, may resist changes
in policing procedure based on their experience on the street. Top-down
approaches often ignore the relative ease with which many implementers
and interest groups can work to subvert the originally established goals.
On the other hand, Paul Sabatier rejects the inevitability of "adaptive"
implementation in which target groups and street level bureaucrats subvert the original program's goals. Sabatier argues that top policy designers do have choices about who implements a policy and what incentives
and sanctions to impose for noncompliance and can influence the expectations and needs of target groups so that adaptive compliance should be
unnecessary or would be counterproductive.[9]

   Finally, top-down approaches assume that policy is contained in a single
statute or other authoritative statement. The fragmented and in some ways
incrementalist nature of policy making in the United States means that,

when one talks about "environmental policy" or "educational policy" or "health policy," one is discussing a wide collection of separate and sometimes contradictory policies. This is related to the tendency of top-down approaches to assume a relatively clear division between policy enactment, on the one hand, and policy implementation on the other. Indeed, many of the studies of implementation from a public administration perspective tend to adopt this distinction, which may be analytically useful but runs the risk of assuming that the same pressures that work to shape policy adoption do not exist in policy implementation.

Bottom-Up Approaches to Implementation

In a reaction to the overly structured top-down approach—in particular, to dissatisfaction with its ability to explain many unsuccessful outcomes—researchers began to view implementation from the perspective not of the topmost implementer, but rather of what Michael Lipsky calls "street level bureaucrats." *Street level bureaucrats* are the teachers, social workers, police officers, and others who implement policies at the point of contact with the policy's target population.[10] Richard Elmore, the key proponent of the bottom-up approach, calls this "backward mapping," in which the implementation process and the relevant relationships are mapped backwards, from the ultimate implementer to the topmost policy designers.[11] This approach is built on a set of assumptions that stand in marked contrast with the implicit assumptions of "forward mapping" or top-down approaches.

First, the bottom-up approach recognizes that goals are ambiguous rather than explicit and may conflict not only with other goals in the same policy area, but also with the norms and motivations of the street level bureaucrats. As Rene Torenvlied notes, "The compliance problem arises when there is a conflict of interest between implementation agencies and politicians."[12] Top-down models are most concerned with compliance, while bottom-up approaches value understanding how conflict can be alleviated by bargaining and sometimes compromise.

Second, the bottom-up approach does not require that there be a single defined "policy" in the form of a statute or other form. Rather, policy can be thought of as a set of laws, rules, practices, and norms, such as "energy policy" or "criminal procedure," that shape the ways in which government and interest groups address these problems. Thus, implementation can be viewed as a continuation of the conflicts and compromises that occur throughout the policy process, not just before and at the point of enactment.

This bottom-up approach has a number of features to commend it. In particular, the lack of a focus on a particular program and on a fixed, top-to-bottom implementation chain means that the bottom-up approach can view implementation as working through a network of actors—much like an issue network or policy community—rather than through some rigidly specified process that fails to account for the richness of the policy making environment. But there are also important shortcomings to consider in the bottom-up approach.[13]

First, Paul Sabatier argues that the bottom-up approach overemphasizes the ability of the street level bureaucrats to frustrate the goals of the top policy makers. Street level bureaucrats are not entirely free agents. They are constrained to act in a particular way based on their professional norms and obligations, by the resources available to them, and by legal sanctions that can be applied for noncompliance. Police officers, for example, who use "too much" discretion and thereby ignore procedural rules for handling suspects or evidence can lose their jobs or face criminal charges; teachers who violate professional norms can be demoted or lose their jobs. Nor do street level bureaucrats necessarily have the resources to thwart policy designers; they may be able to delay, but not entirely subvert, implementation. Of course, the street level bureaucrat may also *want* to follow the lead of the top level designers, supporting the goals handed down from higher up, with no reason to exert discretion to subvert the goals of the policy designers.

Second, bottom-up models of implementation assume that groups are active participants in the implementation process. This is not always true, however. Peter May argues that some policies can be categorized as "policies without publics," which are developed and implemented with relatively little public input, particularly when those policy areas are highly technical.[14] Along these lines, Sabatier also argues that the bottom-up approach fails to take into account the power differences of the target groups.[15] As Anne Schneider and Helen Ingram note, some target populations are more positively constructed than others, with the result that those with greater power can have a greater influence on the impact of policies that affect them than can other groups.[16] Clearly, business interests are going to be treated differently in implementation design than are the poor or prisoners, and these treatments are reflected in the choice of policy tools. The choice of tools is made at the top, based on the desired behavioral change and the nature of the target population itself.

It is worthwhile, however, to consider what these two approaches to implementation design do best. The top-down approach is much more useful when there is a single, dominant program that is being studied. Several times in this book, I have mentioned specific legislative enactments, such as the Oil Pollution Act of 1990 (OPA 90), as important policy changes. It would be appropriate to study the implementation of OPA 90 from the top down, because much of the policy was designed in Congress and the federal executive branch and, regardless of its complexity and the span of issues raised in the law, it is fairly well structured from the outset to be administered by top government officials. Sabatier also argues that top-down approaches are appropriate when one has limited resources to "backward map" the implementation of a particular issue. It is considerably easier to look up statutes and other pronouncements issued by top level policy designers than it is to map all the various interests, agencies, and street level officials that will carry out a policy.

On the other hand, bottom-up modeling makes sense when there is no one dominant program (such as in a state's penal code, which consists of many policy statements regarding the nature and severity of crimes) and when one is more interested in the local dynamics of implementation than in the broad sweep of design. It is useful to consider the local factors, both from practical and academic perspectives, since local experience with implementation success or failure can yield important lessons for policy implementers.

Synthesis: A Third Generation of Implementation Research

Because of the relative strengths and weaknesses of the top-down and bottom-up approaches, researchers have sought to combine the benefits of these approaches into one model or synthesis that can address both the structuring of policy from the top and the likelihood of its subversion or at least its alteration at the ultimate point of implementation.

Richard Elmore has sought to combine his idea of "backward mapping" with a "forward mapping element."[17] By looking both forward and backward, we can understand that top policy makers can make choices of policy instruments or tools to structure implementation while realizing that the motivations and needs of lower level implementers must be taken into account. Paul Sabatier also argues that a conceptual framework should be developed that combines the best of the top-down and bottom-up approaches.[18] The top-down approach is best where there is a dominant program (i.e., law) that is well structured and where the researcher's resources for studying implementation are limited, as when a student is researching the implementation of a program for a term paper or when an implementer needs a quick analysis in discussing with boss and colleagues how to structure a program. By contrast, the bottom-up approach is best where one is interested in the dynamics of local implementation and where there is no single dominant program. One begins by analyzing rather diffuse street level behavior rather than focused, top-down activity. Because of this diffuse behavior, gathering the needed data to tell the implementation story can be challenging, as multiple sources must be consulted and analyzed.

Sabatier's synthesis relies on a framework for studying public policy known as the *Advocacy Coalition Framework*, or ACF, which is discussed at greater length in Chapter 9. In this application of the ACF to implementation, Sabatier's synthesis starts by adopting the bottom-up perspective, which involves looking at "a whole variety of public and private actors involved with a policy problem—as well as their concerns with understanding the perspectives and strategies of all major categories of actors (not simply program proponents)."[19] This contrasts with the top-down focus on the topmost designers of policies. But Sabatier also adopts the top-down perspective by providing a simplified, abstract model of a complex system and by recognizing the importance of the structural features of policy emphasized by the top-down theorists. The primary reason Sabatier uses the ACF to think about implementation is that it reflects the growing sense that implementation does not take place in a one-to-one relationship between the designers, implementers, and targets, but is rather contained within a policy subsystem; the ACF is one way to think about the organization of subsystems.

Refining and reconciling the top-down and bottom-up approaches, Goggin and his colleagues[20] have devised a theory of policy implementation that relies on the sending of *messages* between policy makers and implementers. This study takes into account an important feature of most policy design: that implementation is as much a matter of negotiation and communication as it is a matter of command. Even commands are sometimes resisted because they are unclear or inconsistent with the receiver's expectations. Goggin and his colleagues sum up their argument in two key propositions:

- Clear messages sent by credible officials and received by receptive implementers who have or are given sufficient resources and who implement policies supported by affected groups lead to implementation success.
- Strategic delay on the part of states, while delaying the implementation of policies, can actually lead to improved implementation of policies through innovation, policy learning, bargaining, and the like.

The first of these propositions is a short summary of what has been learned thus far in the study of implementation analysis, but packaged as a matter of communication between various actors. In actual experience, messages are often unclear, officials often lack credibility, implementers are often not receptive or, if they are, do not receive sufficient resources or are opposed by the affected groups. The second proposition counters some of the gloom that had settled around many policy implementation studies. Goggin and his colleagues found, in certain policy areas, that states that "strategically delayed" implementation— in order to seek clarification of a policy, raise more funds, ensure support of affected groups, and so on—often had better success in implementing a policy than did states which immediately implemented a policy. It seems that it would behoove the analyst to take a longer term approach to policy studies, since what may at first blush look like delay on the part of a state or local government may in fact be a period of strategic positioning and adaptation of a policy that actually improves the quality of the service being delivered under the policy, as well as enhancing the likelihood of any implementation.

The debate continues in policy studies over the best approach for the study of implementation and even over whether we should continue studying implementation or focus our attention on other, supposedly more fruitful avenues of study. As long as policies fail, or appear to fail, implementation studies will remain important to policy makers and to students of the policy process.

Summary

The design of policies is at least as important as the decision to do something about a problem in the first place. The features of the political system and the policy process that make deciding to do something so difficult also influence policy implementation. These features also influence the perception of policy success and failure. Many citizens believe that policies fail because of poor design or incompetent administration. This may be true in some cases, but in most cases policies are as well designed as possible given the usual constraints on knowledge and resources, and appear to fail because of unanticipated circumstances, resistance to the policy during implementation but after enactment, and the vagaries of the political process. The challenge for policy designers is to craft policies that meet the broad goals set for them while remaining sufficiently resilient to weather political change, resistance to the policy as implemented, and group conflict. The challenge for students of policy is to understand why policies succeed and fail or, more to the point, why some arguments of success and failure are more effective than others.

The choice of what policies and techniques to use to induce desired outcomes is very difficult. Even if it were merely a technical matter, many variables in implementation, target group behavior, and the policy environment itself influence policy choice. When politics are added to the mix, the policy design process is one of the most interesting to study from the academic perspective, and one of the most difficult tasks facing the practitioner's. Because policy implementation is so difficult, and the reasons for success and failure so variable, policy design and implementation will continue to be rich and important areas, of policy study.

Policy Failure, and Learning from It

For some reason, both journalists and policy scientists like bad news: Journalists will report when the government has lost a lot of money, but will ignore evidence of those instances when the government has saved money through some sort of innovation. At the same time, most of our books on policy implementation describe policy failures. There are probably simple reasons for our concentration on policy failure. The old saying, "If it ain't broke, don't fix it," may dominate our thinking about government: After all, if a government program is reasonably successful, what need is there to describe how it works when we can learn more from failure. I am not sure this is the case: we should and sometimes do learn from failure as well as from success. But because there are so many purported policy failures, and so much written about them, that it is worth considering the reasons for these claims of failure.

No doubt you have asserted, and heard others assert, that a policy has failed. "Our policy against illegal immigrants has failed," you may argue, "because there are still thousands of people coming across the border illegally every day." At this point, let us simply assume that these claims are true. You can then say that the policy has failed to meet its goals: to keep out illegal immigrants and to allow only legal immigrants to come to the country. *Why* might the policy be a failure? You might argue that the Border Patrol is incompetent, that the officers are competent but their managers are not, or that the policy was doomed to fail because of resource deficits. Sometimes we say that a policy is unsuccessful, if not an outright failure, because the policy does not serve enough people or that resources and services are spread too thin among those it does serve.

In other words, we tell causal stories of failure much as we tell causal stories of why problems exist in the first place. The actual idea of "failure" itself is defined implicitly, but not explicitly. In other words, the meaning of "failure" and the context in which it is discussed are never really specified.

Helen Ingram and Dean Mann provide us with a number of useful ways to think about policy failure. They argue that "success and failure are slippery concepts, often highly subjective and reflective of an individual's goals, perception of need, and perhaps even psychological disposition toward life."[21] In other words, failure is perhaps in the eye of the beholder. And the beholder's vision is affected by their immediate perception of the policy in question: as Ingram and Mann argue, labor and management are likely to have very different perspectives on the necessity of the minimum wage. One person may argue that a policy has failed, while another person might look at it as a tentative first step toward a larger goal, such as some health programs for the poor and elderly: Medicare and Medicaid can be viewed as the first step toward more universal health services.

Other reasons for policy failure are listed in Table 8.1, which summarizes Ingram and Mann's argument. If you are active in politics and policy making or even reasonably attentive to politics, you will recognize these reasons for policy failure. There are many possible reasons for policy failure and many possible problems that can cause or contribute to policy failure. Thus, simple storytelling about policy failure may reflect popular dissatisfaction with a policy in particular, or government in general, but fails to take into account the multiple reasons why policies can at least be perceived as failures.

Table 8.1

Explanations for Policy Failure

Alternatives to policies tried	Failure needs to be assessed in terms of the "do nothing" option and in terms of the likelihood that other options would have been more or less successful.
The impact of changing circumstance	Changing circumstances can render policies less successful, such as energy policies that provided price relief before they created dependency on oil and natural gas.
Relationships of one policy to another	Policies are interrelated, and these relationships must be taken into account. For example, a stricter policy against illegal immigrants may endanger broader policy goals surrounding our relations with Mexico, such as oil supplies or drug interdiction.
The boundary question	Political boundaries (between states, for example) will influence policy success.
Excessive policy demand	We may expect too much from policies.
Realizable policy expectations	Policies sometimes fail when they go beyond what we know we can achieve now. But ambitious policy making can be the result of "speculative argumentation"* that seeks to induce innovation. The stated purpose of a policy may not be the actual purpose; there may be more symbolic goals than substance.
Accurate theory of causation	Policy will fail if it is not based on sound causal theory.
Choice of effective policy tools	The choice of ineffective tools will likely yield failure. But the choice of tools is often a function of compromise or ideological predisposition.
The vagaries of implementation	The problems inherent in policy implementation can contribute to policy failure.
Failure of political institutions	"Policy failure is simply a symptom of more profound ailments within our political institutions," such as the breakdown of political party power or devolution of power from congressional leaders to the committees and subcommittees.

Source: Helen Ingram and Dean Mann, "Policy Failure: An Issue Deserving Attention," in *Why Policies Succeed or Fail,* ed. Helen Ingram and Dean Mann (Beverly Hills: Sage, 1980).

Note: *Charles O. Jones, *The Policies and Politics of Pollution Control* (Pittsburgh: University of Pittsburgh Press, 1975).

Policy Success, Failure, and Learning

Given that policies fail, or at least appear to, relatively often, it is likely that, if failure provides an opportunity to learn from mistakes, some sort of policy change or policy design change will result from these failures. It is useful to think about how policy failure induces policy change through a *learning* process. Indeed, many experts and commentators on important public issues claim that certain phenomena can induce organizations to learn from their mistakes.

For some time, social scientists, including those who study complex organizations, have been interested in understanding the extent to which *organizational* learning can take place. Who learns, what is learned, and how learning is employed have been defined rather differently by a number of students of the policy process.[22] The main controversy in the debate over who learns is whether nonhuman entities such as institutions or organizations can "learn" or whether only individual people learn. One can argue that an organization learns through experience: when it develops and implements policies, the evaluation and feedback process provide "learning opportunities" for the organization to change its behavior. While people learn by retaining information and experience in their minds, organizations rely on information storage and retrieval and, perhaps more importantly, on "institutional memory," which, to a large extent, is a function of the experiences and knowledge of key personnel who have been on the job a long time.

This is a rather passive definition of organizational learning. Colin Bennett and Michael Howlett note that learning can be a more active and "deliberate attempt to adjust the goals and techniques of policy in the light of the consequences of past policy and new information so as to better attain" the policy goals.[23] Indeed, organizations make concerted efforts to improve their learning capacity by creating systems to store and disseminate information.

But there are serious conceptual and methodological problems in thinking of organizations as learning agents. Sabatier and May deal with this problem by isolating individuals—agency heads, interest group leaders, academics, journalists, and so on—not institutions, as the unit of analysis in studies of policy making and learning.[24]

Sabatier provides a more specific definition of "policy-oriented learning" as "relatively enduring alterations of thought or behavioral intentions which result from experience and which are concerned with the

attainment (or revision) of policy objectives" (p. 133). Sabatier's definition, by concentrating on individual actors as members of advocacy
coalitions, avoids attributing cognitive processes to organizations, while
broadening policy making to include influential actors, such as academics and journalists, that institutionally focused analyses tend to overlook. This focus on the individual as policy actor also overcomes the
tendency to think of agencies or institutions as the agents of learning.

To summarize, we can think of learning at the organizational and
individual level, but for our purposes it is most useful to consider people
as the agents of learning; these people apply what they have learned in
group policy-making processes.

Types of Learning

The role of focusing events in policy-oriented learning differs with the
different kind of learning that occurs in response to these events. Peter
May divides learning into three categories: instrumental policy learning, social policy learning, and political learning. In all three types of
learning, policy failure—politically and socially defined—provides a
stimulus for learning about how to make better policy.

In the ideal case, learning reflects the accumulation and application
of knowledge to lead to factually and logically correct conclusions.
However, policy makers and their supporters may support policy change
that is not objectively related to change in the political environment or
the nature of the problem. May calls mimicking or copying policy without assessment or analysis *superstitious instrumental learning*. Lotter-
ies and tax policy to attract additional industrial development are
sometimes examples of this sort of mimicking.

Instrumental policy learning concerns learning about "viability of
policy interventions or implementation designs." This sort of learning
centers on implementation tools and techniques. When feedback from
implementation is analyzed and changes to the design are made that
improve its performance, then this suggests that learning has happened
and was successful.

May's article lists what he calls prima facie evidence of these various
forms of learning. In my research, I found that the aftermath of the *Exxon
Valdez* oil spill provides prima facie evidence of instrumental policy learning. Instrumental policy learning involves assessing the efficacy of existing policy instruments. Environmental groups and their allies used the

Exxon Valdez spill to argue, much more strongly than had been possible before the spill, that these policy tools failed to address large oil spills. The resulting legislation, the Oil Pollution Act of 1990, combined aspects of instrumental and social policy learning by establishing new policies regarding oil spill cleanup and liability based on a causal theory involving what it takes to induce oil companies to behave in a less risky way.

Social policy learning involves learning about the "social construction of a policy or program." This type of learning goes beyond simple adjustments of program management to the heart of the problem itself, including attitudes toward program goals and the nature and appropriateness of government action. If successfully applied, social policy learning can result in better understanding of the underlying causal theory of a public problem, leading to better policy responses.

Evidence of social policy learning involves learning the causes of problems and the effectiveness of policy interventions based on those problems. May argues that prima facie indicators of social learning involve "policy redefinition entailing changes in policy goals or scope—e.g., policy direction, target groups, rights bestowed by the policy."[25] There are many examples of such learning. One example concerns the way communities address prostitution. Traditionally, the police tried to control prostitution by arresting prostitutes, and doing so often enough to dissuade women from working in a particular area or community. When this policy was found to be ineffective—and, in many ways, unfair to the prostitutes themselves—communities focused instead on the men who seek out prostitutes, arresting the men and, in some cases, publicizing their arrests and convictions to shame them. In this case, the target of the policy shifted from the prostitute to the "john" because of a new understanding of the problem as being caused at least as much by demand as by supply. A similar logic is sometimes employed against illegal drugs, when attention shifts toward eradication and interdiction of drugs from abroad, rather than making smaller, seemingly less effective arrests of users at home.

Political learning is considerably different from instrumental and social learning. Political learning is learning about "strategy for advocating a given policy idea or problem," leading potentially to "more sophisticated advocacy of a policy idea or problem."

Political learning is learning about effective political advocacy. Political learning can be assumed to have occurred when advocates for or against policy change alter their strategy and tactics to conform to new information that has entered the political system. For example, the breakdown of the nuclear power industry in the United States was due, in part, to the efforts of groups that mobilized against nuclear power; their efforts began before the Three Mile Island (TMI) nuclear power plant accident but were accelerated by that event. Group leaders learned that events like TMI and images like the specter of the "China Syndrome" were highly effective in promoting public and elite concerns about the safety and cost-effectiveness of nuclear power. Indeed, the exploitation of the more frightening or upsetting aspects of any event, from an industrial accident to the nomination of a potential Supreme Court justice, include the sophisticated use of imagery and storytelling to advance a position; these techniques have been learned and honed over time as competing groups seek to improve their competitive positions.

Conclusion

For policy makers and public managers, policy implementation is one of the most difficult aspects of the policy process. For students of public policy, implementation is both frustrating and fascinating. It is fascinating because implementation brings together many actors and forces that cooperate and clash with each other in order to achieve—or to thwart—policy goals. It is frustrating because the process has proven particularly hard to model; contributing to this frustration is the tension between building and testing good theory, on the one hand, while providing useful information to policy makers and implementers on how to structure programs for greater success.

Given the complexity of our political system, it seems that policy failure—or, at best, very limited success—would be the inevitable outcome of any public program. This may not be true, however, because failure is, like so much else in public policy, an subjective condition that is more often grounded in the perceptions of a particular interest than in empirical "fact." However, we can stipulate that some policies are much less successful than others and that policy makers and others concerned with the management of public programs will learn from the purported failure of the policy. In this way, policy development is an ongoing process with no discernible beginning and no obvious end, but with plenty of opportunities for refinement and fine-tuning.

This chapter concludes the discussion of the individual elements of the policy process. The next chapter discusses recent theories, in which all the elements of the policy process are put together into improved models.

9

Putting It All Together: Models of the Policy Process

Thus far in this book we have explored various aspects of the policy process: the history of American policy making, who participates, how they participate, who has the greater power, and so on. This chapter brings these elements together in three ways. The first part is a discussion of a basic "systems" model of the policy process, along the lines first pioneered by David Easton in the mid-1960s. While such systems models are sometimes criticized as simplistic, they are still useful in helping us to make sure that we have taken all aspects of policy making into account. Second is a discussion of how the systems model complements the "stages" heuristic employed by many, if not most, students of the policy process. Finally, I will introduce more recent models of the policy process, to illustrate how social scientists are trying to create more creative, more useful models of the policy process that break free from some of the more rigid aspects of the systems and stages models.

Systems Models of the Policy Process

David Easton's book, *A Systems Analysis of Political Life*, was very important in the development of more sophisticated models of policy making.[1] His book, inspired by the considerable amount of thinking about natural and social systems that occurred in the early 1960s, corresponds with the then-new and growing field of systems analysis.

Easton and the systems modelers argue that we can think of the public policy process as the product of a system, influenced by and influencing the environment in which it operates. The system receives inputs and responds with outputs. The inputs are the various forms of issues, pressures, information, and the like to which the actors in the system react; the outputs are, in simplest terms, public policy decisions to do or not do something. A simplified depiction of this system is shown in Figure 9.1.

The Environment of Policy Making

The policy *environment* contains the features of the structural, social, political, and economic system in which public policy making takes place. Much as a plant or animal is both influenced by and influences its environment, the political process can be thought of as being influenced by and influencing its environment. One must be careful with this analogy, however: the boundary between the political system and its environment is not a fixed line. Rather this boundary is blurry, as the system and the environment overlap to some extent. Within this general notion of the policy environment, we can isolate four "environments" that influence policy making: the structural environment, the social environment, the economic environment, and the political environment.

Structural Environment

We have covered the structural features of American politics and public policy throughout this book. These features include the structure of the three branches of government and the federal system's division of labor between the federal and state governments, with the state's delegation of duties and powers to local governments. Beyond the constitutional framework, there are traditional and legal structures that establish the rules of policy making. The two-party system organizes and structures political actors in Congress and each state legislature. Laws such as the Freedom of Information Act and the Administrative Procedures Act structure the way the government does its business and provide opportunities for public participation in government activities. And legal decisions, particularly those made by the Supreme Court, establish the boundaries of permissible government action. There are many other examples of how the courts have ruled not on the substance of an issue, but on the constitutional meaning of the case: that is, the courts have helped establish the rules under which the policy making process is conducted.

Figure 9.1   A Systems Model of Politics and Policy

The environment—structural, social, political and economic—affects all parts of the system.

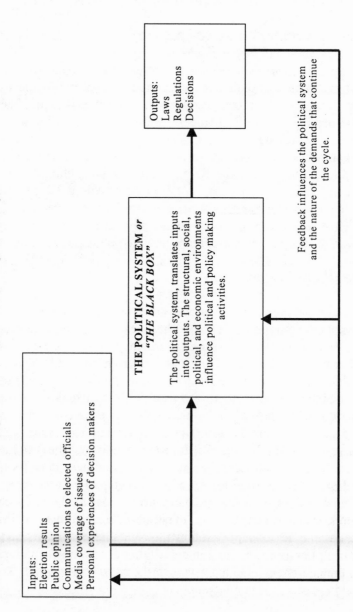

Inputs:
Election results
Public opinion
Communications to elected officials
Media coverage of issues
Personal experiences of decision makers

THE POLITICAL SYSTEM *or*
"THE BLACK BOX"

The political system, translates inputs into outputs. The structural, social, political, and economic environments influence political and policy making activities.

Outputs:
Laws
Regulations
Decisions

Feedback influences the political system and the nature of the demands that continue the cycle.

Social Environment

The social aspect of the policy environment includes the nature and composition of the population and its social structure. *Demographers* study the composition of the population by looking at the distribution of age, race, gender, and other attributes of the population. The founders, by enacting a constitutional mandate that a census be taken every ten years, provided the means by which a vast amount of demographic data are collected and analyzed. Based on trends from the census and other sources, we know that the population of the United States will substantially change in the coming years, as the nation becomes older and comprised of proportionally fewer people of European ancestry. These changes will have significant implications for public policy, including major political issues like the solvency of the Social Security system and seemingly mundane issues such as ensuring that road signs and markings are readable by older drivers.[2] With an increasingly large number of immigrants from Asia and Latin America, cultural changes introduced by these groups will have a discernible influence on policies, particularly in states such as New York, California, Florida, and Texas. These states receive the bulk of immigrants to the United States and are already experiencing change. None of this is to suggest that the change is negative—our national experience shows that immigration often revitalizes the nation and our communities. This trend does reveal, however, that changes are afoot that policy makers must take into account in their future planning.

Another major shift in the social environment that will influence policy is the increasing number of women in professions and roles that were once held by men only. While the Equal Rights Amendment was never made a part of the Constitution, women, who once were literally noncitizens in America, today attend college at a greater rate than men and attend law school at a rate nearly equal to men. While sporting triumphs such as the establishment of the WNBA basketball league and the very closely followed American women's World Cup soccer victory in 1999 seem small in the broader sweep of history, they are highly visible indicators of our society's changing attitudes toward women's roles and capabilities. Still, in many ways, women have not achieved the full benefits of our society that men enjoy, including pay equity and access to corporate and political leadership.

Taken together, these demographic factors will continue to influence public policy. With the increasing independence of women has come a developing political "gender gap" between men and women's political attitudes. With a larger elderly population, we can expect to see increasing demands for policies designed to benefit this segment of society. In addition, greater cultural and ethnic diversity will lead to different types of policy preferences and demands.

Economic Environment

The economic environment includes the distribution of wealth in a society, the nature and distribution of capital, the size and composition of industry sectors, the rate of growth of the economy, inflation, and the cost of labor and raw materials. Economic factors are important because various features of the economy influence the types of policies a society makes. In Keynesian economics (that is, the theories of economics pioneered by the British economist John Maynard Keynes), governments spend more and run budget deficits to stimulate the economy when it is in a recession. When the economy is strong, governments should run budget surpluses to make up for the deficits incurred during the recession.[3] While Keynesian theories have been challenged since their publication in 1936 and came under increasing criticism when so-called supply-side theories of economic stimulus gained primacy in the 1980s, they still have an important influence on policy making. And even some Keynesians and other political actors began to argue, in the 1980s, that the growing federal budget deficit (which contributes to the *national debt*, or the total amount of money owed to the government's creditors) would bankrupt the nation, a prospect that Charles Cochran and Eloise Malone argue is unlikely.[4] As this book was being written, the nation began to experience large budget surpluses, in part as a result of the booming economy, which most Keynesians would argue are completely predictable given the tendency for tax collections to rise and government coffers to fill during good economic times.

The policies a government makes are often a function of the overall wealth of the economy, because the amount of resources available to government (through taxes and through its ability to compel behaviors without gravely negative economic consequences) is influenced by current and continued growth and prosperity. In general, wealthier societies can undertake tasks that less wealthy societies cannot: the United States and the Soviet Union could engage in their space programs because they had more resources available than nations such as Canada or

England. Of course, wealth is not the only determinant of policy choices. For example, the United States has no national health plan and no policies to provide for public employment during economic recessions, even though it is wealthier than many nations that provide these services.

Public policy choices are influenced by the economy, but the policy decisions and the daily operations of government also influence the economic environment; they are very much intertwined. As Peters notes, "approximately 51 percent of all money collected in taxes by the federal government is returned to the economy as transfer payments to citizens."[5] *Transfer payments* involve transfers of money from the government to recipients, such as farm subsidies, disaster relief, and various social welfare programs. The government also buys goods and services from the private sector, ranging from desks and chairs to supercomputers. And tax policies influence economic behavior: The mortgage tax deduction encourages people to buy houses; student loan interest deductions may influence people to start or continue college.[6] These are called *tax expenditures* because allowing people to keep money that would ordinarily go to taxes is fiscally equivalent to taxing people and then giving the money back as subsidies.

People's perceptions of their economic well-being have a significant influence on politics. One reason often cited for President Bush's defeat in the 1992 election was the perception that he was out of touch with the economic downturn then facing the nation. A theory that explains President Clinton's 1996 reelection, in the face of scandal, was the perception that the economy was performing well. In the coming years, as the fruits of the 1990s economic boom are enjoyed by many, the growing wealth gap between the most and least wealthy could create political tensions that may lead to policy change. Such a prospect appears to be, for various reasons, unlikely, as attempts to raise this issue in policy discourse are often dismissed by elected and appointed officials who, like many Americans, are wary of making distinctions or policies based on economic class—unless that class is broadly defined as the "middle class."[7] Most Americans define themselves as being middle-class,[8] making political appeals to the middle class quite popular among interest groups and politicians.

Political Environment

The political environment encompasses a hard to measure but easily understood idea Kingdon calls "the national mood."[9] Kingdon describes the national mood as how we feel about government, public problems, and the effectiveness of government and other institutions in successfully addressing these problems. This notion of the "national mood" is quite vague and considerably controversial among political scientists, who rightly wonder how one would measure and describe something as diffuse as a "mood" among over 250 million people. This is an entirely reasonable critique, but for now let us consider Kingdon's argument on his terms, as it helps us to conceptualize, if not fully explain, important features of politics.

Sometimes, the national mood is generally good, such as when the economy is strong and trust in political institutions and our leaders relatively high. From 1945 to about 1963, the national mood was in many ways optimistic. The United States had emerged from World War II largely unscathed, and the economy boomed after the war. While politics was often characterized by sharp disagreements over policy, fears of communist expansion, fears of nuclear war, and some anxiety about what the social and political scene looked like immediately after World War II,[10] in general, people were optimistic about America's future, believed its social and political system to be superior to other nations,' and trusted its leaders. This sense of optimism was in many ways personified by John F. Kennedy, who symbolized to some Americans the nation's vigor and drive for progress.

By the mid-1960s, however, the national mood began to decay. The Vietnam war began to bog down, and journalists began to report that the official line that the war was being won was not consistent with the actual outcome of the war. By early 1968, President Lyndon Johnson announced that he would not run for reelection because of the intractability of the war and the vehemence of the public protest against it. In the same year, Robert F. Kennedy, brother of the slain president, and the Rev. Dr. Martin Luther King Jr. were murdered, and antiwar protests and urban unrest in the United States and other nations created a sense of crisis in political institutions. The Watergate scandal—which led to President Nixon's resignation in 1974—further shook public trust; at the same time, inflation, unemployment, and the energy crisis combined to erode public faith in the United States' power and its ability to influence world events. By the late 1970s, major American industries were facing severe competitive pressures from Europe and Japan, and one of the "big three" American automakers—Chrysler—sought federal financial aid (some called it a bailout) to remain in business.

The early 1980s saw little improvement in the national mood, as attempts to fight inflation—attempts that were successful in the long run—were largely driven by the Federal Reserve's decision to set economy-crushing interest rates. By the mid-1980s, however, inflation was almost entirely eliminated as a major factor in the economy, and a remarkable economic recovery was under way. Except for a relatively mild recession in the late 1980s and early 1990s, the economy has been remarkably sound by any standard, giving Americans substantial faith in the future of the nation.

Today's national mood is in many ways upbeat—with crime on the decline, the economy booming, and international tensions seemingly much less frightening than they were during the depths of the Cold War. Indeed, some public opinion polls have found that trust in government is inching up somewhat. But many Americans still feel disconnected from government, feel they lack any voice, and, while often angry and upset, are unclear about how to participate in the policy process. This alienation is reflected in low rates of electoral participation and registration (particularly in nonpresidential elections), as shown in Figure 9.2. And while violence against the government or its representatives, such as the catastrophic bombing of the Oklahoma City federal building in 1995, is thankfully quite rare, there is still an undercurrent of antigovernment sentiment that has remained persistently troubling for nearly thirty years.[11]

Why are the national mood and trust in government important for public policy? Because, as Ralph Erber and Richard Lau, referring to David Easton's work, state, "the legitimacy of democratic political systems depends in large part on the extent to which the electorate trusts the government to do what is right at least most of the time."[12]

James Anderson also notes that we can consider *political culture* as an important part of the political environment. Political culture describes the long-standing ways that people think about politics and how they behave in politics. In the United States, key features of our political culture include a strong belief in individual freedom, political equality, self-reliance, free enterprise, and market capitalism. Political culture is much more consistent than national mood and has a substantial influence over the types of issues that are most likely to succeed as policy initiatives. In the United States, any policies that can be portrayed as anticapitalist or that would restrict many people's freedom are unlikely to be enacted.

Figure 9.2 **Rates of Electoral Participation and Registration, 1980–1996**

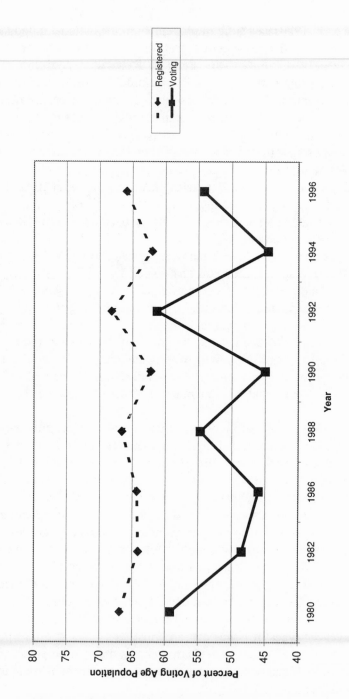

Source: U.S. Department of Commerce, Bureau of the Census, *Statistical Abstract of the United States, 1998*, Table 483.

Inputs

The inputs to the policy making system are the demands placed on the system to do something about a problem. Perhaps the most obvious input is voting: voting is the most common form of political participation, and elected officials and the news media often proclaim the results of elections as providing policy guidance or "mandates" to pursue particular policies.

In some cases, such political guidance may in fact be the result of an election. This is particularly true in states in which there are provisions for citizen *initiatives* or *referenda* that allow people to vote directly on policy proposals. An example is the famous Proposition 13, which California voters approved in 1978; it set limits on property taxes and was the opening act of what apparently became a national tax revolt. Here, the input to the process was the evidence of popular discontent with what was perceived to be onerous levels of taxation. This influenced policy making and politics, and Ronald Reagan won the presidency in 1980, in part, on an antitax campaign.

But interpreting voters' preferences for *candidates* as mandates for particular policy directions is notoriously difficult, and election results rarely have a direct influence on policy outcomes. People have many different reasons for voting for a candidate, ranging from simple name familiarity to appreciation for casework to local political considerations having little to do with broader ideological or policy issues. During election campaigns, candidates can package their policy decisions in a way that they believe is most attractive to voters, realizing that casework and pork may have more of an influence on electoral success than legislative decisions. Furthermore, elections happen at fixed times and politicians have fixed terms: two, four, and six years for the House of Representatives, president, and Senate, respectively. Once the election is held, elected officials need not worry about voters with respect to daily policy decisions.[13] Still, while the connection between voting and policy is sometimes tenuous, elections are important because they do have an influence on the broad policy agenda and because they determine the partisan composition of Congress and other legislative bodies. Parties do have different positions on issues, and the partisan balance in the legislature can influence what policies are most likely to succeed or fail.

Public Opinion

Because Americans believe that political power derives from the consent of the citizens, it is useful and important for us to have a sense of the public's satisfaction with the current situation in general and of its particular preferences on policies. A common way to collect information about public preferences is through public opinion polls. Such polls are conducted by a number of different organizations for a number of different reasons.

Among the better polls are those conducted by academic institutions or in conjunction with them. The National Opinion Research Center collects a great deal of public opinion information, particularly at election time. Most people are familiar with big national polls such as the CBS/*New York Times* and the CNN/*USA Today* polls. Smaller newspapers and broadcasters will subscribe to poll results from national polling firms such as the Gallup and Louis Harris organizations or join forces with polling experts at local universities. In New Jersey, for example, the *Newark Star-Ledger* works with the Eagleton Institute of Politics at Rutgers University to poll residents of New Jersey.

Many people distrust public opinion polls, either because they doubt the reliability of their methods (that is, they doubt that the same results could be achieved if the poll were repeated) or because they can cite classic examples of polls that were, in the end, incorrect in predicting election results. Because of the ways public opinion polls are conducted—in particular, because pollsters only question a sample of the voting population—it is clear that polls will not get the results of every election right. Another common critique of polling is that "pollsters have never called *me* to ask questions," which is often interpreted to mean "If no one asked *me*, how can the results be accurate?" The likelihood of any particular person being called is fairly low because the necessary sample size for reasonably accurate polling is actually quite small: a very accurate national poll can be conducted with just 1,700 respondents, *if* this sample is carefully drawn so as not to introduce the possible biases that poor samples introduce in polling.

Election polling is not the only thing that polling organizations do, of course, and the more issue-oriented polls may be more useful to us in understanding preferences. Pollsters ask citizens about controversial public issues (abortion, school prayer, environmental protection), general political questions (approval ratings of the president, Congress, and the like), and even cultural or entertainment topics. When hot issues arise on the public agenda, such as military action against a country or an economic crisis, polls will ask the public to assess these problems, either on their own merits or in relation to the public's approval of the president, Congress, or other national institutions.

Some of these issue-oriented polls are conducted by political campaigns and parties themselves. They are often used to shape a party's agenda, as the GOP did when formulating its "Contract with America" in the 1994 congressional elections. These poll-driven agendas and policies are often controversial, for some people argue that being driven solely by polls does not equate with the broader goal of creating a good society for all Americans. Other types of issue polling are actually unethical. A technique known as "push polling" was developed in the 1990s to attempt to seed issues on the public agenda. This technique has become controversial in the 2000 presidential campaign, as John McCain and George W. Bush accused each other of using this unethical tactic.[14]

In push polling, the questionnaire is designed not only to elicit information, but also to create responses generated by leading questions. For example, a pollster may ask: "Senator Jones has voted against nearly every anticrime bill that has been introduced in the legislature this year. Does this make you more or less likely to vote for Senator Jones in the fall election?" The pollster, perhaps working for Senator Jones's opponent or a group that opposes him (but representing himself as a "neutral" pollster), is less interested in the answer to this question and more interested in seeding the public with the idea that Senator Jones is "soft on crime." The theme of voting against important legislation (in our example, anticrime legislation) is likely to be repeated in other campaign activities, such as advertising and stump speeches. Push polling is not ethical as *polling* because framing the questions in a manner similar to public opinion poll deceives the respondent and the public at large. The poll is not intended to measure public opinion, but, rather, is intended to set a campaign agenda. Indeed, persistent and unethical polling practices have made legitimate public opinion research difficult to do, as the public progressively loses trust in polling and legitimate pollsters find more and more people refusing to participate in any poll.

In the end, polling can be very useful to interest groups seeking to convey a message to the public. Groups can use polling data to understand what messages will work best in advancing an opinion, and the vast majority of groups want accurate, honestly conducted polls. But we must keep in mind that polls are sometimes crafted to elicit the answers that the group wants to see in the first place. While ethically questionable, some groups justify this practice as a legitimate way of getting their message into public discourse.

Communications to Elected Officials and Public Managers

There are clearly other ways to communicate our individual or group preferences to legislators. Indeed, one of the most popular is expressed in the time-honored admonition to "write your congressman." Congress members do receive thousands of letters, faxes, e-mails, and (in earlier times) telegrams every year. Many of these letters are requests for help in dealing with a problem with the government (called "casework"), but a good proportion of these letters seeks to influence a congressperson's vote on an issue or elicit the member's sponsorship of a bill or an amendment. Indeed, many legislators, in their communications with constituents, argue that a prime source of ideas for legislation is citizen input.

This is true, up to a point. I certainly do not wish to discourage you and other people from writing to elected officials—indeed, at the local level your letters may lead to actual action on an issue, including meeting to discuss your concerns, legislative hearings, and even new legislation. But the sheer volume of communication with members of Congress and most state legislatures suggests that individual letters are likely to be lost in the shuffle. Many times, constituent letters are answered with form letters that are drafted by staff and signed on behalf of the member of Congress or the legislature; such letters are often equivocal and unresponsive and generally do not commit the representative to a particular position. Representatives do not respond this way because they are inattentive; they do so because they know that individual letters and disparate subjects carry relatively little political weight. Rather, focused communications on a single issue are more important to elected officials.

Therefore, to overcome this tendency of letters getting lost in the shuffle, interest groups often mobilize members to send letters or cards to elected officials. This group-generated communication can serve as a rough gauge of public sentiment on an issue, but officials know that the effort it takes to fill in a form letter or postcard is less than the effort it takes to draft an entire letter. Officials can get a very rough idea of interest group activity in their district by, in essence, weighing the pro- and anti-issue mail and using this balance as one of a number of inputs to voting and other decisions.

The News Media

As discussed in Chapter 4, the news media are important participants in policy making, since they highlight some issues and deemphasize others and can therefore shape the public discourse surrounding a policy issue. Indeed, interest groups seek to get their preferred constructions of problems into the media, so as to more broadly affect the debate over the issue; elected and appointed officials also use the media to shape the debate.

Public opinion data expressed in the media are important but sometimes imprecise gauges of how the public and community leaders are thinking about issues. Politicians and policy makers are particularly sensitive to how issues are covered in the media, and, if coverage of their work is going badly, they often lash out at the news media or, more shrewdly, make changes in the course of policy making. A media outcry about a proposed plan of action can stop a policy proposal almost immediately, as in the recent example of OSHA's attempt to regulate workplace safety for telecommuters. Media coverage of issues can also push agendas forward, such as the increased attention to aviation safety that accompanies intensive media coverage of airplane crashes. The agenda setting function of the media is therefore important in shaping the government agenda because it influences people and policy makers to think more about some issues and problems and think less about others.

Policy makers, knowing this, often use the news media as a way of floating "trial balloons" to assess the reaction of the public. Strategic leaks of information are common, particularly when policy makers are preparing large and complex policy initiatives. From public reaction to these trial balloons, policy makers can make adjustments to their proposals or learn whether they are likely to succeed or fail.

It is important to reiterate, however, that although the news media are very important inputs to policy making, they are not the only inputs: decision makers have more sources of information than most citizens, and they can draw upon other information they gather in their jobs to make their decisions. But if we consider citizen demands as important inputs to the policy process, then we must be mindful of the role the news media have in shaping the terms of debate, particularly on the most visible, most controversial issues.

Interest Group Activity

Interest groups have a bad name in American politics. Allan Cigler puts this mildly, saying that "like the public at large, political scientists have often viewed interest groups with ambivalence, recognizing their inevitability but uncomfortable with their impact."[15] More bluntly, politicians and journalists often rail against the power of "special interests" and contrast their activities with a notion of a "public interest."

Regardless of one's attitudes toward interest groups, they are key actors in the policy process. Groups gather together people with similar interests to amplify their voices in policy making; if you belong to an interest group like the National Rifle Association, the International Brotherhood of Teamsters, or Greenpeace, you know firsthand that your group wields more power than you do individually or than even a million unconnected, unorganized people can wield independently.

Decisions

Key to the common definition of "public policy" as being "what government chooses to do or not to do" is the idea of a *decision*. Someone or some institution in the policy process has to make a decision. This can be as complex as President Kennedy's decision, in 1961, that the United States should send an astronaut to the moon and back by 1970. Or it can be as simple as the decision by a police officer to give a motorist a warning rather than a speeding ticket. The decision not to do something is as important as the decision to do something, and a nondecision is also a policy output. In the moon flight example, a considerable amount of momentum had built behind the space program for various reasons, so the decision to not go to the moon, or to mount a more modest space program, would have had a profound influence on future developments in aerospace. At about the same time, the decision to not pursue the Supersonic Transport (SST) airplane program in the late 1960s had profound influences on the aviation and aerospace industries. Our historical decisions not to create a system of national health insurance have as profound an effect on our national health system as would a decision to create such a system.

Indeed, our constitutional system is structured in a way that often prevents decisions from being made. The numerous points that bills must pass before they become laws, that proposed regulations must pass before they become actual regulations, and that laws must pass before they are effectively implemented make any sort of final and authoritative decision very difficult to reach. Thus, when analyzing policies, it is as important to specify what has not been done, as it is to specify what was done.

In this section, I briefly explain some key concepts in the study of how decisions are made about what to do, once the decision has been reached that something is to be done. While public policy is as much about what government chooses not to do as it is about what government actually does, for illustrative purposes I will focus primarily on how decisions to do *something* are reached. And, as is true throughout this book, when I discuss Congress or the presidency, we can apply the same ideas to the state legislatures and governors.

For simplicity's sake, we can say that the decision making process begins after an issue or problem is placed on the agenda and as it makes its way through the legislative process until it comes close to the *decision agenda*. The decision agenda is that relatively small collection of things about which an organization must make a decision. In Congress's case, it usually begins by winnowing down a set of alternatives that are, for the most part, debated and formulated in the committees. The goal is to link potential problems to potential solutions.

Many of the models of decision making presented here are both *positive* models (that is, neutral explanations of how a system works) and *normative* models (explanations of how decisions *should* be made). Because my goal in this book is to explain public policy making, I will not delve deeply into the normative dimensions of these issues; that is, I will not spend much time on whether the rational comprehensive decision making model is superior or should be used in making governmental decisions. This is a task for you, the reader, to decide as you weigh the relative merits of these perspectives both as normative models and as reasonable models of how the policy process works. What's more, like so much of public policy studies, it is difficult to argue any model or perspective holds true across all time and circumstances.

Rational Comprehensive Decision Making

Most discussions of decision making begin with a discussion of the "rational comprehensive" or "rational actor" as an "ideal type" of decision making that is rarely, if ever, achieved.[16] Yet for years the rational actor model was widely assumed to be a primary method of decision making in public and private organizations, and the quest for this sort of rationality persists today. After all, wouldn't it be best if all our decisions were made rationally, based on the best information we have available?

There are several assumptions that underlie the rational model.[17] The main assumptions of the rational actor model are that decision makers are presented with a problem and a goal (involving solving or ameliorating the problem) and are set to the task of solving or addressing, to the extent possible, the problem. In so doing, decision makers gather all the possible information they can on the problem—its societal and economic costs, for example—and on possible solutions to the problem. Multiple options are analyzed, including the option to take no action at all. The goal, Dye argues, is to achieve "maximum social gain" through the agreed-upon policy.

This model is often set up as a straw man against which other models of decision making are compared; an example of this straw man is Model I (the rational actor model) in Graham Allison's *Essence of Decision.*[18] The reason for this is simple: several features of the rational model render it an unrealistic model of decision making.

First is the problem of goal consensus. Often, when a problem is identified, it is hard to understand what goals the various proponents of policies have in mind. Often, goals are left purposefully ambiguous so that legislation can gain passage; it is then left to the implementers to try to figure out what the most important goal or goals are. Because solutions are so often tied to goals, some solutions to a problem will foster political conflict, even if the solution seems the most "rational." For example, liberals might see welfare as a form of societal compassion to help less fortunate people overcome the conditions that lead to poverty. Conservatives, on the other hand, may view welfare as a temporary boost to help people while they look for employment; the conservatives' support is based more on economics than compassion. Thus, the same problem can be seen as having two rather different goals.

Another problem with the rational model is that the information processing demands are too great for human minds in human institutions. It is impossible to gather all the information about a particular problem; one could spend a lifetime doing so and not find a final answer. Even with today's vastly improved information storage and retrieval systems, it is very difficult for decision makers, confronted as they are with significant resource constraints and time pressure, to gather all the information needed, weigh the information, and make a decision.

An additional problem with attempts at highly rational decision making comes with the nature of information itself. Because decision makers deal with social phenomena, and social phenomena are notoriously difficult to track and analyze, it is difficult to find the proper information about goals, values, costs, and benefits needed to make a rational decision. This is one of the key criticisms of *cost-benefit analysis*, abbreviated CBA. In CBA, the analyst tries to count up, often in monetary terms, the cost of pursuing a certain policy and the benefits to be derived from it. The problem is that the costs of an action are sometimes easier to count up than are the benefits. For example, we might know that the cost of cleaning up a toxic waste site is $50 million dollars, and the result is that we might reduce the rate of cancers and other illnesses by somewhere between 2 and 10 percent. What is the benefit, in dollar terms, of this reduction? How can we make this reduction more certain? This depends on our calculation of how much each life is worth, a very difficult thing to calculate. Again, this does not mean we should not try to use CBA. And, as Dye makes quite clear, we should not forget that rational analysis is also about values and preferences, not simply about dollar costs and benefits.[19]

Many of the critiques of the rational actor model suggest that rationality is so difficult, or nearly impossible, that other models of decision making are more accurate. But it is important to keep rationality in mind as, at least, a *goal*, if not the realistic end. After all, *if* complete rationality were possible—that is, if we had complete (or very nearly complete) access to all relevant information, and that information was adequate, we would be able to make better decisions. This is why people continue to develop information systems and analytic techniques: to move us toward improved, more rational decision making.

Incrementalism and Bounded Rationality

James March and Herbert Simon provide us with a way of thinking about rationality that recognizes the limits on resources and human abilities to process information. This concept is called *bounded rationality*.[20] To be boundedly rational means that one behaves as rationally as one can within certain bounds or limits, including limited time, limited information, and our limited human ability to recognize every feature and pattern of every problem; we can try to enhance these skills, but they are still inherently limited.

Charles Lindblom applied these ideas in a now-classic article, "The Science of 'Muddling Through,'" which appeared in *Public Administration Review* in 1959.[21] In this article, Lindblom argued that people make decisions in relatively small increments, rather than in big leaps. They do so because key sources of information include what we know about the current nature of an existing problem, our accumulated knowledge about what steps have been taken before, if any, to address the problem, and whether those steps appeared to be successes or failures. This description of the policy process is both a model of how decisions are made and a description of how contending interests behave in making policy.

An overview of Lindblom's comparison between rational comprehensive and incremental decision making is shown in Table 9.1. Lindblom calls the rational comprehensive method of decision making the "root" method, because decisions start from the "root" of the issue or problem; incrementalism is the "branch," he argues, because it uses and builds on what is already known, without relying on reanalyzing everything about what is currently being done. In this way, the incremental method allows the decision maker to take a fair number of short cuts: it eliminates the need to explicitly separate means from ends, to pick the analytically "best" policy, and to rely heavily on theories that the decision maker may have neither the time nor the inclination to use.

Two major problems with the theory (and to some extent the practice) of incrementalism are, first, that some problems demand bold decisions and, second, that some goals simply cannot be met with incremental steps. For example, President Franklin Roosevelt was elected on a pledge to tackle the grave social and economic problems associated with the Great Depression. His flurry of activity—the banking holiday, new banking and finance laws, the promotion of various measures such as the National Industrial Recovery Act—as a rather sharp departure from prior governmental practice. These innovations were occasioned, in large part, by the public's demand that the government do *something*; the gravity of the Depression was such that aggressive measures needed to be adopted.

A second example starts with President Kennedy's address to Congress in 1961, in which he urged that the United States put an astronaut on the moon and safely return him to earth before 1970. Paul Schulman calls this a "major national commitment," and the federal government, after some years of organizational and political confusion, responded to Kennedy's challenge by appropriating money and causing the rapid

Table 9.1

Rational Comprehensive Decision Making and Bounded Rationality
(incremental decision making)

Rational comprehensive	Bounded rationality
1a. Clarification of values or objectives distinct from and usually prerequisite to empirical analysis of alternative policies.	1b. Selection of value goals and empirical analysis of the needed action are not distinct from one another but are closely intertwined.
2a. Policy formulation is therefore approached through means-end analysis: First the ends are isolated, then the means to achieve them are sought.	2b. Since means and ends are not distinct, means-end analysis is often inappropriate or limited.
3a. The gist of a "good" policy is that it can be shown to be the most appropriate means to desired ends.	3b. The test of a "good" policy is typically that various analysts find themselves directly agreeing on a policy (without their agreeing that it is the most appropriate means to an agreed objective).
4a. Analysis is comprehensive; every important relevant factor is taken into account.	4b. Analysis is drastically limited: (i) Important possible outcomes are neglected; (ii) Important alternative potential policies are neglected; (iii) Important affected values are neglected.
5a. Theory is often heavily relied upon.	5b. A succession of comparisons greatly reduces or eliminates reliance on theory.

growth of the National Aeronautics and Space Administration and other agencies to meet the goal.[22] Because this task—putting someone on the moon—was undertaken even before the first American astronaut had simply orbited the earth, the space program serves as an example of a nonincremental, all-or-nothing decision. While the landing on the moon might have resulted from a more incrementalist space policy, it is likely that it would have taken longer and would have been achieved rather differently than it was.

Another example of sudden, nonincremental policy is the decision to mobilize for all-out war. Before the United States was drawn into to World War II, it pursued an incremental policy of pressure on Japan to halt its expansionism and on Germany to protect shipments of war material to Great Britain. When Japan attacked Pearl Harbor in December 1941, and Germany and Italy declared war, the United States had to move from incrementalist economic and diplomatic policies to a very sudden commitment to build a large military to win a two-front war. Of course, some military commitments are incremental, such as the slowly building American involvement in Vietnam in the 1960s, followed by the slow disengagement from Vietnam in the early 1970s.

Other Models of Decision Making

The rational comprehensive and incrementalist models of decision making are perhaps the two most commonly reviewed models in public policy, but other models, borrowing from these and other theories, exist to help explain how decisions are made.

Michael Cohen, James March, and Johan Olsen developed the *garbage can* model to explain decision making in what they call "organized anarchies."[23] They use universities as an example of organized anarchies because, as you may have experienced or be experiencing as you read this, universities are not rigidly organized and managed institutions. Indeed, members of the faculty demand and usually receive considerable autonomy in the management of their own work and of their departments. Students enjoy a degree of autonomy in their choices of which courses and majors to take, how to structure living arrangements, and what to do during free time. And administrators must manage the various interests— faculty, alumni, students, and members of the broader community—without violating the traditional prerogatives of any of these groups.

There are three elements or streams in the garbage can model: problems, solutions, and participants. In each of these streams, various elements of decision making float about; what is perhaps most important about this model is the idea that there are solutions looking for problems as much as vice versa, and participants floating about looking for a way to participate in putting together these problems and solutions. Cohen, March, and Olsen call the decision opportunities "garbage cans" into which the three streams are mixed together. For example, the selection of a new dean is an opportunity for participants to come together in a garbage can and use the hiring to link perceived problems in the college with perceived solutions.

An important point to stress in the garbage can model of decision making or problem solving is that it is not a model in which a problem is identified, and then people go out to develop or invent solutions and bring them back. Rather, many solutions already exist, and the role of participants is to advance their solution to a problem, even when it seems that they are simply carrying a solution in search of a problem. For example, Secretary of Housing and Urban Development Jack Kemp, in the Bush administration, strongly suggested that Urban Enterprise Zones (UEZs)—zones in which tax laws and other regulations are relaxed to encourage development—be created in cities to provide jobs while slowing urban decay. Kemp promoted other ideas for public housing and job creation as well. In 1992, when Los Angeles exploded in rioting in the wake of the acquittal of police accused of beating a black motorist, Kemp tied the UEZ solution to the problem of urban unrest and alienation. The fact that the riots happened gave Kemp an opportunity to link his potential solutions to the problem of rioting.[24]

It is important to realize, however, that not all organizations are as anarchic and unmanaged as universities; universities may very well be the extreme example. But John Kingdon's very successful application of the idea to policy making in the federal system suggests the considerable value of this way of thinking; this streams and garbage cans model will, I hope, be clearer after we review Kingdon's model of the agenda setting process.

Two other models of decision making are considered in Allison's *Essence of Decision*. He labels them Organizational Process and Governmental Politics, or Models II and III (Model I is the rational actor model). We might also call Model II the bureaucratic politics model.

The major tenets of the two models are as follows. Model II is a model of organizational process grounded in a notion of *bounded rationality*. Allison argues that decisions are the result of bureaucrats applying standard operating procedures (SOPs) to problems. The model assumes that such procedures are relatively simple and that outcomes from these models are predictable. In addition, as Jonathan Bendor and Thomas Hammond note,[25] the model suggests that SOPs will largely condition behavior in such a way that if we know the SOP we can make relatively good guesses about decision makers' future behavior. Finally, the model assumes that individuals seek information, that information carries with it relatively high costs, and that reducing the cost of information is therefore an important goal. From this we can conclude that incrementalism is a key feature of this style of decision making, remembering that information deficits make bold steps difficult if not impossible.

Model III, the governmental politics model, is a model of political conflict. The model echoes Neustadt's argument in *Presidential Power* that the power of any chief executive rests in his or her persuasive abilities.[26] Decisions in this model are the product of competition and negotiation among the president, top government executives, bureaucrats, legislators, and other interested parties. American politics is thus characterized by a high degree of fragmentation and competition, and decision making is slow, competitive, and likely to reflect the power of the relative actors more than the ultimate desirability of the decision at hand. One can easily imagine that if the *president's* power is mainly limited to persuasion; the power of other actors (who do not have the powers and prestige of the president) will be even more limited.

Outputs

Laws

When studying public policy, we are often interested in *statute law*: the laws that are drafted and passed in the legislature and codified in the statute books, such as the Oregon Revised Statutes or the United States Code. Statute laws are just the beginning of public policy, however. *Case law* is also a policy output of the government, in this case, the judicial branch. While many people decry "lawmaking by unelected judges" and seek measures to curb such activity, it is true that judge-made law has long been a feature of American government and of the British legal system on which it is based. Case law often determines the constitutional bounds under which the legislature and executive operate or explains how the Constitution requires them to make or not make particular sorts of policies. The landmark Supreme Court case *Brown v. Board of Education*, for example, prohibited states from requiring that schools be segregated based on race and indeed required that states desegregate their schools "with all deliberate speed." *Roe v. Wade* did *not* make abortion legal in the United States—several states had already legalized abortion in some way, and other states did not before 1973. But *Roe* did say that states must take into account a woman's interests and the states' interests in regulating—but not outright prohibiting—abortions.

These are controversial decisions, which is why they are famous. And, like controversial policies created in statutes, controversial case law takes time to implement. For example, *Roe* began a series of arguments, often decided in court, over how states can and cannot regulate abortion. *Brown* was an important part of the civil rights movement in the United States, which led to considerable social upheaval in the South and the North, as some communities resisted the Court's command to desegregate schools and to meet their duty under the Fourteenth Amendment to the Constitution. Like statutes, case law is therefore not self-implementing; unlike statutes, the courts, lacking, as Hamilton put it in *Federalist* 78, "the power of the purse or the sword," often rely on persuasion and the prestige of the court to compel compliance. But their decisions, once codified, implemented, and obeyed, are as much policy as any statute.

Both case laws and statute laws require that agencies of government implement them. Implementation was considered in more detail in Chapter 7, but for now it is important to think about rules and regulations as an important output of government.

Regulations are the rules that government agencies make to administer the various activities of government. The federal government is a vast enterprise, and laws exist that regulate everything from commercial aviation to shrimp fishing, from toy safety to nuclear power plants. With such a broad range of responsibilities, one might guess that the number of regulations is vast. The current *Code of Federal Regulations* (CFR) takes up at least fifteen feet of shelf space (fortunately, much of this is now available on CD-ROM or online).[27] Much of what it contains is highly technical—it is unlikely that you would understand 14 CFR 121 (that is, Title 14, part 121 of the *Code of Federal Regulations*), the regulations governing various operational aspects of commercial aviation, unless you are a pilot or other aviation professional. But if you are a professional or a well-informed citizen in a particular policy area, you can and should track the *Federal Register*—the daily newspaper of federal regulatory activity—to keep abreast of the key regulatory issues in your field.

Laws, rules, and regulations are often thought of as burdensome and challenged on those grounds. And these claims are usually quite true: laws and regulations *do* impose burdens on some people or interests. The key factor for policy makers is who bears the burden and how heavy the burden is. That a law or regulation imposes a burden on someone is an insufficient reason for supporting or opposing a rule without understanding who benefits and who pays for a given policy.

Finally, it is important to note that a great volume of policy making is what is called "symbolic" policy making. Symbolic policies are policies that do not make any substantive changes to the law or policy outcomes, such as improved health or welfare. Examples of symbolic policies include laws to declare holidays, prevent flag desecration, honor national heroes, and the like. Other symbolic policies include renaming or reorganizing agencies: the Veterans Administration was renamed the Department of Veterans Affairs and elevated to cabinet level status in 1990. It is important, however, not to discount the importance of symbolic policies. While they may not have sweeping benefits, symbolic policies often satisfy the desires of groups for recognition of their values and causes. Seemingly symbolic acts like changing the name of an agency can also signal a shift in the role of the agency, which *is* a substantive policy change, as when the Atomic Energy Commission (AEC) was broken up and a main unit of the former commission was named the Nuclear Regulatory Commission: along with the name change came a greater commitment to *regulate* nuclear power, rather than simply promote it as under the old AEC.

Oversight

An increasingly important part of Congress's work is the *oversight* function. Oversight involves "overseeing" programs that Congress has already enacted to ensure that they are being run efficiently and effectively, following *legislative intent*. Oversight is an important output of the policy process because it influences how policies are carried out. Most agencies are sensitive to legislative intent. Oversight activities, such as hearings and investigations, help the legislature determine whether its intent was followed and provide cues to administrators to change policies to more closely conform to legislative intent.

Oversight has become a more common activity in Congress for at least three reasons. First, policies passed by Congress are often complex, yet delegate a considerable amount of discretion to administrators, who decide how to implement laws passed by Congress and, in particular, what aspect of a law to emphasize. Congress may engage in oversight to review these choices and offer its advice as to what aspects to emphasize.

Second, there has been greater pressure, in the past twenty years, to ensure the efficacy of current laws rather than simply make new ones. Calls for more gun control policies, for example, are countered with calls to more effectively enforce the laws that are already on the books. Oversight often seeks to understand whether laws are being effectively enforced and, if not, how they can be made more effective.

Finally, greater partisan polarization in Congress—in particular, the shift in power in the Congress from the Democrats to the Republicans—

has made oversight an important way for Republicans to scrutinize programs that are less popular with their partisans than with the more liberal Democrats. Whether this has been a significant outcome of this shift in power is not well known, but we should be alert to its possibility.

Evaluation

Related to the oversight activity is policy evaluation. Evaluation is the process of determining whether and to what extent a program is achieving some benefit or achieving its explicit or implicit goals. Policy evaluation is an important aspect of policy studies, and entire textbooks and professional courses are designed to teach the skills necessary to do good policy evaluation.[28] I will leave the techniques of evaluation to these sources. In this section, I focus on evaluation as an important output of the policy process.

All of us are familiar with some form of evaluation, because we engage in policy evaluation just about every day. If you see cars routinely parking illegally or running red lights, you may do a quick evaluation of the traffic laws and conclude that the laws themselves or their enforcement are inadequate to meet the goal of maximum traffic safety. If you read a newspaper or magazine article about how the government has spent millions of dollars to give unemployed people job training but few of these people actually found work, then you are reading the results of a journalistic evaluation of policy. Often, these accounts rely on the work of experts inside and outside of government, who undertake policy evaluations when asked to do so by the sponsoring agencies or affected target groups or, sometimes, simply out of curiosity about the way a program works. This latter type of evaluation is primarily confined to academe, where there is greater flexibility in choosing one's research topics.

In a perfect world, these evaluation studies would work like the best possible social science, involving unlimited research resources and sophisticated research designs, statistical controls, and neutral, scientifically detached observers who have no particular stake in the outcome of an evaluation. In the real world of public policy, however, there are some important impediments to effective policy analysis.[29] Data are often difficult to find because they may not exist, are too time-consuming to acquire, or their owner may not want to reveal it for fear it will be used in a negative evaluation. The best research methods are often hard to employ because the characteristics of the people or processes being studied are constantly changing.

These are primarily scientific problems that the best evaluators have learned to overcome. There are also important political problems associated with policy evaluation. Often, policy evaluation is couched in highly technical terms, such as "cost-benefit analysis," that cloak the studies in a veneer of scientific objectivity while failing to make clear that the very methods themselves are controversial. By cloaking studies in science, analysts, intentionally or by accident, will exclude the public from assessing the quality and relevance of evaluation research and the meaning of the results. In the heat of debate, various interests will use misleading or incomplete statistics or conclusions based on reports that the evaluators themselves depict as preliminary or suggestive, not final. And perhaps the most disturbing abuse is the use of evaluation and analysis as a delaying tactic to prevent decision making. It has become a running joke in Congress and the state legislatures that if one wants to kill an idea without coming out as wanting to kill it, one need only call for "further study" of the problem and hope it then fades from the agenda.

Finally, it is very important to bear in mind that policy evaluation is, by itself, unlikely to carry the day in policy debate. As Giandomenico Majone notes, evidence from the natural and social sciences is used by the participants in policy debate to buttress their sides of a debate, not as the final word on whether a policy is or is not working.[30] How many times have you encountered policy debates in which each side rounds up its best scientific evidence to "prove" that certain programs have been successes or failures? Such debates are played out daily in the media. Often, the decision of which evidence to use to prove a point is driven primarily by a group's ideological commitments more than a commitment to sound social science.

With these caveats in mind, good policy analysis has an important role in the policy process. Even if analysis is primarily used by various interests as evidence of the correctness of a certain course of action, the analysis still can be useful if the underlying science is sound. In most cases, however, policy evaluation is at best both a social scientific, evaluative process and a political process that involves policy disputants working to achieve a particular goal.

Opening the Black Box: Inputs into Outputs

The challenge in thinking about policy as the product of a system comes not in the specification of inputs and outputs, which are fairly clear and derived almost intuitively. Rather, the challenge is in understanding how sets of inputs are translated by policy makers into outputs. In this section, I review some ways that policy scholars describe the making of public policy.

The major criticism of Easton's notion of a systems model is that most depictions of this model treat the political system as a "black box" (that is, a system in which the internal workings are unexplained), rather than opening the box to understand the processes that occur within it. This is not a fatal flaw of the model, though, as hundreds of scholars have sought to open up the box. The more important question is whether one can think of the political system as "systematically" as Easton poses it.

No new model is offered here because a new model would go beyond the scope of this book. Rather, this section is a review of three current major approaches to the study of the policy process. While these different models have important weaknesses, they also have strengths that must be taken into account when considering different political and policy-making situations.

The simplest model of policy making is the classic "how a bill becomes a law" model, which is familiar to just about anyone who had a high school civics class. While a good functional model of the process, this model does not really specify the various factors involved in the translation of demands into policies.

The Stages Model of Policy Making

Related to Easton's systems model is perhaps the preeminent model of the policy process depicted in most introductory public policy textbooks. In the stages model, policy making is assumed to proceed in stages, from *issue emergence and* agenda setting to *implementation* and then to *evaluation* and *feedback*. This process is depicted in Figure 9.3.

A main critique of the stages or "textbook model" of policy making is that it implies that policy making proceeds in a step-by-step way, starting at the beginning and ending at the end.[31] Critiques of this thinking point out that a policy idea may not reach every stage: that a policy concept may reach the agenda, but that any ideas generated may not get beyond mere discussion. Others argue that one cannot separate the implementation of a policy from its evaluation, because evaluation happens all the time as a policy is being implemented.

Figure 9.3 **The Stages Model of the Policy Process**

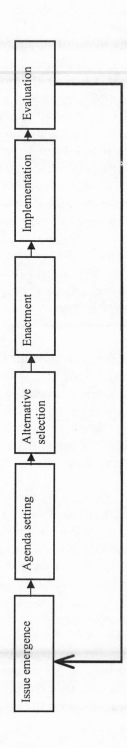

But there is still life in the notion of the stages, for at least one important reason: it is a remarkably helpful way of structuring our thinking about the policy process. As political scientist Peter deLeon notes, each stage of the process is represented in the literature by numerous classics in the field.[32] Agenda setting classics like E.E. Schattschneider's *The Semisovereign People* through classics on agenda setting and alternative selection (John Kingdon's *Agendas, Alternatives and Public Policies*) and implementation (notably Jeffrey Pressman and Aaron Wildavsky's *Implementation*)[33] have all contributed mightily to our understanding of the policy process. Most importantly, these books do what Easton hoped systems thinking would do: they carefully and closely analyze elements of a system; the system, in its way, therefore directed research to important and analytically compact parts of a broader system.

To summarize, thinking about systems helps focus our thinking. So while the stages heuristic, as Paul Sabatier calls it, is not a model in the strictest sense of the term, it is a good way of at least seeing how all the pieces of the policy process fit together.

Recent Models of the Policy Process

In the past twenty years, as dissatisfaction with the stages model of the policy process has grown, political scientists have sought to provide more sophisticated and useful models of the policy process. Because there are so many models, and because they are analytically quite rich, space permits only a summary of three prominent models here: John Kingdon's "streams" metaphor of public policy, Paul Sabatier's "Advocacy Coalition Framework," and Frank Baumgartner and Bryan Jones's "punctuated equilibrium" model of agenda and policy processes.

Kingdon's Streams Metaphor

John Kingdon's book *Agendas, Alternatives and Public Policies* is now a classic in policy studies.[34] Kingdon argues that issues gain agenda status, and alternative solutions are selected, when elements of three "streams" come together. Each of these three streams contains various individuals, groups, agencies, and institutions that are involved in the policy-making process. One stream encompasses the state of politics and public opinion (the *politics stream*). A second stream contains the potential solutions to a problem (the *policy stream*). The third, the *prob-*

lem stream, encompasses the attributes of a problem and whether it is getting better or worse, whether it has suddenly sprung into public and elite consciousness through a focusing event, and whether it is solvable with the alternatives available in the policy stream.

Within any particular problem area, these streams run parallel and somewhat independently of each other in a policy area or domain until something happens to cause two or more of the streams to meet in a "window of opportunity." This window is the possibility of policy change, but the opening of the window does not guarantee that policy change will occur. That trigger can be a change in our understanding of the problem, a change in the political stream that is favorable to policy change, a change in our understanding of the tractability of the problem given current solutions, or a focusing event that draws attention to a problem and helps open a window of opportunity. The streams metaphor is graphically represented in Figure 9.4.

Paul Sabatier argues that the streams metaphor may be an incomplete description of policy making because it does not describe the policy process beyond the opening of the window of opportunity.[35] In contrast, Nikolaos Zahariadis argues that the streams approach can be applied to decision opportunities, not simply agenda setting opportunities; a *decision* to make new or change existing policy may be more likely when the streams come together.[36]

Thus, Kingdon provides a rich and multilayered metaphor of policy making from the early acceptance of new ideas about public problems to the active considerations of solutions as new public policy. Kingdon's metaphor is important to my thinking about focusing events because he introduces the idea of focusing events in a much clearer way than prior policy theory. The three streams thus suggest different types of event variables that can be examined for their influence on the agenda.

The Advocacy Coalition Framework

Sabatier's Advocacy Coalition Framework (ACF) is an important model of the policy process, based on the idea that interest groups are organized in policy communities within a policy domain. The most recent version of this framework is depicted in Figure 9.5. In the ACF, two to four advocacy coalitions typically form in a particular policy domain when groups coalesce around a shared set of core values and beliefs. These groups engage in policy debate, competing and compromising on

Figure 9.4 **Kingdon's Streams Metaphor**

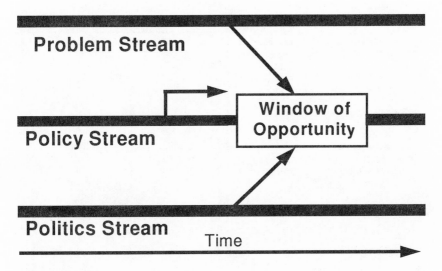

solutions based on their core values and beliefs. Competition between coalitions is mediated by policy brokers who have a stake in resolving the problem, either on substantive grounds or because of their interest in maintaining political harmony in the system. These brokers are more likely to succeed when they can develop compromises that do not threaten either advocacy coalition's core beliefs and values. Policy change is much less likely if polarization of advocacy coalitions is so great that there is no room in the periphery of the groups' belief systems in which compromise can be found.

Like the streams metaphor, Sabatier's ACF encompasses a variety of individual and institutional actors, and it views policy making as an iterative process that runs over years or decades. The ACF also considers the mechanisms for policy change (not simply the possibility for change, as in the streams metaphor) and more consciously encompasses the influence of implementation and feedback on the system.

In the ACF, policy making is influenced both by "relatively stable" system parameters and by "dynamic (system) events," with the interaction between the two promoting or inhibiting policy making. The stable parameters include the basic attributes of the problem area, the basic distribution of natural resources in the society, the fundamental cultural

Figure 9.5 **The Advocacy Coalition Framework**

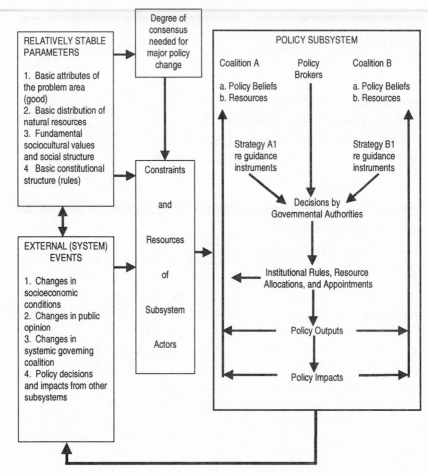

Source: From *Theories of the Policy Process*, by Paul Sabatier. Copyright © 1999 by Westview Press, a member of the Perseus Books Group. Reprinted by permission of Westview Press, a member of Perseus Books, L.L.C.

values and social structure, and the basic legal structure, which in the United States is the constitutional framework and judicial norms.

The dynamic features of the system include changes in socioeconomic conditions and technology, changes in public opinion, changes in systemic governing coalitions (partisan balance in the legislature or the executive branch, for example), and policy decisions and impacts from other subsystems. Change in the governing coalition corresponds to one example of change in the politics stream in Kingdon's model, while changes in socioeconomic and technological conditions influence the problem and policy streams. The activities of other subsystems can influence the policy, politics, and problem streams as their activities spill over into other policy domains.

Punctuated Equilibrium

Baumgartner and Jones borrow the concept of "punctuated equilibrium" from evolutionary biology to describe the process by which policy is made in the United States.[37] They argue that the balance of political power between groups of interests remains relatively stable over long periods of time, punctuated by relatively sudden shifts in public understanding of problems and in the balance of power between the groups seeking to fight entrenched interests.

Key to their theory of equilibrium is the idea of the *policy monopoly*, which corresponds with the idea of policy subsystems. A policy monopoly is a fairly concentrated, closed system of the most important actors in policy making. Such a monopoly has an interest in keeping policy making closed, because a closed system benefits the interests of those in the monopoly and keeps policy making under some measure of control. Under the iron triangle notion of policy making, this system will remain closed and stable for a long time. But Baumgartner and Jones argue that there are instances when the "equilibrium" maintained by policy monopolies will break down, greater and more critical attention to issues will follow, and rapid policy change will be the immediate result. The policy monopolies themselves can break down or at least become more open issue networks.

How do policy monopolies and their dominant construction of problems break down? First, greater media attention to an issue can begin to break open policy monopolies. Media attention to issues can grow when a small but compelling or influential group of people tell of problems with a policy to which members of the policy community do not effectively respond. Baumgartner and Jones and Jeffrey Berry use the breakdown of the nuclear power monopoly to illustrate the effect of greater attention on a problem.[38] The nuclear policy monopoly consisted of the Atomic Energy Commission (AEC), the nuclear utilities, the builders of nuclear power plants, the civil and military nuclear establishment, and the Joint Committee on Atomic Energy (JCAE), a very powerful joint committee of the U.S. House and Senate. This monopoly began to break down as interest groups and, in time, the public voiced greater concern about the safety and cost of nuclear power, and by the mid-1970s the JCAE had been disbanded, the AEC broken up, and the Nuclear Regulatory Commission created, all due to reformist tendencies in government in the early 1970s and the greater media and public attention paid to nuclear power.

This example also illustrates an important finding of Baumgartner and Jones's study: that increased attention to a problem usually means greater *negative* attention to it. In this way, the "policy image" of various issues and policies can change. In the nuclear power case, the increased scrutiny of the industry began to break down the image of nuclear power as "the peaceful atom" creating power "too cheap to meter" to an image of danger and expense. This negative image was reinforced by the accident at the Three Mile Island nuclear plant in Pennsylvania in 1979 and the multi-billion-dollar default on bonds sold to build nuclear power plants in Washington State in 1982.

Policy monopolies also break down as groups that seek access to and change in the policy making process go venue shopping to find the best venue in which to press their claims. The media are one venue, and groups can seek access to the courts or other units of government to gain access to policy debate. The reform of the congressional committee system and, most important, the increasing autonomy of subcommittees starting in the early 1970s have led to a greater number of venues in Congress for groups to find a sympathetic ear to influence policy making.

An important aspect of this way of thinking about policy is the long periods of stability followed by rapid change, followed again by long periods of stability. In this way, Baumgartner and Jones argue, policy change is not merely incremental and not in a state of constant flux: rather, policy remains stable, followed by a period of rapid change, then stability again.

Conclusion

So far, we have discussed various models of the policy process without seriously considering what a model of the policy process *is* or how to assess whether, in Thomas Dye's words, a model "is helping or not." Dye considers this question in some detail. He says that "a model is merely an abstraction or representation of political life."[39] We can clarify this idea by thinking about the difference between, say, a model airplane and a real airplane. A model airplane is merely an approximation of the real thing: while the model airplane has wings, a propeller, a tail, landing gear, and the like, it is a much simplified version of the "real thing": it may not have a working engine or may not even actually fly. But it tells us enough to help us learn about an airplane. So models vary in their complexity and faithfulness to the actual thing they represent based on the use to which we want to put the model. And, of course, if the model becomes as complex as the thing it is modeling, it may not help much at all.

This is because good models, according to Dye, seek to order and simplify reality, identify what is significant about a system, are congruent with reality, communicate meaningful information about the policy process, direct inquiry and research, and suggest explanations of public policy. On this last point, Dye argues that models "should suggest hypotheses about the causes and consequences of public policy."[40]

In the end, I hope you can adapt all the models we have described here to help you think about what is most important in the policy process, particularly if they help you make better political arguments. If these models help you, your allies, and even your opponents think about how policy is made—and how you can get involved to make better policy—then an important function of the models will have been served.

Appendix:
Public Policy Research
on the Web

Because the World Wide Web and the Internet are important and remarkably useful research tools, it seems entirely appropriate to provide a short appendix with tips and ideas on how to use the Internet for researching public policy issues. The World Wide Web, or Web for short, is a particularly rich arena in which public policy positions are advanced, arguments made, and claims supported or debunked.

If you are a student or even a casual user of the Web, I probably do not need to convince you of the remarkable value of the Internet as a research tool—in the past five years, the Web and the Internet have, among my students, evolved from a technical curiosity to a vital aspect of daily life. Students and faculty alike are using the Web to facilitate what were once remarkably tedious research practices. Unfortunately, the Web has also spawned a considerable degree of laziness in research among some students and academics, as people have come to forget that there are many resources in the library that are unavailable on-line, either because they do not exist at all on a computer system or because they do exist, but access is prohibitively expensive. In this appendix, I will share with you some ideas and thoughts on using the Web for research, but I will urge you not to forget to become proficient in the use of a library.

This approach to Internet research is motivated by three key facts of the World Wide Web. The first is that the Web is constantly in flux, changing daily or even hourly. Because of this flux, the proliferation of books and magazines that provide directories to the Web, often organized like telephone directories, seem rather silly to me today. After all, what good are these books when they tend to go out of date in a matter of weeks? Of course, many sites remain in place, but many do not, and such books are less useful than they seem. Even the list of Web sites found at the end of this appendix will eventually go out of date, as some sites go off-line and other, often better resources come on-line.

The second fact of Web life is that the Web is *vast*. There are thousands of Web servers hosting thousands of Web pages, ranging from official government information to interest group advocacy pieces to individual pages of people's pets, families, vacations, and hobbies. In this way, the Web is the world's biggest reference library, the biggest (and seemingly the dullest) vacation photo slide show, and, at times, the scariest collection of hate literature, conspiracy theories, and unintelligible rants ever assembled. The size and ease of use of the Web are its biggest strengths. You have no doubt read or heard news stories about how kids learn to build bombs on the Web, or how parents need to shield their kids from sex and violence on the Web, or how efforts to do so often block users from finding good sources of information. Much of what you hear about the Web is news-driven hype, often written by journalists with a very limited understanding of how the Web works or why it even exists. While some problems have arisen from the Web, most can be easily handled and will be as more people become informed users of the Web. My goal in this appendix is to help you be an informed user of the Web as you research public policy issues.

The Web's vast size and its constantly changing shape have led directly to the proliferation of *search engines*. Search engines are among the most important sites on the Web, and they tend to be the most often visited as well, because they allow users to simply enter some key words and search the Net for whatever comes up. You have probably heard of the most popular search engines, such as hotbot.com, lycos.com, and yahoo.com. Perhaps the best search site is http://www.google.com, which uses a rather different logic than other search pages to guarantee a greater likelihood of successful searching. You will also want to be familiar with the search engines that allow you to submit a search to multiple search engines simultaneously, such as www.metacrawler.com or www.dogpile.com. However, the world of search engines is changing almost daily, and today's favorite will be tomorrow's has-been. Try multiple search engines to pick the ones you like best. An excellent list of search engines (including those I had never heard of!) is found at http://www.albany.edu/library/internet/engines.html, and you might want to learn more about search engines and how they work at http://www.searchenginewatch.com.

In the end, no search engine is perfect, and none of them will find every page relevant to your search, because of capacity and technological limits and because many sites are not open to being found by search engines. Do not worry, however, if your search engine does not find everything on the Web: the challenge in the use of search engines is not in finding enough information on the Web, but comes in finding *too much* information, much of which is junk that you cannot use or will decide not to use.

The size of the Web is related to the third important fact of Web life: that it is really easy and really cheap to post just about anything on the World Wide Web and to induce other people to look at it. Let's consider the economics.

Let us say that you are the director of a small interest group—*Pets Everywhere ComforT Society*, with a catchy Web address like petsnow.org or petseverywhere.org (pets.com, pets.org, and pets.net won't work! They are all owned by pets.com, the on-line pet supply store)—and you are lobbying state and federal governments to pass laws to prevent landlords from banning cats and dogs in apartments, because of the health and social benefits of pet ownership for individuals and the community at large, you claim.

We will assume that PETS has 500 members, that you want to send out a four-page quarterly newsletter to each member, and that you would like other people to learn about your cause and to join. Here is how the costs would break down if we compare the costs of mailing the newsletter to simply posting it on your Web site:

Printing	500 members × 4 pages × 5 cents a page × 4 times a year	$ 400.00
Postage	500 × 4 times a year × 50 cents (estimate)	$1,000.00
Total		$1,400.00

To set up a Web site, PETS will arrange with one of hundreds of companies that host Web pages on their computers, but that allow you to use your own address for people to find the page. A small group like

PETS could have its site hosted for about $50 a month, or $600 a year. Thus, PETS saves $800 per year. At the same time, the page can be viewed by many more than 500 people—thousands of people may look at your page, particularly when your issue or your Web site (which can conceivably contain much more information than your newsletter) gains press coverage, or when the issue of the social benefits of pet ownership is somehow elevated on the agenda. This is why many groups are abandoning paper newsletters entirely and are posting their newsletters on the Web, sending them to their members via e-mail, or both. Of course, if PETS does not already own a computer, you will need to buy one, which would cost about $1,000, and Internet service (which PETS is likely to have anyway) is about $200 a year.

What is the value of this exercise? Simply put, access to the Web is so easy that *anyone, regardless of the quality of their argument or of their evidence,* can put material on the Web and reach far more people for far less money that was possible before. Many people seem to think that Web pages are somehow authoritative or "official" because they have a Web address (technically called a URL, for Uniform Resource Locator) and may look as slick as well-known sites such as the *New York Times* (www.nytimes.com) or CNN (www.cnn.com). Thus, as both a teacher and a researcher, I have found that the biggest pitfall of the Internet is that too many people assume that too much of it is prima facie useful or accurate. Related to this pitfall is the idea that the Internet has somehow replaced traditional libraries as a source of information. Indeed, the lure of the Internet is powerful, and, in many ways, it is beginning to supplant library research. But with this new tool comes a higher level of sophistication and care demanded of its users. In summary, there are many ways to go about using the Web for research; however you go about it, it is best to be organized and selective in your searching rather than taking a scattershot approach. This is why I have included links to information that will help you evaluate a site's credibility and quality.

The Web As a Complement to Your Library

Most people start their research on any topic by going to one of the popular Web search engines. I do not recommend this approach, because this sort of search strategy is based on the assumption that the Web and its search engines are replacements for traditional libraries.

Rather, I urge you to think of the Web as a *complement* to or an *extension* of your library. This is because many of the most valuable sources of information that you can access from your desktop—academic journal articles, newspaper and magazine articles, reports, and the like—are primarily accessible from college, university, and some public libraries. These resources are available through electronic databases that can be accessed only at the library, or through print, microfilm, microfiche, or electronic resources that are physically located at the library. Thus, the best way to start a search may be from your university or public library's Web site. These libraries pay fees to firms like EBSCO Information Services, OCLC, and Lexis-Nexis to allow qualified users (students, faculty, library cardholders) access to many indexes, several with full text references.

You should also use libraries because librarians are today's information experts. Many of us still hold the image of librarians as dour, bookish sorts who shush people in the library. The reality is much different—librarians are now information experts who know the most current techniques for searching for and retrieving all kinds of information, from the most common to the most obscure. They exist to help you find what you need, whether it is available in print or electronically.

Depending on your topic, you might first want to read or skim books in the library. Books are particularly important because they synthesize a considerable amount of information and provide a useful summary of knowledge in a particular field at the time that the book was written. Books are often authoritative because they are written by experts in a field, such as college professors, professional practitioners, or well-informed journalists. For fast-moving topics, you may find that books become obsolete too soon; in other fields, such as many of the sciences, you may find that journals are more commonly used to disseminate information than are books. But it is often hard to know this until you look at some books in the field to see if they are out of date.

Many students avoid looking at books out of fear that they will have to read the whole book. In some cases it is important to do so, but it is also important to look at books strategically, to glean the most information from them in the least amount of time. You generally need not read an entire book to glean the desired information. Rather, through careful reviewing of the index and table of contents and through quick skimming, you can find useful information. Of course, you should also carefully review the reference list for ideas on other sources. In this way, your references can grow.

Some of the most important books on public policy are reference books, such as the *Statistical Abstract of the United States*, the *Congressional Quarterly Almanac*, and the *Almanac of American Politics*. Many of these resources are available on-line, but it is often easier to browse the printed versions in your library. Your librarian can help you find these and related books.

Searching the Web

You can find a considerable amount of up-to-date information that is not yet available in magazines, academic journals, or books by searching the Web. This can be a slow and sometimes frustrating process, but it can also be very rewarding and even thrilling when you find that hard-to-find nugget of information you have searched all over for.

The first step in a Web search is to use some of the popular search engines. For searches that are likely to return hundreds, thousands, or hundreds of thousands of links, there are ways to construct the search syntax of your search so that fewer results are found. This is usually done by learning what is called *Boolean logic*. Boolean logic involves finding things in a search engine or database based on three *operators*: "and," "or," and "not." Many pages on the Internet explain how Boolean operators and searches work: there is a good one at www.albany.edu/library/internet/boolean.html. You should also consult any "search tips" provided by the search engine; there is often an obvious link to them on the page.

The next step in your Web search is looking at the sites that have been found by your search engine. Often times you will get a whole lot of junk that you do not want. This is sometimes a result of a poor search strategy. For example, if I go to the AltaVista search engine and search for the term "environmental policy," the first five hits (that is, sites) I get are a scientific site on global warming with a tendency to deny that the problem exists (a form of bias); a link to a new research center on agriculture and environmental policy; Princeton University's site on its program in Science, Technology, and Environmental Policy (university sites are often highly credible); an environmental organization that addresses issues involving "standing" to go to court to protect the environment and the "takings" issue involving land use and the Constitution (biased in a particular direction); and a politically conservative (that is, biased in a particular way) site on "free market environmentalism." Searches on other major search engines yield similar results.

If your interest is in, say, policies that seek to promote biodiversity—that is, the diversity of life on the planet—then these links would do you very little good. Indeed, a broad search such as "environmental policy" will require you to look through many sites. This is fine if you have a great deal of time, but you will want to devise a more specific Web search, such as "biodiversity and public policy" or even "biodiversity and state law" to find what you need. Even then, these searches are unlikely to be very precise. The search for "biodiversity and state law" yields thousands of pages, most of which fall into about twelve general categories. However, at least one search engine, Northern Light (www.northernlight.com), will organize the sites it finds in "folders" that allow you to further narrow your search. Better search engines, such as google.com, are more likely to display what you're looking for at the top of the results list. Each search engine is a little different in how it handles searches. For help on how to narrow your search, look for a "help" or "hints" link on the search engine page.

In essence, searching the Web is not a simple, shortcut way of avoiding using traditional resources in the library. It has its own quirks, and Web searching is sometimes frustrating. Plus, Web searches are much less "filtered" than information that you can get from your library: no publisher has decided whether a Web page is good or full of inaccurate information, nor has any group of experts reviewed most Web pages for scientific and technical accuracy, as most scholarly journals are reviewed. When searching the Web, you must do so at your own peril, because *you* are serving as editor and expert reviewer. Failing to carefully assess the quality and relevance of materials found on the Web will result in research that is biased, full of inaccurate or unverified information, and unhelpful to you and to those who may seek to benefit from your research. To protect your own credibility, use care in finding and using on-line resources.

Selected Internet Resources

All this being said, there are a number of remarkably useful sources available to you on the Web. I have collected here a list of my favorite Web sites for doing general research on politics and public policy. Much of this list extends a list maintained by Professor Peter May at the University of Washington for his course on public policy. I am grateful for his permission to use and extend his Web page. This is by no means a comprehensive list, but, rather, is intended to provide a set of important starting points in policy research. Many of these links are simply links to other sources, many of which are considered credible sources in their fields, but users should apply the same care to the use of these sites as to any other site on the Web.

In the links listed below, you will find a period at the end of a link that ends a sentence. Remember to *not* enter the period at the end of the link— no links end with periods. You will find this to be true of links published in magazines and newspapers as well. If a link does not work, try again without a period ("dot") at the end of the link. If it still does not work, please e-mail me at birkland@albany.edu and let me know. If you have a new or better link to the same information, also please let me know at this address.

This list of resources is also available at http://www.albany.edu/~birkland/links.htm, from which you can point and click to these resources. On that page, you will find a way to report out-of-date or broken links as well. Since this page is evolving and growing, please send me suggestions for new links to important Web pages, and I will post them for the benefit of future readers of this book.

Assessing the Quality of Web Resources

Evaluating Information Found on the Internet
http://milton.mse.jhu.edu:8001/research/education/net.html
A site at Johns Hopkins University, this is a good guide to how to assess all kinds of information, including information found on the Internet. There is also a good link here to information about copyright and intellectual property, which is very important to avoid plagiarism, which is copying words or ideas written or expressed by others.

Assessing the Credibility of Online Sources
http://leo.stcloudstate.edu/research/credibility1.html
Another good guide on how to effectively and carefully assess the quality of Web pages. Also from St. Cloud State University (Minnesota) is a worksheet on assessing Web sources, at http://www.stcloudstate.edu/~burkec02/ENGL552/screening.html. This worksheet is far better than the one I originally drafted for this book!

Search Engines: General Information

Journalist's Guide to Web Searches
http://www.newslink.org/web/
The Journalist's Guide covers many of the issues mentioned in this appendix, such as Web site reliability and searching strategies. Since most journalists are sticklers for reliability, this site will help you find sound sources.

Search Engine Watch
http://www.searchenginewatch.com
This is a site that covers the latest news and information about search engines. You can learn about the newest search engines, how to search them, and how to maximize the success of your searches. This site contains a great deal of interesting technical information as well.

The Major Search Engines

www.altavista.com
Best suited for searches on pop culture sites, such as celebrity photos, music, and the like.

www.dogpile.com
A "metacrawler" site that searches multiple search engines.

www.excite.com
www.google.com
As of this writing, the best search engine available.

www.hotbot.com
www.lycos.com
www.northernlight.com
www.webcrawler.com
A metacrawler that searches multiple search engines.

www.yahoo.com
Excellent for looking by topic heading, as in a telephone directory.

Library Research

Information and links compiled by or about libraries.

Library of Congress
http://www.loc.gov
Catalog and links to other databases.

Political Science and Public Affairs Reference and Web Resources
http://faculty.washington.edu/alvin/PolBib.htm
Compiled by library staff at the University of Washington.

Social Sciences
http://www.ksg.harvard.edu/library/sosci_polisci.htm
Political science and public policy from Harvard University libraries.

U.S. and Foreign Government Information
http://www.albany.edu/library/divs/gov/government.html
From the University at Albany, State University of New York.

OCLC WorldCat
http://firstsearch.oclc.org
A database of books held by libraries throughout the United States and Canada. This database will indicate the nearest library that holds this item (including yours). This is usually available through your library.

Also, do not forget to check your college or university Web page, or your local public library's page, which will likely have similar and often more current links to library sources.

Journals, Periodicals, and Newspapers

JSTOR
http://www.jstor.org
Perhaps the best full-text source available, with access to journals in political science, economics, sociology, and several other disciplines. This site displays the text of journal articles in the same format as paper journals.

Project Muse
http://muse.jhu.edu
Full-text access to journals published by the Johns Hopkins University Press. This tends to be oriented toward the humanities.

EBSCO Information Services
http://www.ebsco.com
A subscription database service found primarily in academic libraries. This contains brief and full-text references.

OCLC Public Affairs Information Service
http://www.pais.org
This is the online version of the printed PAIS index and its CD-ROM product—any version is remarkably useful for finding substantive policy information, including books, reports, and government documents as well as journals.

General Political Resources

Lists with links to governmental, media, and interest groups.

Poly-Cy
http://pslab11.polsci.wvu.edu/PolyCy/
Internet resources for political science—an extensive set of links relating to politics and policy, including links to educational institutions, interest groups, the media, think tanks, and the like.

Project Vote Smart
http://www.vote-smart.org/

Yahoo Government and Politics
http://www.yahoo.com/Government/Politics/

National Political Index
http://www.politicalindex.com/
An extensive collection of links, many unusual or obscure, relating to politics and policy.

Atlantic Monthly Political Resources
http://www.theatlantic.com/politics/resource.htm

Public Policy Resources

Lists with links to government, media, and interest groups with a specific reference to public policy.

Public Policy links at Poly-Cy
http://pslab11.polsci.wvu.edu/PolyCy/pspubpol.html
Also look for other subfields at the main Poly-Cy page for additional resources and ideas.

Policy.com
http://www.policy.com

intellectualcapital.com
http://www.intellectualcapital.com
Both of these sites are general policy sites with links to interest groups, news articles, and other resources.

Public Agenda
http://www.publicagenda.org/
A nonpartisan organization that seeks to improve policy makers' knowledge of public opinion on issues while improving citizens' knowledge of the issues.

St. Martin's Press: Public Policy and Interest Groups
http://www.smpcollege.com/SMP_GOVT/POLICY.HTM
A site maintained by this well-known publisher of politics and policy texts. Includes a number of links to topical information on many policy topics, as well as links to other sets of Internet resources.

Policy Research Initiative (Canada)
http://policyresearch.schoolnet.ca/
A site for research in Canadian public policy, which is very important to American researchers as well, because many comparisons are made with Canada in fields such as education, health care, and environmental policies.

Governmental Resources

Links to federal, state, and local sources.

University of Michigan Documents Center
http://www.lib.umich.edu/libhome/Documents.center/
Links to local, state, national, foreign, and international resources, legislation, laws, regulations, proposed regulations: a stellar gateway to governmental information.

Frequently Used Sites Related to U.S. Federal Government Information
http://www.library.vanderbilt.edu/central/staff/fdtf.html
From Vanderbilt University.

U.S. Government Documents
http://www.cc.columbia.edu/cu/libraries/indiv/dsc/readyref.html
Links to invaluable information published by the federal government.
This is a good supplement to traditional sources of information available from your library.

GovBot Search Engine
http://www.nwbuildnet.com/nwbn/govbot.html
A search engine for governmental Web pages and resources.

Federal Government Search
http://regional.searchbeat.com/fed-usa.htm
Another search engine of governmental and media resources.

Congressional Information Service
http://web.lexis-nexis.com/congcomp/form/cong/overview.html
Gateway to legislation, bills, and other documents by this well-respected
private organization. This is a subscription service that may be accessible only from your library.

Congress.org
http://www.congress.org
Another private gateway to legislation.

State Law Watch
http://www.statelawwatch.com
An excellent collection of links to state government and business information.

State and Local Government on the Net
http://www.piperinfo.com/state/index.cfm
A state-by-state list of government information; primarily links to various resources.

State government Web sites
The typical syntax for finding state Web sites is http://www.state.xx.
us, where xx is the two-letter postal service abbreviation for a state.
Thus, http://www.state.ak.us is the State of Alaska Web site, http://
www.state.wy.us is Wyoming's, and so on.

Legal Research

Sites that will help you find specific federal and state laws and regulations.

Lawguru.com legal research page
http://www.lawguru.com/search/lawsearch.html
A commercial site, generally oriented toward lawyers but easily used by laypeople, that allows free access to federal and state laws and regulations. Navigation could be clearer, but it is an excellent resource.

Legal Information Institute at Cornell University Law School
http://www.law.cornell.edu
This is an extremely useful site, providing legal research tools that were once only affordable by big law firms. Search federal and state laws, constitutions, regulations, and other legal materials. This site is particularly good at summarizing and reporting the most recent U.S. Supreme Court decisions—if you read about it in the newspaper, you can read an authoritative summary here.

FedLaw from the General Services Administration
http://www.legal.gsa.gov
A site developed for federal employees who need to do legal research, but available for public use. Some links to important aspects of state law, but for serious research use the other resources.

Lexis-Nexis
http://www.lexis-nexis.com
Consult your library to see if this resource is available to you. This and Westlaw are the best-known on-line legal research tools.

Westlaw
http://www.westlaw.com
This subscription service may be available through your library, university, or county law library. Ask your librarian. The subscription fee is prohibitive for individual users, but you may know a lawyer or law student who could help you use this tool.

Media and Interest Groups

Links to news sites and information about interest groups.

Lexis/Nexis Academic Universe
http://web.lexis-nexis.com/universe/
Article search and news database. This link may not work if you are connecting from home, but may work if you are using a computer at your college or public library. Ask your librarian for details or for information as to where you can access this service.

Newslink
http://www.newslink.org
Links to newspapers, magazines, radio/TV, and other resources by the American Journalism Review.

PathFinder
http://www.pathfinder.com
Time Warner link to CNN, *Time*, *Fortune*, and other Time-Warner sites.

CNN
http://www.cnn.com
The Cable News Network site.

MSNBC
http://www.msnbc.com
The Microsoft and NBC Internet site.

The New York Times
http://www.nytimes.com
The on-line edition of the *New York Times*.

Washington Post
http://www.washingtonpost.com

Los Angeles Times
http://www.latimes.com

Wall Street Journal
http://www.wsj.com
The Website for the *Wall Street Journal*. Please note that this is a pay site.

USA Today
http://www.usatoday.com

Salon
http://www.salon.com
An on-line magazine.

Slate
http://www.slate.com
An on-line magazine, owned by Microsoft but fairly independent of Bill Gates and Microsoft.

http://dir.yahoo.com/News_and_Media/Newspapers
Yahoo's directory page for finding local newspapers in the United States.

Associations on the Net
http://www.ipl.org/ref/AON/
Extensive links to organizations, interest groups, and think tanks.

Public Opinion

Public Agenda Online
http://www.publicagenda.org/
Polls and discussion of current issues on the public agenda.

University of North Carolina IRSS Poll Database
http://www.irss.unc.edu/data_archive/pollsearch.html
Questionnaire search for opinion surveys.

Gallup Poll
http://www.gallup.com
Extensive on-line access to polls concerning elections and current events.

General Social Survey
http://www.icpsr.umich.edu/GSS99/index.html
Archive of survey results and on-line search for this national survey about attitudes, values, and behaviors.

Roper Center for Public Opinion Research
http://www.ropercenter.uconn.edu/
Index to polls.

National Election Studies
http://www.umich.edu/~nes/nesguide/nesguide.htm
Guide to public opinion and electoral behavior from one of the most respected public opinion organizations in the nation.

Governmental and Other Statistics

Sites with links to statistics compiled by governmental agencies and other organizations.

Statistical Abstract of the United States
http://www.census.gov/prod/www/statistical-abstract-us.html
The standard reference work for national-level statistics. Some statistics are broken out by state or other region, and there is a considerable amount of time-series (yearly) data. This is also available in printed form in most academic and public libraries.

Fedstats
http://www.fedstats.gov/index.html
One-stop shopping for governmental statistics; links to sources of U.S. governmental statistics.

Dismal Scientist
http://www.dismalscientist.com
Current and historical economic information at the national and regional level.

The Census Bureau
http://www.census.gov

The Census Bureau Web site. Here you can find population and other demographic information from the national to the local level and learn how to buy CD-ROMs with extensive local-level data.

Economic Statistics Briefing Room
http://www.whitehouse.gov/fsbr/esbr.html

Links to a wide range of current economic information.

Economic Data
http://www.econdata.net/index.html

Regional economic data links.

International Statistical Agencies
http://www.census.gov/main/www/stat_int.html

U.S. Census Bureau links to statistical agencies of foreign governments.

National Priorities Project
http://www.natprior.org/

Analysis of federal budget spending priorities for states and cities.

Notes

Notes to Chapter 1

1. Daniel C. McCool, *Public Policy Theories, Models, and Concepts: An Anthology* (Englewood Cliffs, N.J.: Prentice Hall, 1995), 1.

2. McCool, *Public Policy Theories*, 1; Harold D. Lasswell, *Politics: Who Gets What, When, How* (New York: Meridian Books, 1958).

3. This theme is persistent in most advanced treatments of public policy. A good discussion of this can be found in chapter 1 of Michael Howlett and M. Ramesh, *Studying Public Policy: Policy Cycles and Policy Subsystems* (Toronto: Oxford University Press, 1995).

4. A considerable amount of information on such programs can be found at the National Association of Schools of Public Affairs and Administration Web site, www.naspaa.org.

5. Ronald Paul Hill and Sandi Macan, "Consumer Survival on Welfare with an Emphasis on Medicaid and the Food Stamp Program," *Journal of Public Policy and Marketing* 15, no. 1 (Spring 1996): 118–127.

6. McCool, *Public Policy Theories*, 7; Thomas S. Kuhn, *The Structure of Scientific Revolutions*, 2nd ed. (Chicago: University of Chicago Press, 1970).

7. Thomas R. Dye, *Understanding Public Policy*, 7th ed. (Englewood Cliffs, N.J.: Prentice Hall, 1992).

8. George D. Greenberg et al., "Developing Public Policy Theory: Perspectives from Empirical Research," *American Political Science Review* 71, no. 4 (1977): 1532–1543.

9. Paul A. Sabatier, "Political Science and Public Policy," *PS: Political Science and Politics* 24, no. 2 (1991): 144–147; Paul A. Sabatier, "Toward Better Theories of the Policy Process," *PS: Political Science and Politics* 24, no. 2 (1991): 147–156.

10. Paul A. Sabatier and Hank C Jenkins-Smith. *Policy Change and Learning: An Advocacy Coalition Approach.* (Boulder, Colo.: Westview, 1993).

11. Frank Baumgartner and Bryan D. Jones, *Agendas and Instability in American Politics* (Chicago: University of Chicago Press, 1993).

12. McCool, *Public Policy Theories,* 10.

13. David Weimer and Aidan Vining, *Policy Analysis: Concepts and Practice* (Englewood Cliffs, N.J.: Prentice Hall, 1992); Edith Stokey and Richard Zeckhauser, *A Primer for Policy Analysis* (New York: W.W. Norton, 1978).

14. Giandomenico Majone, *Evidence, Argument and Persuasion in the Policy Process* (New Haven: Yale University Press, 1989).

15. Clarke E. Cochran et al., *American Public Policy: An Introduction*, 6th ed. (New York: St. Martin's Press, 1999).

16. Majone, *Evidence, Argument*; Deborah Stone, *Policy Paradox: The Art of Political Decision Making* (New York: W.W. Norton, 1997); Deborah A. Stone, "Causal Stories and the Formation of Policy Agendas," *Political Science Quarterly* 104, no. 2 (1989): 281–300.

17. Anne Larason Schneider and Helen Ingram, *Policy Design for Democracy* (Lawrence: University Press of Kansas, 1997), 2.

18. See, for example, Martha Shirk and Nancy Klepper, "Olympic National Park: An Ancient Forest Unlike Any Other in U.S.," *St. Louis Post-Dispatch,* May 19, 1991, Travel Section, page 1; and Tom Kenworthy, "Showdown in Big Sky Country," *Washington Post Magazine*, September 27, 1992, W24.

19.Cochran et al., *American Public Policy*; James E. Anderson, *Public Policymaking*, 4th ed. (Boston: Houghton Mifflin, 2000).

Notes to Chapter 2

1. David B. Robertson and Dennis R. Judd, *The Development of American Public Policy: The Structure of Policy Restraint* (Glenview, Ill.: Scott, Foresman and Company, 1989).

2. That is, relatively homogeneous among the European population that colonized the nation. In the south in particular, blacks and Native Americans constituted a large proportion of the population, and blacks were numerically in the majority in some southern districts. But by law and social practice blacks and Native Americans were considered outside the political community and therefore generated few demands for policies to address the needs and aspirations of this population. And, of course, until 1920 women were not allowed to vote, and until recently in our history women had relatively little influence on the policy process.

3. Robertson and Judd, *Development of American Public Policy,* 42.

4. *A.L.A. Schechter Poultry Corp. v. United States*, 295 U.S. 495 (1935).

5. 300 U.S. 379 (1937).

6. See, for example, Martha Derthick, *New Towns in Town* (Washington, D.C.: Urban Institute, 1972).

7. An article about the administration of Head Start in New York City calls the program "highly regarded." See Joe Sexton, "Critics Warn That Moving Head Start Is Endangering Two Child-Care Programs," *New York Times*, March 3, 1996, 38. The *Philadelphia Inquirer* calls it "one of the most successful legacies" of the Johnson administration. See Kimberly J. Mclarin, "The Promise of Head Start Still Out of Reach for Many," *Philadelphia Inquirer*, January 26, 1992, C1. On the doubts about the ESEA's success, see James E. Anderson, *Public Policymaking*, 4th ed. (Boston: Houghton Mifflin, 2000), 293.

8. Robert S. Erikson, Gerald C. Wright, and John P. McIver, *Statehouse De-*

mocracy: Public Opinion and Policy in the American States (New York: Cambridge University Press, 1993).

9. James E. Anderson, *Public Policymaking.*

10. One of the best books that explore these contradictions or "paradoxes" is Deborah Stone, *Policy Paradox: The Art of Political Decision Making* (New York: W.W. Norton, 1997).

11. For an early assessment of Clinton's problems in advancing policy initiatives, see Fred I. Greenstein, "The Presidential Leadership Style of Bill Clinton: An Early Appraisal," *Political Science Quarterly* 108, no. 4 (Winter 1993): 589–601.

12. David Osborne, *Laboratories of Democracy: A New Breed of Governor Creates Models for National Growth* (Cambridge, Mass.: Harvard Business School Press, 1988).

13. James R. Tallon, Jr., and Lawrence D. Brown, "Who Gets What? Devolution of Eligibility and Benefits in Medicaid," in *Medicaid and Devolution: A View from the States,* ed. Frank J. Thompson and John J. DiIulio, Jr. (Washington, D.C.: Brookings Institution Press, 1998), 249.

14. Charles A. Beard, *An Economic Interpretation of the Constitution of the United States* (New York: Macmillan, 1956).

15. Robert D. Plotnick and Richard F. Winters, "A Politico-Economic Theory of Income Redistribution," *American Political Science Review* 79, no. 2 (1985): 458–473.

16. Harrell R. Rodgers Jr., "Civil Rights and the Myth of Popular Sovereignty," *Journal of Black Studies* 12, no. 1 (1981): 66.

17. Barrington Moore, *Social Origins of Dictatorship and Democracy: Lord and Peasant in the Making of the Modern World* (Boston: Beacon Press, 1966); James H. McPherson, *Abraham Lincoln and the Second American Revolution* (New York: Oxford University Press, 1990).

18. Beard, *Economic Interpretation of the Constitution.*

19. Robert G. McCloskey, *The American Supreme Court,* ed. Sanford Levinson, 2nd ed. (Chicago: University of Chicago Press, 1994).

20. Robertson and Judd, *Development of American Public Policy.*

21. For more general treatments of these dynamics in environmental policy, see Walter A. Rosenbaum, *Environmental Politics and Policy,* 2nd ed. (Washington, D.C.: CQ Press, 1991); Daniel J. Fiorino, *Making Environmental Policy* (Berkeley, Calif.: University of California Press, 1995); Norman Vig and Michael Kraft, *Environmental Policy in the 1990s* (Washington, D.C.: CQ Press, 1996).

22. Malcolm L. Goggin et al. *Implementation Theory and Practice: Toward a Third Generation* (Glenview, Ill.: Scott Foresman/Little Brown, 1990).

23. See, for example, Randall Rosenberg, *The Hollow Hope* (Chicago: University of Chicago Press, 1991).

24. Malclom L. Goggin et al., *Implementation Theory and Practice.*

Notes to Chapter 3

1. B. Dan Wood, "Federalism and Policy Responsiveness: The Clean Air Case," *Journal of Politics* 53, no. 3 (1991): 851–859.

2. According to the 1999 edition of the *Statistical Abstract of the United States,* table 566, there were 30,474 people working for the federal legislative branch in

1998. While this is a substantial number, we should keep in mind that many of these people work for the General Accounting Office, the Library of Congress, and other agencies that serve members in their legislative duties and the public at large. The size of Congress's staff is substantially smaller than it was in the mid-1980s, when the total number of legislative employees peaked at around 40,000. An older article that explains the problems of the size and power of congressional staff is Gregg Easterbrook, "What's Wrong With Congress," *Atlantic Monthly,* December 1984, 57–84.

3. To a considerable extent, these features of Congress apply to the state legislatures as well. Most state legislatures are not as large and complex as Congress, but Texas, New York, and California have legislatures that rival Congress in size and complexity.

4. Jack L. Walker, "Setting the Agenda in the U.S. Senate: A Theory of Problem Selection," *British Journal of Political Science* 7 (1977): 423–445.

5. Bills in Congress are numbered with designators that indicate the body in which they were introduced. H.R. indicates the House of Representatives (not House Resolution) and S. indicates a Senate bill. Other types of legislation are numbered differently; for details, refer to http://thomas.loc.gov.

6. Some often-cited texts on Congress include Ross K. Baker, *House and Senate* (New York: W.W. Norton, 1989); Roger H. Davidson and Walter J. Oleszek, *Congress and Its Members*, 7th ed. (Washington, D.C.: CQ Press, 1999); R. Douglas Arnold, *The Logic of Congressional Action* (New Haven: Yale University Press, 1990). Morris P. Fiorina, *Congress: Keystone of the Washington Establishment* (New Haven: Yale University Press, 1989); and Randall Ripley and Grace Franklin, *Congress, Bureaucracy, and Public Policy*, 5th ed. (Pacific Grove, Calif.: Brooks-Cole, 1991). The latter book explores the policy-making relationship between Congress and the bureaucracy.

7. The electoral influence of casework is controversial, although most members of Congress at least perceive it to be important, which, in the end, may be really all that matters when explaining the choices they make. For more on this controversy, see Diana Evans Yiannakis, "The Grateful Electorate: Casework and Congressional Elections," *American Journal of Political Science* 25, no. 3 (1981): 568–580; Morris Fiorina, "Some Problems in Studying the Effects of Resource Allocation in Congressional Elections," *American Journal of Political Science* 25, no. 3 (1981): 543–567; John C. McAdams and John R. Johannes, "Does Casework Matter? A Reply to Professor Fiorina," *American Journal of Political Science* 25, no. 3 (1981): 581–604; John R. Johannes and John C. McAdams, "The Congressional Incumbency Effect: Is It Casework, Policy Compatibility, or Something Else? An Examination of the 1978 Election," *American Journal of Political Science* 25, no. 3 (1981): 512–542; and David W. Romero, and "The Case of the Missing Reciprocal Influence: Incumbent Reputation and the Vote," *Journal of Politics* 58, no. 4 (1996): 1198–1207.

8. The most important book on oversight in recent years is Joel D. Aberbach, *Keeping a Watchful Eye: The Politics of Congressional Oversight* (Washington, D.C.: Brookings Institution, 1990).

9. In "Accidents, Scandals, and Political Support for Regulatory Agencies," *Journal of Politics* 46, no. 2 (1984): 401–427, Kathleen Kemp looks more systematically at accidents and scandals to see how they affect Congress's (and the president's) relationships with regulatory agencies.

10. Thomas A. Birkland, *After Disaster: Agenda Setting, Public Policy and Focusing Events* (Washington, D.C.: Georgetown University Press, 1997), Chapter 4.

11. In this book, "house of Congress" refers to either the House of Representatives or the Senate. "Congress" refers to the entire Congress, both the House and the Senate together. "House" used by itself refers to the House of Representatives.

12. Fiorina, *Congress: Keystone of the Washington Establishment.*

13. Richard Fenno, *Homestyle: House Members in Their Districts* (Boston: Little, Brown, 1978).

14. John W. Kingdon, *Agendas, Alternatives and Public Policies,* 2nd ed. (New York: Harper Collins, 1995.) I use the pronoun *he* to refer to the president because we have not yet elected a woman as president, although the likelihood of this happening seems to be growing as women, such as Governor Christine Todd Whitman of New Jersey and former cabinet member Elizabeth Dole, become more nationally prominent.

15. See, for example, Doris A. Graber, *Mass Media and American Politics,* 5th ed. (Washington, D.C.: CQ Press, 1997), Chapter 9.

16. Richard E. Neustadt, *Presidential Power and the Modern Presidents: The Politics of Leadership from Roosevelt to Reagan* (New York: Free Press, 1990).

17. Arthur Schlesinger, *The Imperial Presidency* (Boston: Houghton Mifflin, 1973).

18. Paul C. Light, *The President's Agenda: Domestic Policy Choice from Kennedy to Carter (with Notes on Ronald Reagan)* (Baltimore: Johns Hopkins University Press, 1982), 423.

19. Jonathan Weisman, "Clinton: Lame Duck on a Roll," Louisville *Courier-Journal,* June 20, 1999, 1D.

20. Amy Wallace and Faye Fiore, "Hollywood Surprised by Clinton's Violence Inquiry," *Los Angeles Times*, June 7, 1999, Home Edition, A1.

21. Max Weber, "Bureaucracy," in *From Max Weber: Essays in Sociology*, ed. and trans. H.H. Gerth and C. Wright Mill (New York: Oxford University Press, [1946] 1973).

22. B. Guy Peters, *American Public Policy: Promise and Performance* (Chappaqua, N.Y.: Chatham House/Seven Rivers, 1999).

23. Charles L. Cochran and Eloise F. Malone, *Public Policy: Perspectives and Choices* (New York: McGraw Hill, 1995), 17.

24. Woodrow Wilson, "The Study of Administration," *Political Science Quarterly* 2, no. 2 (June 1887), 210, 212.

25. For an illuminating discussion of Wilson's article and the assumptions underlying it, see Charles H. Levine, B. Guy Peters, and Frank J. Thompson, *Public Administration: Challenges, Choices, Consequences* (Glenview, Ill.: Scott, Foresman/Little Brown, 1990), 105–107.

26. Kenneth J. Meier, *Regulation, Politics, Bureaucracy and Economics* (New York: St Martin's Press, 1985) excerpted in *Public Policy: The Essential Reading,* ed. Stella Z. Theodoulou and Matthew A. Cahn (Englewood Cliffs, N.J.:Prentice Hall, 1995), 275.

27. Mary Schiavo, *Flying Blind, Flying Safe* (New York: Avon Books, 1997).

28. Peters, *American Public Policy*, 94–95.

29. I thank Professor Scott Barclay, who wrote the initial draft of this section and reviewed my additions to it.

30. 1 Cranch 137 (1803).

31. David Easton, *A Systems Analysis of Political Life* (New York: John Wiley and Sons, 1965).

32. 347 U.S. 483 (1954).

33. 109 U.S. 3 (1883).

34. 163 U.S. 537 (1896).

35. Edward Levi, *An Introduction to Legal Reasoning* (Chicago: University of Chicago Press, 1949).

36. Donald Horowitz, *The Courts and Social Policy* (Washington, D.C.: Brookings Institution, 1977), 3, emphasis in original.

37. Robert A. Dahl, "Decision-Making in a Democracy: The Supreme Court as a National Policy-Maker," *Journal of Public Law* 6 (Fall 1957): 279–295.

Notes to Chapter 4

1. James Chesney and Otto Feinstein, "Making Political Activity a Requirement in Introductory Political Science Courses," *PS: Political Science and Politics* 26, no. 3 (1993): 535–538; Hindy Lauer Schachter, *Reinventing Government or Reinventing Ourselves: The Role of Citizen Owners in Making a Better Government* (Albany: State University of New York Press, 1997).

2. Morris P. Fiorina, *Congress: Keystone of the Washington Establishment* (New Haven: Yale University Press, 1989).

3. Theodore Lowi, *The End of Liberalism: The Second Republic of the United States*, 2nd ed. (New York: W.W. Norton, 1979).

4. Andrew McFarland, "Interest Groups and Theories of Power in America," *British Journal of Political Science* 16 (1978): 129–147.

5. Michael Howlett and M. Ramesh, *Studying Public Policy: Policy Cycles and Policy Subsystems* (Toronto: Oxford University Press, 1995), 57.

6. All quotes from Howlett and Ramesh, *Studying Public Policy,* 57.

7. Mancur Olson, *The Logic of Collective Action* (Cambridge: Harvard University Press, 1971).

8. Olson, *The Logic of Collective Action.*

9. Decided January 24, 2000. For the opinion, see http://supct.law.cornell.edu/supct/html/98-963.ZO.html. When this opinion is published in its final form, you will be able to find a formal citation to *United States Reports* (U.S.) at http://supct.law.cornell.edu; search on either party's name.

10. Randall Rosenberg provides a critical view of the use of litigation as a means of inducing policy change in *The Hollow Hope* (Chicago: University of Chicago Press, 1991). The term "venue shopping" in the policy process is described in some detail in Frank Baumgartner and Bryan D. Jones, *Agendas and Instability in American Politics* (Chicago: University of Chicago Press, 1993).

11. Samuel J. Eldersveld, *Political Parties in American Society* (New York: Basic Books, 1982); John C. Green and Daniel M. Shea, eds., *The State of the Parties: The Changing Role of Contemporary American Parties* (Lanham, Md.: Rowman and Littlefield, 1999); Ronald Hrebenar, *Political Parties, Interest Groups, and Political Campaigns* (Boulder, Colo.: Westview, 1999).

12. Policy.com, an excellent Web site on policy issues, maintains a list of the well-known and less well known think tanks at http://www.policy.com/community/ttank.html. For a lively history of think tanks, see policy.com's first issue of "In the

Tanks," at http://www.policy.com/community/inthetanks.html.

13. Dean E. Alger, *The Media and Politics*, 2nd ed. (Belmont, Calif.: Wadsworth, 1996); Doris A. Graber, *Mass Media and American Politics*, 5th ed. (Washington, D.C.: CQ Press, 1997); W. Lance Bennett, *News: The Politics of Illusion*, 3rd ed. (New York: Longman, 1995).

14. Nicholas Varchaver, "CNN Takes Over the World," *Brill's Content*, June 1999. Available at http://www.brillscontent.com/features/cnn_0699.html.

15. Conrad Smith, *Media and Apocalypse: News Coverage of the Yellowstone Forest Fires, Exxon Valdez Oil Spill, and Loma Prieta Earthquake* (Westport, Conn.: Greenwood Press, 1992).

16. E.E. Schattschneider, *The Semisovereign People* (Hinsdale, Ill.: The Dryden Press, [1960] 1975).

17. Roger W. Cobb and Charles D. Elder, *Participation in American Politics: The Dynamics of Agenda-Building*, 2nd ed. (Baltimore: Johns Hopkins University Press, 1983).

18. Baumgartner and Jones, *Agendas and Instability.*

19. Cobb and Elder, *Participation*, 142–143.

20. Felicity Barringer, "Los Angeles Times Issues Unsparing Report on Itself," *New York Times,* December 21, 1999, C2.

21. See, for example, Lawrie Mifflin, "An ABC News Reporter Tests the Boundaries of Investigating Disney and Finds Them," *New York Times,* October 19, 1998, 8C; and "Timid Media Giants," *Phoenix Gazette*, December 9, 1995, B6.

22. My thinking on this point is particularly influenced by Bennett, *News: The Politics of Illusion.*

23. One of the first and still one of the classic treatments of pack journalism is Tim Crouse, *The Boys on the Bus* (New York: Random House, 1973).

24. John W. Kingdon, *Agendas, Alternatives and Public Policies*, 2nd ed. (New York: Harper Collins, 1995), 57–61.

25. Howlett and Ramesh, *Studying Public Policy,* 59.

26. Baumgartner and Joines, *Agendas and Instability.*

27. Edward O. Laumann and David Knoke, *The Organizational State: Social Choice in National Policy Domains*. (Madison: University of Wisconsin Press, 1987).

28. Kingdon, *Agendas*, 190–194.

29. Baumgartner and Jones, *Agendas and Instability.*

30. Hugh Heclo, "Issue Networks and the Executive Establishment," in *The New American Political System*, ed. Anthony King (Washington: American Enterprise Institute, 1978), 88.

31. Baumgartner and Jones, *Agendas and Instability.*

32. Heclo, "Issue Neworks."

33. Randall Ripley and Grace Franklin, *Congress, the Bureaucracy and Public Policy*, 5th ed. (Pacific Grove, Calif.: Brooks-Cole, 1991).

34. Sabatier and his colleagues have written extensively on this framework. The most comprehensive treatment is Paul Sabatier and Hank C. Jenkins-Smith, *Policy Change and Learning: An Advocacy Coalition Approach* (Boulder, Colo.: Westview, 1993).

35. Thomas A. Birkland, *After Disaster: Agenda Setting, Public Policy and Focusing Events* (Washington, D.C.: Georgetown University Press, 1997); Kingdon, *Agendas,* 94–100.

36. Regina Lawrence, *The Politics of Force: Media and the Construction of Police Brutality* (Berkeley: University of California Press, 2000).

37. David B. Robertson and Dennis R. Judd, *The Development of American Public Policy: The Structure of Policy Restraint* (Glenview, Ill.: Scott, Foresman, 1989).

38. Most of this information on MADD comes from its Web site, www.madd.org.

39. Keven A. Hill and John E. Hughes, *Cyberpolitics: Citizen Participation in the Age of the Internet* (Lanham, Md.: Rowman and Littlefield, 1998).

40. Robertson and Judd, *Development of American Public Policy.*

Notes to Chapter 5

1. E.E. Schattschneider, *The Semisovereign People* (Hinsdale, Ill.: The Dryden Press, [1960] 1975), 66.

2. James Hilgartner and Charles Bosk, "The Rise and Fall of Social Problems: A Public Arenas Model," *American Journal of Sociology* 94, no. 1 (1988): 53–78.

3. Roger W. Cobb and Charles D. Elder, *Participation in American Politics: The Dynamics of Agenda-Building*, 2nd ed. (Baltimore: Johns Hopkins University Press, 1983), 85.

4. Cobb and Elder, *Participation in American Politics*, 85–86.

5. Hilgartner and Bosk, "Rise and Fall;" Laurence J. O'Toole, "The Public Administrator's Role in Setting the Policy Agenda," in *Handbook of Public Administration*, ed. James L. Perry (San Francisco: Jossey Bass, 1989).

6. Peter Bachrach and Morton Baratz, "The Two Faces of Power," *American Political Science Review* 56 (1962): 952.

7. Anne Schneider and Helen Ingram, "The Social Construction of Target Populations: Implications for Politics and Policy," *American Political Science Review* 87, no. 2 (1992): 334–348.

8. Rachel Carson, *Silent Spring* (Greenwich, Conn.: Fawcett, 1962).

9. Schattschneider, *Semisovereign People*, 71, emphasis in original.

10. John Gaventa, *Power and Powerlessness: Quiescence and Rebellion in an Appalachian Valley* (Urbana: University of Illinois Press, 1980).

11. Herbert G. Reid, "Review of John Gaventa, *Power and Powerlessness: Quiescence and Rebellion in an Appalachian Valley*," *Journal of Politics* 43, no. 4 (November 1981): 1270–1273.

12. Frank Baumgartner and Bryan D. Jones, *Agendas and Instability in American Politics* (Chicago: University of Chicago Press, 1993).

13. Gaventa, *Power and Powerlessness.*

14. Schattschneider, *Semisovereign People*, 35.

15. John W. Kingdon, *Agendas, Alternatives and Public Policies*, 2nd ed. (New York: Harper Collins, 1995)

16. Baumgartner and Jones, *Agendas and Instability.*

17. Kingdon, *Agendas, Alternatives.*

18. These figures are from the *Statistical Abstract of the United States*, 1999, table 742. This book is available in most libraries, and a very useful version is available on line from the U.S. Census Bureau at http://www.census.gov/prod/www/statistical-abstract-us.html. For more discussion of this issue, see Kevin P. Phillips, *The Politics of Rich and Poor: Wealth and the American Electorate in the Reagan Aftermath* (New York: Random House, 1990).

19. Baumgartner and Jones, *Agendas and Instability*, 31

20. On the idea that the courts are constrained in their ability to promote social change, see Randall Rosenberg, *The Hollow Hope*. (Chicago: University of Chicago Press, 1991). For critiques of his position see Michael W. McCann, "Reform Litigation on Trial." *Law and Social Inquiry* 17, no. 4 (1992): 715–743.

21. Cobb and Elder, *Participation in American Politics*.

22. Deborah Stone, *Policy Paradox: The Art of Political Decision Making* (New York: W.W. Norton, 1997).

23. Joseph Gusfield, *The Culture of Public Problems: Drinking-Driving and the Symbolic Order* (Chicago: University of Chicago Press, 1981)

24. Alan Lifson, "Vaccines Have Made World a Different, Better Place," *Minneapolis Star-Tribune*, February 5, 2000, 15A; "Agency Recommends Shot Replace Oral Polio Vaccine," *Indianapolis Star*, January 21, 2000, A9.

25. Ray Lilley, "Mayor Warns Blackout Could Continue for 10 Days in New Zealand," Associated Press, February 23, 1998, accessed via Lexis-Nexis, http://www.lexis-nexis.com.

26. Stone, *Policy Paradox*, 137. Perhaps the preeminent student of symbolic politics is Murray Edelman. His major works are *The Symbolic Uses of Politics* (Urbana: University of Illinois Press, 1967); *Political Language: Words That Succeed and Policies That Fail* (New York: Academic Press, 1977); and *Constructing the Political Spectacle* (Chicago: University of Chicago Press, 1988).

27. See, for example, "OSHA Won't Hold Companies Responsible for Safety of Home-Offices," *CNN Interactive*, January 27, 2000, available at http://cnn.com/2000/US/01/27/homeworker.safety.ap; "Red-Faced OSHA Drops Rules for Home Workers," *Human Events*, January 14, 2000, 4.

28. Stone covers this topic in Chapter 8 of *Policy Paradox*; she also explores the topic in "Causal Stories and the Formation of Policy Agendas," *Political Science Quarterly* 104, no. 2 (1989): 281–300.

29. The oil companies promised, among other things, to clean ballast water, to preserve local air quality from oil vapors, and to be prepared for an oil spill. See Thomas A. Birkland, *After Disaster: Agenda Setting, Public Policy, and Focusing Events* (Washington, D.C.: Georgetown University Press, 1997), Jeff Wheelwright, *Degrees of Disaster: Prince William Sound: How Nature Reels and Rebounds* (New York: Simon and Schuster, 1994), and Art Davidson, *In the Wake of the Exxon Valdez*. (San Francisco: Sierra Club Books, 1990).

30. On this point, see Gary Newman, "Bluffs Leads State in Violent Crime: The city's police chief says the FBI report makes the situation appear worse than it is," *Omaha World-Herald*, December 8, 1999, 19; on the general point, see Adella Jones (Communications Director, St. Louis Metropolitan Police Department), letter to the editor in *St. Louis Post-Dispatch*, June 14, 1999, D14, and Carol Napolitano, "Why We Didn't Use FBI Numbers," *Omaha World-Herald*, November 8, 1999, 2.

31. On the environmentalist take on the GDP as a measure of well-being, see Jonathan Rowe and Mark Anielski, *The Genuine Progress Indicator: 1998 Update—Executive Summary* (San Francisco: Redefining Progress, 1999).

32. Another example of this problem of statistical outliers, also from King County, is described in Roberto Sanchez, "Medina? For Homes It Can't Be Finer," *Seattle Times*, February 20, 2000 (Sunday night final edition), B1.

33. Edward Tufte, *The Visual Display of Quantitative Information* (Cheshire,

Conn.: Graphics Press, 1983); *Envisioning Information* (Cheshire, Conn.: Graphics Press, 1990); and *Visual Explanations* (Cheshire, Conn.: Graphics Press, 1997).

Notes to Chapter 6

1. Theodore J. Lowi, "American Business, Public Policy, Case Studies, and Political Theory," *World Politics* 16 (July 1964): 667–715.

2. Randall Ripley and Grace Franklin, *Congress, Bureaucracy, and Public Policy*, 5th ed. Pacific Grove, Calif.: Brooks-Cole, 1991).

3. While budgeting is a very important element of the policy process, it is also somewhat technical and is not taken up in this book. James Anderson's *Public Policymaking*, 4th ed. (Boston: Houghton Mifflin, 2000) contains an excellent introduction to the federal budget process. There are also specialized texts on budgeting, such as Aaron Wildavsky, *The New Politics of the Budgetary Process* (New York: HarperCollins, 1992); John Cranford, *Budgeting for America* (Washington, D.C.: CQ Press, 1989); and John F. Cogan, *The Budget Puzzle: Understanding Federal Spending* (Stanford, Calif.: Stanford University Press, 1994).

4. Theodore Lowi, *The End of Liberalism: The Second Republic of the United States*, 2nd ed. (New York: W.W. Norton, 1979).

5. Ripley and Franklin, *Congress, Bureaucracy, and Public Policy*, 20.

6. Ripley and Franklin, *Congress, Bureaucracy, and Public Policy*, 21.

7. See, for example, Kevin P. Phillips, *The Politics of Rich and Poor: Wealth and the American Electorate in the Reagan Aftermath* (New York: Random House, 1990).

8. James Q. Wilson, *Bureaucracy* (New York: Basic Books, 1989), 79. Many of the examples in this discussion are drawn from this book. See also James Q. Wilson, *Political Organizations* (Princeton: Princeton University Press, 1995), Chapter 16.

9. Richard J. Stillman, *The American Bureaucracy*, (Chicago: Nelson-Hall, 1996), 135–136.

10. Lowi, "American Business," 707.

11. Peter J. Steinberger, "Typologies of Public Policy: Meaning Construction and the Policy Process," *Social Science Quarterly* 61 (September 1980): 185–197.

12. The following section on different policy types relies largely on Anderson, *Public Policymaking*, Chapter 1.

13. For a general discussion of the rulemaking process under the APA, see Charles H. Levine, B. Guy Peters, and Frank J. Thompson, *Public Administration: Challenges, Choices, Consequences* (Glenview, Ill.: Scott, Foresman/Little Brown, 1990), 169–170.

14. 491 U.S. 397 (1989).

Notes to Chapter 7

1. An excellent discussion of the importance of outcomes is provided by Dennis P. Affholter, "Outcome Monitoring," in *Handbook of Practical Program Evaluation*, ed. Joseph S. Wholey, Harry P. Hatry, and Kathryn E. Newcomer (San Francisco: Jossey Bass, 1994

2. Deborah Stone, *Policy Paradox: The Art of Political Decision Making* (New York: W.W. Norton, 1997).

3. Stone, *Policy Paradox*, 83.

4. Helen Ingram and Dean Mann, "Policy Failure: An Issue Deserving Attention." In *Why Policies Succeed or Fail*, ed. Helen Ingram and Dean Mann (Beverly Hills: Sage, 1980).

5. Edward O. Laumann and David Knoke, *The Organizational State: Social Choice in National Policy Domains* (Madison: University of Wisconsin Press, 1987): Chapter 1.

6. Frank Reissman, "Full Employment Now?" *Social Policy* 29, no. 4 (Summer 1999): 4; Jody Lipford, "Twenty Years After Humphrey-Hawkins," *Independent Review* 4, no. 1 (Summer 1999): 41–63. Both available via EBSCO Academic Search Elite, http://www.epnet.com/ehost/login.html.

7. Matthew Wald, "Experts Begin a Hard Look at Air Safety," *New York Times*, January 9, 1995, A12; Paul Hoverston, "Airlines, FAA Try for Zero Accidents," *USA Today*, February 10, 1995, A1.

8. Deborah A. Stone, "Causal Stories and the Formation of Policy Agendas," *Political Science Quarterly* 104, no. 2 (1989): 281–300.

9. Stone, *Policy Paradox*, 189.

10. Anne Larason Schneider and Helen Ingram, *Policy Design for Democracy* (Lawrence: University Press of Kansas, 1997), p. 93.

11. James E. Anderson, *Public Policymaking*, 4th ed. (Boston: Houghton Mifflin, 2000).

12. Lester M. Salamon and Michael S. Lund, "The Tools Approach: Basic Analytics," in *Beyond Privatization: The Tools of Government Action*, ed. Lester M. Salamon (Washington, D.C.: Urban Institute Press, 1989), 29.

13. Salamon and Lund, "The Tools Approach," 28.

14. Michael Howlett and M. Ramesh, *Studying Public Policy: Policy Cycles and Policy Subsystems* (Toronto: Oxford University Press, 1995), 157–163.

15. Howlett and Ramesh, *Studying Public Policy*, 158.

16. *United States v. Lopez*, 514 U.S. 549 (1995).

17. Charles H. Levine, B. Guy Peters, and Frank J. Thompson. *Public Administration: Challenges, Choices, Consequences*. Glenview, Ill.: Scott, Foresman/Little Brown, 1990.

18. Salamon and Lund, "The Tools Approach," 41.

Notes to Chapter 8

1. Neal Ryan, "Unraveling Conceptual Developments in Implementation Analysis," *Australian Journal of Public Administration* 54, no. 1 (1995): 65–81. Available via EBSCO Academic Search Elite, http://www.epnet.com/ehost/login.html.

2. Jeffery Pressman and Aaron Wildavsky, *Implementation* (Berkeley: University of California Press, 1973); Martha Derthick, *New Towns in Town* (Washington, D.C.: Urban Institute, 1972).

3. Van Horn, Carl E., and Donald S. Van Meter, "The Implementation of Intergovernmental Policy," in *Public Policy Making in a Federal System*, ed. Charles O. Jones and Robert D. Thomas (Beverly Hills: Sage, 1976); Carl Van Horn, *Policy Implementation in the Federal System: National Goals and Local Implementers* (Lexington, Mass.: Lexington Books, 1979); Daniel Mazmanian and Paul Sabatier, *Implementation and Public Policy* (Lanham, Md.: University Press of America, 1989).

4. Ryan, "Unravelling Conceptual Developments."

5. Caroline Dyer, "Researching the Implementation of Educational Policy: A Backward Mapping Approach," *Comparative Education* 35, no. 1 (1999): 45–62. Available via EBSCO Academic Search Elite, http://www.epnet.com/ehost/login.html.

6. James E. Anderson, *Public Policymaking*, 4th ed. (Boston: Houghton Mifflin, 2000), 205–210.

7. Paul A. Sabatier, "Top-Down and Bottom-Up Approaches in Implementation Research: A Critical Analysis and Suggested Synthesis," *Journal of Public Policy* 6, no. 1 (1986), 21–48.

8. Malcolm L. Goggin, Ann O'M. Bowman, James P. Lester, and Laurence J. O'Toole Jr., *Implementation Theory and Practice: Toward a Third Generation* (Glenview, Ill.: Scott Foresman/Little Brown, 1990).

9. Sabatier, "Top-Down and Bottom-Up," 25.

10. Michael Lipsky, "Street Level Bureaucracy and the Analysis of Urban Reform," *Urban Affairs Quarterly* 6 (1971): 391–409.

11. Richard Elmore, "Backward Mapping: Implementation Research and Policy Decisions," *Political Science Quarterly* 94, no. 4 (1979): 601–616.

12. Rene Torenvlied, "Political Control of Implementation Agencies," *Policy Sciences* 8, no. 1 (1996): 25–57. Available via EBSCO Academic Search Elite, http://www.epnet.com/ehost/login.html.

13. Sabatier, "Top-Down and Bottom-Up."

14. Peter J. May, "Reconsidering Policy Design: Policies and Publics," *Journal of Public Policy* 11, no. 2 (1990): 187–206.

15. Sabatier, "Top Down and Bottom Up."

16. Anne Schneider and Helen Ingram, "The Social Construction of Target Populations: Implications for Politics and Policy," *American Political Science Review* 87, no. 2 (1993): 334–348.

17. Richard Elmore, "Forward and Backward Mapping," in *Policy Implementation in Federal and Unitary Systems*, ed. K. Hanf and T. Toonen (Dordrecht: Martinus Nijhoff, 1985), 33–70.

18. Sabatier, "Top-Down and Bottom-Up," 37–38. Indeed, at the same time that Sabatier was writing, Laurence O'Toole argued that better thinking on implementation was needed precisely to provide policy makers and designers with useful advice. See Laurence O'Toole, "Policy Recommendations for Multi-Actor Implementation: An Assessment of the Field," *Journal of Public Policy* 6, no. 2 (1986): 181–210.

19. Sabatier, "Top-Down and Bottom-Up," 39.

20. Goggin et al., *Implementation Theory and Practice.*

21. Helen Ingram and Dean Mann, "Policy Failure: An Issue Deserving Attention," in *Why Policies Succeed or Fail*, ed. Helen Ingram and Dean Mann (Beverly Hills: Sage, 1980), 12

22. Colin J. Bennett and Michael Howlett, "The Lessons of Learning: Reconciling Theories of Policy Learning and Policy Change," *Policy Sciences* 25, no. 3 (1992): 275–294.

23. Bennett and Howlett, "The Lessons of Learning."

24. Paul A. Sabatier, "An Advocacy Coalition Framework of Policy Change and the Role of Policy-Oriented Learning Therein," *Policy Sciences* 21 (1988): 129–

168; Peter J. May, "Policy Learning and Failure," *Journal of Public Policy* 12, no. 4 (1992): 331–354.

25. May, "Policy Learning and Failure," 336.

Notes to Chapter 9

1. David Easton, *A Systems Analysis of Political Life* (New York: John Wiley, 1965).

2. These issues are discussed in Clarke E. Cochran et al., *American Public Policy: An Introduction*, 6th ed. (New York: St. Martin's Press, 1999), 14–18.

3. Keynes's original work on this subject and perhaps his most famous is *The General Theory of Employment, Interest and Money* (London: Macmillan, 1936). For a readable discussion of economic ideas, see Robert L. Heilbroner, *The Worldly Philosophers: The Lives, Times, and Ideas of the Great Economic Thinkers* (New York: Simon and Schuster, 1999). Keynes's ideas are discussed in Charles L. Cochran and Eloise F. Malone, *Public Policy: Perspectives and Choices* (New York: McGraw Hill, 1995), 160.

4. Cochran and Malone, *Public Policy*, 160.

5. B. Guy Peters, *American Public Policy: Promise and Performance* (Chappaqua, N.Y.: Chatham House/Seven Rivers, 1999).

6. Vicki Kember, "Home Inequity," *Common Cause Magazine* 20, no. 2 (Summer 1994): 14–20.

7. For example, Senator John McCain was castigated by Governor George W. Bush for proposing a tax plan that clearly benefited the upper classes more than it helped lower class people. See, for example, Robert Reno, "Of Course He's Conservative; What More Must McCain Do to Preserve His Credentials?" *Minneapolis Star-Tribune*, January 25, 2000, 13A.

8. For example, conservative commentator Dinesh d'Souza notes the seeming "middle-class" nature of some of the nation's newest high-tech millionaires in "The Billionaire Next Door," *Forbes*, October 11, 1999, 50–59. Consider this passage: "Interestingly, most Americans think of themselves as middle-class but only 34 million households, about a third of the population, belong to this group. Middle-class people have a net worth between $55,000 and $500,000, most of it in home equity and in retirement accounts."

9. John W. Kingdon, *Agendas, Alternatives and Public Policies*, 2nd ed. (New York: Harper Collins, 1995), 146–149.

10. This anxiety was perhaps best expressed in a William Wyler film, *The Best Years of Our Lives*, which deals with the postwar letdown experienced by three servicemen, their families, and their communities. Indeed, this film is one of the few post–World War II films that address these issues.

11. Cochran et al., *American Public Policy*, 12.

12. Ralph Erber and Richard R. Lau, "Political Cynicism Revisited: An Information-Processing Reconciliation of Policy-Based and Incumbency-Based Interpretations of Changes in Trust in Government," *American Journal of Political Science* 34, no. 1 (February 1990): 236.

13. A discussion of the relationship of voting to policy making is found in Michael Howlett and M. Ramesh, *Studying Public Policy: Policy Cycles and Policy Subsystems* (Toronto: Oxford University Press, 1995), 53–54.

14. Don VanNatta Jr., "The 2000 Campaign: The Polling; Years Ago, Bush Adviser in Texas Helped Draft a Poll Using Disputed Method," *New York Times,* February 15, 2000, A22; Doyle McManus and Judy Pasternak, "No Clear Signs Back Up McCain's Claims of Bush 'Push Poll,'" *Los Angeles Times*, February 16, 2000, A14.

15. Allan J. Cigler, "Interest Groups: A Subfield in Search of an Identity," in *Political Science, Looking to the Future: Volume IV: American Institutions*, ed. William Crotty (Evanston, Ill.: Northwestern University Press, 1991), 99.

16. Charles H. Levine, B. Guy Peters, and Frank J. Thompson. *Public Administration: Challenges, Choices, Consequences* (Glenview, Ill.: Scott, Foresman/Little Brown, 1990), 82.

17. See, for example, Thomas R. Dye, *Understanding Public Policy,* 7th ed. (Englewood Cliffs, N.J.: Prentice-Hall, 1992), 33.

18. Graham Allison, *Essence of Decision: Explaining the Cuban Missile Crisis* (Boston: Little, Brown, 1971).

19. Dye, *Understanding Public Policy*.

20. James G. March and Herbert A. Simon, *Organizations* (New York: John Wiley, 1958).

21. Charles E. Lindblom, "The Science of 'Muddling Through,'" *Public Administration Review* 19 (1959): 79–88. His follow-up to this article is Charles Lindblom, "Still Muddling, Not Yet Through," *Public Administration Review* 39 (1979): 517–526.

22. Paul R. Schulman, "Nonincremental Policy Making: Notes Toward an Alternative Paradigm," *American Political Science Review* 69, no. 4 (December 1975): 1354–1370.

23. Michael D. Cohen, James G. March, and Johan P. Olsen, "A Garbage Can Model of Organizational Choice," *Administrative Science Quarterly* 17 (1972): 1–25.

24. See, for example, William Claiborne, "Kemp Calls on Mayors for 'Audacious' Effort; Enterprise Zones, New War on Poverty Urged," *Washington Post*, June 23, 1992, A19; David Lauter, "Administration Again Divided on Urban Aid," *Los Angeles Times*, home edition, May 25, 1992, A24.

25. Jonathan Bendor and Thomas H. Hammond, "Rethinking Allison's Models," *American Political Science Review* 86, no. 2 (1992): 301–322.

26. Richard E. Neustadt, *Presidential Power and the Modern Presidents: The Politics of Leadership from Roosevelt to Reagan* (New York: Free Press, 1990).

27. At the time of this writing, the *Code of Federal Regulations* is available at http://www.access.gpo.gov/nara/cfr/index.html. If not at this link, simply find the online *Code of Federal Regulations* through any search engine. It is also available through the Lexis-Nexis and Westlaw information services.

28. See, for example, Edith Stokey and Richard Zeckhauser, *A Primer for Policy Analysis* (New York: W.W. Norton, 1978); Joseph S. Wholey, Harry P. Hatry, and Kathryn E. Newcomer, eds. *Handbook of Practical Program Evaluation* (San Francisco: Jossey Bass, 1994).

29. A considerable amount of the following discussion is based on James Anderson's discussion of policy evaluation in chapter 7 of *Public Policymaking*, 4th ed. (Boston: Houghton Mifflin, 2000).

30. Giandomenico Majone, *Evidence, Argument, and Persuasion in the Policy Process*. (New Haven: Yale University Press, 1989).

31. Robert T. Nakamura, "The Textbook Policy Process and Implementation Research," *Policy Studies Journal* 7, no. 1 (1987): 142–154.

32. Peter deLeon, "The Stages Approach to the Policy Process: What Has It Done? Where Is It Going?" in *Theories of the Policy Process*, ed. Paul A. Sabatier (Boulder, Colo.: Westview, 1999).

33. E.E. Schattschneider, *The Semisovereign People* (Hinsdale, Ill.: The Dryden Press, [1960] 1975); Kingdon, *Agendas, Alternatives and Public Policies*; Jeffrey Pressman and Aaron Wildavsky, *Implementation* (Berkeley: University of California Press, 1973).

34. Kingdon, *Agendas, Alternatives and Public Policies*.

35. Paul A. Sabatier, "Political Science and Public Policy," *PS: Political Science and Politics* 24, no. 2 (1991): 144–147.

36. Nikolaos Zahariadis, "To Sell or Not to Sell? Telecommunications Policy in Britain and France," *Journal of Public Policy* 12, no. 4 (1993): 355–376.

37. Frank Baumgartner and Bryan D. Jones, *Agendas and Instability in American Politics* (Chicago: University of Chicago Press, 1993).

38. Jeffrey M. Berry, "Subgovernments, Issue Networks, and Political Conflict," in *Remaking American Politics*, ed. Richard and Sidney Milkis Harris (Boulder, Colo.: Westview Press, 1989).

39. Dye, *Understanding Public Policy*, 44.

40. Dye, *Understanding Public Policy*, 45.

Glossary

Note: Each entry contains the chapter in which the term is most thoroughly discussed, although the term may be mentioned in earlier and subsequent chapters.

Administrative Procedure Act. A federal law (5 U.S.C. 551 et seq) that requires regulatory agencies to follow particular procedures in rule making, such as public notice of new rules, public comment periods, publication of rule making activity in the *Federal Register*, and the like (Chapter 4).

Advocacy Coalition Framework (ACF). A model or framework for understanding the interactions of groups and coalitions of groups called advocacy coalitions. In the framework, typically two to four coalitions form based on shared beliefs on policy issues. Paul Sabatier is the primary developer of the ACF, which has been applied to studies of implementation, policy change, and learning (Chapter 9).

agenda. The list of things that are being discussed and sometimes acted upon by an institution, the news media, or the public at large (Chapter 5).

agenda setting. The process by which problems and alternative solutions gain or lose public and elite attention, or the activities of various actors and groups to cause issues to gain greater attention or to prevent them from gaining attention (Chapter 5).

agenda setting (in the media). The process by which the news media devote greater attention to issues, thereby resulting in greater public attention (Chapter 4).

agenda universe. The list of all the possible ideas that could ever be advanced in any society. Compare to the *systemic agenda* (Chapter 5).

aggregate data. Data based on the adding up, or aggregation, of smaller data points. For example, data on the average family income of Canada is based on smaller data elements gathered all over Canada and then aggregated for analysis (Chapter 5).

anecdotal evidence. Evidence offered in policy debates that is based on stories and personal experience rather than empirical evidence (Chapter 1).

behaviorism. The approach, pioneered in the late 1930s and 1940s, to study social phenomena based on the postulated and observed behavior of individuals. Behaviorism was a response to the more common approach of its day known as *institutionalism* (Chapter 3).

bounded rationality. A term, used most prominently by James March and Herbert

Simon, that describes how decision makers seek to act as rationally as possible within certain bounds or limits; these limits include limited time, limited information, and our limited human ability to recognize every feature and pattern of every problem (Chapter 9).

budget deficit. The difference between what a government spends and what it receives in revenue. When a national government runs a deficit, it must often borrow to make up the difference, thereby increasing the *national debt* (Chapter 9).

bureaucracy. (1) A term of derision used for any complicated, cumbersome process characterized by paperwork, unresponsiveness, and slow results; (2) a system of social organization in which tasks are divided among bureaus, each of which follows particular procedures to evenhandedly administer rules; (3) the organization that administers government through rules and procedures (Chapter 3).

casework. The tasks undertaken by a legislator (or, more commonly, the legislator's staff) to help constituents with problems with government. Examples include writing letters of recommendation for admission to military academies, resolving immigration or passport problems, and resolving problems with federal benefits, such as Social Security (Chapter 3).

causal theory. A theory about what causes a problem and how particular responses would alleviate that problem (Chapter 7).

classical liberalism. In political theory, the ideological system that emphasizes individual liberty and the ownership and acquisition of private property as means by which to improve overall wealth and happiness, and to discourage social strife. Liberalism is the political ideology on which the American political system is based.

***Code of Federal Regulations* (CFR).** The compilation (in print and on-line) of all federal regulations. These regulations are first published in the *Federal Register*, and public comment is taken into account, before the regulations are codified in the CFR (Chapter 9).

commerce clause. Article I, section 8, clause 3, of the Constitution, which gives the Congress (and, by extension, the federal government) the power "to regulate commerce with foreign nations, and among the several states, and with the Indian tribes" (Chapter 2).

condition. A fact or situation that may be unpleasant but about which nothing can be done. For example, the weather can be thought of as a condition. Compare with a *problem* (Chapter 5).

cost-benefit analysis. Sometimes called cost-benefit-risk analysis, a technique of policy analysis that seeks to understand the costs of a course of action and its benefits. When risk is introduced, the risk of something bad happening is also taken into account (Chapter 9).

decision agenda. The agenda that contains items that are about to be acted upon by a governmental body, such as bills, court cases, or regulations (Chapter 5).

depression. Any severe economic downturn, but, in particular, the one suffered by the United States and other nations from approximately 1929 to the outbreak of World War II in 1939 (referred to as the Great Depression). A depression is accompanied by extremely high unemployment and significant reductions in the gross domestic product (GDP).

devolution. The process by which federally designed and administered programs are turned over, in whole or in part, to the states for them to manage as they see fit, based on their needs and conditions. This is often justified by the sense that the states are more innovative and responsive than the too-large federal government (Chapter 2).

discretion. The judgment or choices that bureaucrats exercise in the administration of policies. To exercise discretion is to make choices about how certain decisions will be made, based on the bureaucrat's experience and preferred outcomes (Chapter 3).

efficiency. Gaining the most output for a given level of input, or getting "more bang for the buck" (Chapter 9).

elitism. In studies of groups and politics, the theory or belief that policy making is dominated by the best educated, wealthiest, and most powerful elites. This position is most closely associated with sociologist C. Wright Mills. Contrast with *pluralism* (Chapter 5).

empirical evidence. Evidence based on observation and the collection of data, usually gathered to test a hypothesis about a scientific phenomenon. Compare with *anecdotal evidence* (Chapter 1).

enactment. The act of putting a decision, such as legislation or regulation, into effect. Statute laws are generally enacted in the United States when the president or a state governor signs a bill presented by the legislature (Chapter 5).

Enlightenment. Term used to describe the early eighteenth century, in which numerous theorists and philosophers developed new political and social philosophies based on reason and on insights from the natural sciences. From the Enlightment developed the thinking that spurred the American and French Revolutions, among other changes (Chapter 1).

evaluation. The process of investigating whether and to what extent a program has its desired effect (Chapter 9).

Federal Register. The daily journal of federal rule making and other administrative activity. Many notices of federal administrative activity are published in the *Federal Register*, the most important of which are codified in the *Code of Federal Regulations* (Chapter 6).

federalism. A system of government in which power is shared between a central or federal government and other governments, such as states or provinces. Key federal systems in the world include the United States, Canada, and Germany, among others (Chapter 2).

feedback. In systems models of the policy process, feedback is the information that reenters the system and shapes another round of policy making, thus completing the policy cycle.

field (of study). A particular area of study, often thought of as a subset of a discipline, such as public policy, which is a field under political science and some other disciplines (Chapter 1).

field hearing. A legislative hearing held outside Washington, D.C., often for the purpose of highlighting a local issue, capitalizing on an accident, disaster, or scandal, or providing local residents with an opportunity to make their views known to their elected officials (Chapter 3).

Freedom of Information Act. Federal law that allows citizens to gain information about government programs through a specified procedure. This act is often invoked by journalists and researchers when the government is at first unwilling to provide information; it is sometimes but not always successful in compelling the government to provide information. Of course, national security information is often unavailable (Chapter 3).

Great Society. The package of domestic programs advanced by President Lyndon Johnson to alleviate poverty, improve education, and foster civil rights during the 1960s. These programs were quite controversial, and while some, like Head Start, were considered successful, others, like urban renewal, were widely considered less successful (Chapter 2).

gross domestic product. The total value of all goods and services produced in a country (Chapter 3).

implementation. The process by which policies enacted by government are put into effect by the relevant agencies (Chapter 8).

incrementalism. A model of decision making in which policy change is accomplished through small, incremental steps that allow decision makers to adjust policies as they learn from their successes and failures (Chapter 9).

institutional agenda. That list of issues that is being currently considered by a governmental institution, such as an agency, legislature, or court (Chapter 4).

institutionalism. The study of politics and policy based on the interaction of formal institutions in government, such as the legislative, executive, and judicial branches. Compare with *behaviorism* (Chapter 3).

interest group. A collection of people or organizations that unite to advance their desired political outcomes in government and society (Chapter 4).

iron triangle. A particular style of *subgovernment* in which there are mutually reinforcing relationships between a regulated interest, the agency charged with regulation, and the congressional subcommittee charged with policy making in that issue area. This way of characterizing policy making relationships has largely given way to more sophisticated *issue networks* and *subgovernment* concepts (Chapter 4).

issue emergence. The point at which an issue becomes more visible and important to citizens and policy makers, when some stirrings of government and interest group activity begin to be evident (Chapter 9).

issue network. A term that describes the relationships between the various actors and interests in a particular policy issue. Hugh Heclo promoted this term because it describes a more open policy making system that contains more actors and relationships than the older *iron triangle* concept (Chapter 3).

judicial review. The power of the courts to review the acts of the legislature and executive branch and to strike them down if the courts find them to be unconstitutional. This power was first proclaimed by the court in *Marbury v. Madison* in 1803 (Chapter 3).

Laissez-faire economics. A system of economic regulation in which government leaves business totally or almost totally unfettered (Chapter 7). This term has negative connotations, referring as it does to the freewheeling and sometimes abusive business practices of the late nineteenth century (Chapter 2).

logrolling. The legislative practice of trading commitments to vote for members' pet policies (Chapter 4).

mobilization. The process by which people or groups are motivated to take action —lobbying, protest, or any other form of expression—in response to an issue or problem (Chapter 4).

national debt. The total amount of money owed to the nation's creditors, such as those who hold Treasury bills and savings bonds (Chapter 9).

New Deal. The program of policy changes and reforms associated with the Franklin Roosevelt administration; in particular, this term describes the policies intended to alleviate the Great Depression during his first two terms (Chapter 2).

open public meetings laws. Laws, most often passed at the state level, that mandate that most public meetings and hearings be open to the public, in order to promote citizen access to government and participation in decision making (Chapter 2).

outcomes. The results of the implementation of a policy. Outcomes can be intended or unintended, positive or negative (Chapter 7).

outputs. (1) The things that the policy process produces, such as laws, regulations, rules, and the like; (2) the effort that government expends to address problems. For example, more teaching hours provided by a school district is an output; the outcome would be, one hopes, an improvement in students' educational achievement (Chapter 7).

peak associations or peak organizations. The largest and most influential groups in a policy domain. These tend to be the groups that lead other like-minded groups in advocacy coalitions. The American Medical Association and the National Rifle Association are examples of peak organizations (Chapter 4).

peer review. A process in which articles published in academic journals have been submitted to other experts in the same field to determine the suitability of the article for publication, based on the existing norms and body of knowledge of the profession (Chapter 1).

pluralism. In group theories of politics, the theory, assumption, or belief that there are many groups that compete with each other in a reasonably open political system and that policy results from this group competition. Contrast with *elitism* (Chapter 5).

policy. A statement by government of what it intends to do or not to do, such as a law, regulation, ruling, decision, or order, or a combination of these (Chapter 6).

policy community. The group of actors—such as interest groups, government agencies, the media, and elected officials—who are actively involved in policy making in a particular domain. This group is generally thought of as being more open and dynamic than an iron triangle or subgovernment (Chapter 4).

policy design. The process by which policies are designed, both through technical analysis and the political process, to achieve a particular goal (Chapter 7).

policy domain. The substantive area of policy over which participants in policy making compete and compromise, such as the environmental policy domain or the health policy domain (Chapter 4).

policy monopoly. A term coined by Frank Baumgartner and Bryan Jones to describe a fairly concentrated, closed system of the most important actors in a domain, who dominate or monopolize policy making in the domain; this is similar to the idea of the *iron triangle*.

policy network. Another term for *issue network* (Chapter 4).

policy subsystem. Another term for *policy network* or *issue network,* although the term *subsystem* implies a somewhat less open, more mutually accommodating set of relationships between members of the subsystem (Chapter 4).

politics. In this book, I define politics the same way that Harold Lasswell does: the process by which society determines who gets what, when they get it, and how they get it (Chapter 1).

problem. A usually undesirable situation that, according to people or interest groups, can be alleviated by government action. Compare with *condition* (Chapter 5).

public goods. Goods that, once provided for one user, are provided for everyone, such as national defense or police services; economists say that public goods are indivisible and nonexclusive, because they cannot be divided into parts for individuals to consume and because one person's use of the good does not deny others the use of the good (Chapter 3).

public policy. There are many definitions, but for this book, I most like Thomas Dye's definition: "Whatever governments choose to do or not to do" (Chapter 1).

rational comprehensive decision making. A model of decision making in which it is assumed that decision makers have nearly all information about a problem, its causes, and its solutions at their disposal, whereupon a large number of alternatives can be weighted and the best one selected. Contrast with *incrementalism* and *bounded rationality* (Chapter 8).

recession. A period of economic contraction, when the value of the *gross domestic product* shrinks for two consecutive quarters (Chapter 9).

science. Knowledge, or a field of human endeavor that values the accretion of knowledge, both for its own sake and for practical purposes (Chapter 1).

scientific method. The system for gaining knowledge most commonly used in Western science, involving identifying a problem, gathering data, and testing hypotheses (Chapter 1).

separation of powers. The constitutional division of powers between the legislative, executive, and judicial branches of the government (Chapter 2).

social construction. The process by which issues and problems are defined in society (Chapter 5).

social movement. A broad-based group of people that come together to press for political or policy goals. A social movement is broader than an interest, often encompassing many groups and otherwise politically unorganized people. Recent social movements include the civil rights movement and the women's rights movement (Chapter 4).

social science. The branch of the sciences that studies the actions and behavior of people, groups, and institutions. Political science, sociology, anthropology, and economics are social sciences, and history is sometimes considered a social science (Chapter 1).

street level bureaucrats. A term coined by Michael Lipsky to describe the actors at the lowest end of the implementation chain, such as teachers, police officers, and social workers, who implement policies at the point of contact with the policy's target population (Chapter 8).

subgovernment. Policy network or subsystem that is most involved in making policy in a particular policy domain.

subsystem. A small group of actors in a policy domain, much like an issue network, although the term *subsystem* implies a somewhat closer relationship between these actors than does the issue network. Iron triangles are one kind of subsystem (Chapter 3).

systemic agenda. Any issue, problem or idea, that could possibly be considered by participants in the policy process, provided that the idea does not fall outside well-established social, political, ideological, and legal norms (Chapter 5).

tax expenditures. Government payments or subsidies in the form of tax deductions or credits; they are called "expenditures" because not collecting a tax is similar to collecting it and spending it (Chapter 9).

think tanks. Independent research organizations, sometimes ideologically neutral but often identified with a particular political perspective (Chapter 4).

transfer payments. Transfers of money from the government to individual recipients, such as farm subsidies, disaster relief, and various social welfare programs (Chapter 9).

venue shopping. A term used by Frank Baumgartner and Bryan Jones to describe how groups lobby the branch or agency of government that is most likely to give their concerns a sympathetic hearing (Chapter 4).

References

Aberbach, Joel D. *Keeping a Watchful Eye: The Politics of Congressional Oversight*. Washington, D.C.: Brookings Institution, 1990.

Affholter, Dennis P. "Outcome Monitoring." In *Handbook of Practical Program Evaluation*, ed. Joseph S. Wholey, Harry P. Hatry and Kathryn E. Newcomer. San Francisco: Jossey Bass, 1994.

Alger, Dean E. *The Media and Politics*. 2nd ed. Belmont, Calif.: Wadsworth, 1996.

Allison, Graham. *Essence of Decision: Explaining the Cuban Missile Crisis*. Boston: Little, Brown, 1971. This classic text explores various ways of explaining American and Soviet decision-making processes during the Cuban missile crisis. The book's value is in its development of three models of decision making and their application to the missile crisis case.

Anderson, James E. *Public Policymaking*. 4th ed. Boston: Houghton Mifflin, 2000. A reliable standard text on the policy process; its strength is its theoretical richness combined with practical examples, without providing a series of disconnected chapters on substantive policy topics.

Arnold, R. Douglas. *The Logic of Congressional Action*. New Haven: Yale University Press, 1990.

Bachrach, Peter, and Morton Baratz. "The Two Faces of Power." *American Political Science Review* 56 (1962): 947–952. A now-classic article on how political power is used by groups to advance their ideas while preventing other groups' ideas from gaining attention.

Baker, Ross K. *House and Senate*. New York: W.W. Norton, 1989.

Baumgartner, Frank, and Bryan D. Jones. *Agendas and Instability in American Politics*. Chicago: University of Chicago Press, 1993. This book uses the idea of "punctuated equilibrium" to explain how policies often remain at a standstill for a long time and then suddenly gain attention and undergo rapid change. This book is remarkable for both its method and the sweep of its analysis.

Beard, Charles A. *An Economic Interpretation of the Constitution of the United States*. New York: Macmillan, 1956. This book presents the controversial argument that the founders of the Constitution structured the document, and thus the

American system of government, largely to protect their own economic interests and the interests of their economic class.

Bendor, Jonathan, and Thomas H. Hammond. "Rethinking Allison's Models." *American Political Science Review* 86, no. 2 (1992): 301–322. A review and critique of Graham Allison's decision-making models in *Essence of Decision*. The article is useful both for its careful summary of Allison's argument and its reasoned critique of it.

Bennett, Colin J., and Michael Howlett. "The Lessons of Learning: Reconciling Theories of Policy Learning and Policy Change." *Policy Sciences* 25, no. 3 (1992): 275–294. A review of the literature on policy learning and its relationship to change.

Bennett, W. Lance. *News: The Politics of Illusion*. 3rd ed. New York: Longman, 1995. A very readable text on how the news media cover and present the news. Bennett argues that the information provided by news media is insufficient for people to use to make decisions in a democracy.

Berry, Jeffrey M. "Subgovernments, Issue Networks, and Political Conflict." In *Remaking American Politics*, ed. Richard and Sidney Milkis Harris. Boulder, Colo.: Westview Press, 1989.

Birkland, Thomas A. *After Disaster: Agenda Setting, Public Policy and Focusing Events*. Washington, D.C.: Georgetown University Press, 1997. A book on how the politics of focusing events differ depending on the nature of the event and the type of policy community that mobilizes, or fails to do so, to change policy in response to the event.

Carson, Rachel. *Silent Spring*. Greenwich, Conn.: Fawcett, 1962. This book is about the environmental damage done by pesticides. The publication of Carson's book is widely acknowledged as one of the most important events in the history of the environmental movement, which in many ways elevated the environmental issue to the institutional agenda.

Chesney, James, and Otto Feinstein. "Making Political Activity a Requirement in Introductory Political Science Courses." *PS: Political Science and Politics* 26, no. 3 (1993): 535–538.

Cigler, Allan J. "Interest Groups: A Subfield in Search of an Identity." In *Political Science, Looking to the Future: Volume IV: American Institutions*, ed. William Crotty. Evanston, Ill.: Northwestern University Press, 1991.

Cobb, Roger W., and Charles D. Elder. *Participation in American Politics: The Dynamics of Agenda-Building*. 2nd ed. Baltimore: Johns Hopkins University Press, 1983. Cobb and Elder view agenda setting, or, as they put it, "agenda-building," as "a particularly critical phase in the policy process." This book is a rich description of how problems are defined and how groups interact and compete to build their own agendas and deny others access to the agenda.

Cochran, Charles L., and Eloise F. Malone. *Public Policy: Perspectives and Choices*. New York: McGraw Hill, 1995.

Cochran, Clarke E., Lawrence Mayer, T.R. Carr, and N. Joseph Cayer. *American Public Policy: An Introduction*. 6th ed. New York: St. Martin's Press, 1999.

Cogan, John F. *The Budget Puzzle: Understanding Federal Spending*. Stanford, Calif.: Stanford University Press, 1994.

Cohen, Michael D., James G. March, and Johan P. Olsen. "A Garbage Can Model of Organizational Choice." *Administrative Science Quarterly* 17 (1972): 1–25. The "garbage can model" was developed to describe decision making and agenda setting in "anarchic" settings, such as universities. John Kingdon adopted and modified the streams and garbage cans concept in his book *Agendas, Alternatives and Public Policies.*

Cranford, John. *Budgeting for America.* Washington, D.C.: CQ Press, 1989.

Crouse, Tim. *The Boys on the Bus.* New York: Random House, 1973. An amusing and readable journalistic account of the 1972 presidential primaries, in which pack journalism became evident as a major problem in the news media.

Dahl, Robert A. "Decision Making in a Democracy: The Supreme Court as a National Policy-Maker." *Journal of Public Law* 6 (Fall 1957): 279–295. An investigation into the extent to which the Supreme Court makes policy that differs meaningfully from the preferences of the public, as measured by the composition of the "governing coalition" in Congress. Dahl found that the Supreme Court's decisions did not stray too far from the policy choices made by Congress, although later research has questioned his conclusions.

Davidson, Art. *In the Wake of the Exxon Valdez.* San Francisco: Sierra Club Books, 1990.

Davidson, Roger H., and Walter J. Oleszek. *Congress and Its Members.* 7th ed. Washington, D.C.: CQ Press, 1999.

deLeon, Peter. "The Stages Approach to the Policy Process: What Has It Done? Where Is It Going?" In *Theories of the Policy Process,* ed. Paul A. Sabatier. Boulder, Colo.: Westview, 1999.

Derthick, Martha. *New Towns in Town.* Washington, D.C.: Urban Institute, 1972. An early study of policy implementation, describing, in this case, the "New Towns in Town" program initiated during the Johnson Administration.

Dye, Thomas R. *Understanding Public Policy.* 7th ed. Englewood Cliffs, N.J.: Prentice Hall, 1992.

Dyer, Caroline. "Researching the Implementation of Educational Policy: A Backward Mapping Approach." *Comparative Education* 35, no. 1 (1999): 45–62. Available via ESBCO Academic Search Elite, http://www.epnet.com/ehost/login.html. A very useful article showing how the key concepts of implementation research can be applied to a particular case and to nations outside the United States and Europe—in this case, India.

Easterbrook, Gregg. "What's Wrong with Congress." *Atlantic Monthly,* December 1984, 57–84.

Easton, David. *A Systems Analysis of Political Life.* New York: John Wiley, 1965. The book that introduced systems thinking and modeling to political science and policy studies; while the models it inspired are no longer in vogue among political scientists, the concepts and terminology that it developed are still employed today.

Edelman, Murray J. *The Symbolic Uses of Politics.* Urbana: University of Illinois Press, 1967.

———. *Political Language: Words That Succeed and Policies That Fail.* New York: Academic Press, 1977.

———. *Constructing the Political Spectacle.* Chicago: University of Chicago Press, 1988. Edelman's work is the foundation for almost all the work on the importance of symbols and symbolic rhetoric in politics and policy making. His work has influenced students of the news media, agenda setting, and social construction.

Eldersveld, Samuel J. *Political Parties in American Society*. New York: Basic Books, 1982.

Elmore, Richard. "Backward Mapping: Implementation Research and Policy Decisions." *Political Science Quarterly* 94, no. 4 (Winter 1979): 601–616.

———. "Forward and Backward Mapping." In *Policy Implementation in Federal and Unitary Systems*, ed. K. Hanf and T. Toonen. Dordrecht: Martinus Nijhoff, 1985. In his 1979 article, Richard Elmore describes the backward mapping technique for analyzing policy implementation, arguing that it is important to take into account the motivations and actions of lower level implementers when designing and implementing policies. The 1985 article is an effort to combine top-down (forward mapping) and bottom-up approaches in the study of implementation.

Erber, Ralph, and Richard R. Lau. "Political Cynicism Revisited: An Information-Processing Reconciliation of Policy-Based and Incumbency-Based Interpretations of Changes in Trust in Government." *American Journal of Political Science* 34, no. 1 (February 1990): 236–253.

Erikson, Robert S., Gerald C. Wright, and John P. McIver. *Statehouse Democracy: Public Opinion and Policy in the American States*. New York: Cambridge University Press, 1993.

Fenno, Richard. *Homestyle: House Members in Their Districts*. Boston: Little, Brown, 1978. A major study of how members of the House of Representatives work in their home districts to gain the support of constituents and voters.

Fiorina, Morris P. "Some Problems in Studying the Effects of Resource Allocation in Congressional Elections." *American Journal of Political Science* 25, no. 3 (1981): 543–567.

———. *Congress: Keystone of the Washington Establishment*. New Haven: Yale University Press, 1989. A lively and assertive book in which Fiorina argues that there exists a "Washington establishment" of interest groups, bureaucrats, the media, lobbyists and others, but that the focal point or "keystone" of all this activity is in Congress.

Fiorino, Daniel J. *Making Environmental Policy*. Berkeley, Calif.: University of California Press, 1995. An excellent introductory text on environmental policy, written by an insider in the federal environmental community.

Gaventa, John. *Power and Powerlessness: Quiescence and Rebellion in an Appalachian Valley*. Urbana: University of Illinois Press, 1980. Chapter 1 of this book is a remarkably concise and insightful discussion of three levels of political power. The remainder of the book describes how these levels of power work to keep coal miners from mobilizing to improve their position in their jobs and communities.

Goggin, Malcom L., Ann O'M. Bowman, James P. Lester, and Laurence J. O'Toole, Jr. *Implementation Theory and Practice: Toward a Third Generation*. Glenview, Ill.: Scott Foresman/Little Brown, 1990. This volume, which has unfortunately gone out of print, is a synthesis of top-down and bottom-up approaches to implementation in what the authors call a "communications" model of implementation. In their model, the top policy designers send implementation messages that are received and interpreted by targets and intermediaries.

Graber, Doris A. *Mass Media and American Politics*. 5th ed. Washington, D.C.: CQ Press, 1997. This is a balanced, readable, and comprehensive text on political communications written by one of the primary experts in the field.

Green, John C., and Daniel M. Shea, eds. *The State of the Parties: The Changing Role of Contemporary American Parties*. Lanham, Md.: Rowman and Littlefield, 1999.

Greenberg, George D. , Jeffrey A. Miller, Lawrence B. Mohr, and Bruce C. Vladeck. "Developing Public Policy Theory: Perspectives from Empirical Research." *American Political Science Review* 71, no. 4 (1977): 1532–1543. This article argues that more efforts at theory building should give way to, or at least by accompanied by, greater efforts at empirical testing of theory.

Greenstein, Fred I. "The Presidential Leadership Style of Bill Clinton: An Early Appraisal." *Political Science Quarterly* 108, no. 4 (Winter 1993): 589–601.

Gusfield, Joseph. *The Culture of Public Problems: Drinking-Driving and the Symbolic Order*. Chicago: University of Chicago Press, 1981.

Hall, Peter A. "Policy Paradigms, Social Learning and the State." Paper presented at the Annual Meeting of the International Political Science Association, Washington, D.C., 1988.

Heclo, Hugh. "Issue Networks and the Executive Establishment." In *The New American Political System*, ed. Anthony King. Washington, D.C.: American Enterprise Institute, 1978. In this article, Hugh Heclo argues that the iron triangle concept of policy "was not so much wrong as it is disastrously incomplete." He argues that the issue network is a better way of describing the more competitive and contentious relationships between interests, regulators, and lawmakers.

Heilbroner, Robert L. *The Worldly Philosophers: The Lives, Times, and Ideas of the Great Economic Thinkers*. 7th revised edition. New York: Simon and Schuster, 1999. This very readable book is a good starting point for those interested in the history of economic ideas, ranging from Adam Smith to John Maynard Keynes.

Hilgartner, James, and Charles Bosk. "The Rise and Fall of Social Problems: A Public Arenas Model." *American Journal of Sociology* 94, no. 1 (1988): 53–78. Hilgartner and Bosk argue "that public attention is a scarce resource, allocated through competition in a system of public arenas." Because public attention is scarce, the competition to gain a place on the agenda is often fierce.

Hill, Kevin A., and John E. Hughes. *Cyberpolitics: Citizen Participation in the Age of the Internet*. Lanham, Md.: Rowman and Littlefield, 1998. Most people believe intuitively that the Internet and other new media are already having a profound effect on politics in general and carry with them the potential of greater public participation in policy and politics. This book is a balanced introduction to what will be a fruitful area of study for years to come.

Hill, Ronald Paul, and Sandi Macan. "Consumer Survival on Welfare With an Emphasis on Medicaid and the Food Stamp Program." *Journal of Public Policy and Marketing* 15, no. 1 (Spring 1996): 118–127.

Horowitz, Donald. *The Courts and Social Policy*. Washington, D.C.: Brookings Institution, 1977.

Howlett, Michael, and M. Ramesh. *Studying Public Policy: Policy Cycles and Policy Subsystems*. Toronto: Oxford University Press, 1995. Howlett and Ramesh have written one of the most sophisticated texts on the public policy process in recent years. As Canadians, the authors bring a comparative perspective to the study of public policy that is not often seen in texts by American writers.

Hrebenar, Ronald. *Political Parties, Interest Groups, and Political Campaigns*. Boulder, Colo.: Westview, 1999.

Ingram, Helen, and Dean Mann. "Policy Failure: An Issue Deserving Attention." In *Why Policies Succeed or Fail*, ed. Helen Ingram and Dean Mann. Beverly Hills: Sage, 1980. This introductory essay explores some reasons why policies fail—or are claimed to have failed. The authors argue that the question of policy failure deserves further study to determine whether policies are really failing, why they fail, and to what extent their failure is influenced by other, overlapping policies and goals.

Johannes, John R., and John C. McAdams. "The Congressional Incumbency Effect: Is It Casework, Policy Compatibility, or Something Else? An Examination of the 1978 Election." *American Journal of Political Science* 25, no. 3 (1981): 512–542.

Kemp, Kathleen. "Accidents, Scandals, and Political Support for Regulatory Agencies." *Journal of Politics* 46, no. 2 (1984): 401–427.

Keynes, John Maynard. *The General Theory of Employment, Interest and Money*. London: Macmillan, 1936. This is Keynes's most famous book, and launched the Keynesian movement in economics. Adherents of Keynesian economics argue, among other things, that government should spend money during recessions to stimulate the economy, and collect tax surpluses during periods of growth to prepare for the inevitable economic downturns that characterize the business cycle.

Kingdon, John W. *Agendas, Alternatives and Public Policies*. 2nd ed. New York: Harper Collins, 1995. This text, first published in 1984, outlines a "streams" metaphor of public policy making, in which policy change is more likely to occur when changes in the politics, policy, and problem streams lead to the opening of a "window of opportunity" for change. This book has become very influential in policy studies and is used to explain policy making in many different fields.

Kuhn, Thomas S. *The Structure of Scientific Revolutions*, 2nd ed. Chicago: University of Chicago Press, 1970. This book, first published in 1962, is a major work in the history of science. Kuhn argues that science does not progress through the steady accretion of knowledge, but, rather, though the adoption and destructions of "paradigms" in which researchers perform "normal science" until the contradictions between their findings and the paradigm lead to a revolution and the creation of a new paradigm.

Lasswell, Harold D. *Politics: Who Gets What, When, How*. New York: Meridian Books, 1958.

Laumann, Edward O., and David Knoke. *The Organizational State: Social Choice in National Policy Domains*. Madison: University of Wisconsin Press, 1987.

Lawrence, Regina. *The Politics of Force: Media and the Construction of Police Brutality*. Berkeley: University of California Press, 2000. This book is a social constructionist understanding of how the public, with the help of the news media, come to understand the nature of actual and alleged police brutality.

Levi, Edward. *An Introduction to Legal Reasoning*. Chicago: University of Chicago Press, 1949.

Levine, Charles H., B. Guy Peters, and Frank J. Thompson. *Public Administration: Challenges, Choices, Consequences*. Glenview, Ill.: Scott, Foresman/Little Brown, 1990. This is a basic undergraduate text on public administration, a field that shares a considerable amount of research and thinking with public policy. This book is particularly strong in understanding and explaining the relationships between politics, policy, and public management.

Light, Paul C. *The President's Agenda: Domestic Policy Choice from Kennedy to Carter (with Notes on Ronald Reagan)*. Baltimore: Johns Hopkins University Press, 1982. A groundbreaking book in the tradition of Neustadt's *Presidential Power*. Light argues that the power of the presidency is in the power to set the agenda—that is, to cause Congress, the media, interest groups, and the public to focus on the issues he finds most important. Nevertheless, the president's power is limited; he must gather resources to advance his chosen issues on the agenda early in his term, before those resources are expended.

Lindblom, Charles E. "The Science of 'Muddling Through.'" *Public Administration Review* 19 (1959): 79–88.

———. "Still Muddling, Not Yet Through." *Public Administration Review* 39 (1979): 517–526. These two articles discuss the idea of *incrementalism* as a way of understanding why policy decisions seem so small and timid.

Lipford, Jody. "Twenty Years After Humphrey-Hawkins." *Independent Review* 4, no. 1 (Summer 1999): 41–63. Available via ESBCO Academic Search Elite, http://www.epnet.com/ehost/login.html.

Lipsky, Michael. "Street Level Bureaucracy and the Analysis of Urban Reform." *Urban Affairs Quarterly* 6 (1971): 391–409. This article introduces the idea of the "street level bureaucrat" as an important element of policy implementation. Street level bureaucrats are the teachers, police officers, and social workers charged with the direct delivery of services; their exercise of professional discretion in the delivery of services can significantly influence the extent to which policy goals are met.

Lowi, Theodore J. "American Business, Public Policy, Case Studies, and Political Theory." *World Politics* 16, no. (July 1964): 667–715. Lowi introduces the distributive–redistributive–regulatory policy typology in this article.

———. *The End of Liberalism: The Second Republic of the United States*. 2nd ed. New York: W.W. Norton, 1979.

Majone, Giandomenico. *Evidence, Argument, and Persuasion in the Policy Process*. New Haven: Yale University Press, 1989.

March, James G., and Herbert A. Simon. *Organizations*. New York: John Wiley, 1958.

May, Peter J. "Reconsidering Policy Design: Policies and Publics." *Journal of Public Policy* 11, no. 2 (1990): 187–206. Peter May discusses the policy design implications of "policies without publics"—that is, policy for which there is little or no public demand or mobilization to cause policy to be made, such as policies intended to mitigate natural hazards.

———. "Policy Learning and Failure." *Journal of Public Policy* 12, no. 4 (1992): 331–354.

Mazmanian, Daniel, and Paul Sabatier. *Implementation and Public Policy*. Lanham, Md.: University Press of America, 1989.

McAdams, John C., and John R. Johannes. "Does Casework Matter? A Reply to Professor Fiorina." *American Journal of Political Science* 25, no. 3 (1981): 581–604.

McCann, Michael W. "Reform Litigation on Trial." *Law and Social Inquiry* 17, no. 4 (1992): 715–743.

McCloskey, Robert G. *The American Supreme Court*, ed. Sanford Levinson. 2nd ed. Chicago: University of Chicago Press, 1994. This is one of the best books on the Supreme Court, because it links the historical development of the United States to the legal doctrines that were being developed by the Court. The book proceeds chronologically, from the founding until 1960. This second edition, edited by Sanford Levinson, updates McCloskey's original work with chapters on the Court and civil rights and other topics.

McCool, Daniel C. *Public Policy Theories, Models, and Concepts: An Anthology.* Englewood Cliffs, N.J.: Prentice Hall, 1995. An anthology of classic readings in public policy that stands apart by including excellent introductory essays that place the readings in context and bring the theories up to date.

McFarland, Andrew. "Interest Groups and Theories of Power in America." *British Journal of Political Science* 16 (1978): 129–147.

McPherson, James H. *Abraham Lincoln and the Second American Revolution.* New York: Oxford University Press, 1990.

Meier, Kenneth J. *Regulation, Politics, Bureaucracy and Economics.* New York: St. Martin's Press, 1985, excerpted in *Public Policy: The Essential Readings*, ed. Stella Z. Theodoulou and Matthew A. Cahn. Englewood Cliffs, N.J.: Prentice Hall, 1995.

Moore, Barrington. *Social Origins of Dictatorship and Democracy: Lord and Peasant in the Making of the Modern World.* Boston: Beacon Press, 1966.

Nakamura, Robert T. "The Textbook Policy Process and Implementation Research." *Policy Studies Journal* 7, no. 1 (1987): 142–154. Nakamura argues that the stages model or what he calls "the textbook policy process" is unrealistic, because the process is not step-by-step and orderly in the way implied by most depictions of this model.

Neustadt, Richard E. *Presidential Power and the Modern Presidents: The Politics of Leadership from Roosevelt to Reagan.* New York: Free Press, 1990.

Olson, Mancur. *The Logic of Collective Action:* Cambridge: Harvard University Press, 1971. This is the classic book on why collective action—that is, joining and taking action in groups—is so difficult to achieve unless there are powerful incentives for group formation and action. This book serves as a reaction to the pluralist claim that people will often join groups to advance their claims and serve as counterweights to other interest groups.

Osborne, David. *Laboratories of Democracy: A New Breed of Governor Creates Models for National Growth.* Cambridge, Mass.: Harvard Business School Press, 1988.

O'Toole, Laurence J. "The Public Administrator's Role in Setting the Policy Agenda." In *Handbook of Public Administration*, ed. James L. Perry. San Francisco: Jossey Bass, 1989.

———. "Policy Recommendations for Multi-Actor Implementation: An Assessment of the Field. " *Journal of Public Policy* 6, no. 2 (1986): 181–210.

Peters, B. Guy. *American Public Policy: Promise and Performance.* Chappaqua, N.Y.: Chatham House/Seven Rivers, 1999. A public policy textbook, this book combines theory with a series of case studies. Perhaps the best balance between theory and case studies in any undergraduate textbook.

Phillips, Kevin P. *The Politics of Rich and Poor: Wealth and the American Electorate in the Reagan Aftermath.* New York: Random House, 1990. Kevin Phillips, a political commentator long associated with Republican causes, surprised many people with this well-documented discussion of the growing concentration of wealth at the top of society and the growing wealth gap between the rich and poor. He argues that this gap will have significant political consequences.

Plotnick, Robert D., and Richard F. Winters. "A Politico-Economic Theory of Income Redistribution." *American Political Science Review* 79, no. 2 (1985): 458–473.

Pressman, Jeffrey , and Aaron Wildavsky. *Implementation*. Berkeley: University of California Press, 1973. Still required reading in many courses on public policy and policy implementation, this book describes the problems that accompanied the implementation of economic development projects at the Port of Oakland and the Oakland International Airport. The authors find that implementation is made difficult by the "complexity of joint action."

Reid, Herbert G. "Review of John Gaventa, *Power and Powerlessness: Quiescence and Rebellion in an Appalachian Valley.*" *Journal of Politics* 43, no. 4 (November 1981): 1270–1273.

Reissman, Frank. "Full Employment Now?" *Social Policy* 29, no. 4 (Summer 1999): 4. Available via ESBCO Academic Search Elite, http://www.epnet.com/ehost/login.html.

Ripley, Randall, and Grace Franklin. *Congress, Bureaucracy, and Public Policy*, 5th ed. Pacific Grove, Calif.: Brooks-Cole, 1991. This book adopts and extends Lowi's distributive–redistributive–regulatory policy typology to illustrate the relationships between Congress, the bureaucracy, and interest groups in the policy process.

Robertson, David B., and Dennis R. Judd. *The Development of American Public Policy: The Structure of Policy Restraint*. Glenview, Ill.: Scott, Foresman, 1989. This book adopts a historical and structural analysis of the constitutional system to show how American government and politics were explicitly designed to restrain policy making, particularly when that policy making is supported by mass publics rather than by elites.

Rodgers, Harrell R., Jr. "Civil Rights and the Myth of Popular Sovereignty." *Journal of Black Studies* 12, no. 1 (1981): 53–70.

Romero, David W. "The Case of the Missing Reciprocal Influence: Incumbent Reputation and the Vote." *Journal of Politics* 58, no. 4 (1996): 1198–1207.

Rosenbaum, Walter A. *Environmental Politics and Policy*, 2nd ed. Washington, D.C.: CQ Press, 1991. Rosenberg, Randall. *The Hollow Hope*. Chicago: University of Chicago Press, 1991. A well-researched, clearly argued, and very controversial book in which the author argues that the Supreme Court and the lower courts are not the powerful protector of civil rights and venue for policy change that many social movement leaders and laypeople believe.

Rowe, Jonathan and Mark Anielski. *The Genuine Progress Indicator: 1998 Update—Executive Summary*. San Francisco: Redefining Progress, 1999.

Ryan, Neal. "Unraveling Conceptual Developments in Implementation Analysis." *Australian Journal of Public Administration* 54, no. 1 (1995): 65–81. Available via ESBCO Academic Search Elite, http://www.epnet.com/ehost/login.html.

Sabatier, Paul A. "Top-Down and Bottom-Up Approaches in Implementation Research: A Critical Analysis and Suggested Synthesis." *Journal of Public Policy* 6, no. 1 (1986): 21–48.

———. "An Advocacy Coalition Framework of Policy Change and the Role of Policy-Oriented Learning Therein." *Policy Sciences* 21 (1988): 129–168.

————. "Political Science and Public Policy." *PS: Political Science and Politics* 24, no. 2 (1991): 144–147.

————. "Toward Better Theories of the Policy Process." *PS: Political Science and Politics* 24, no. 2 (1991): 147–156.

Sabatier, Paul A., and Hank C. Jenkins-Smith. *Policy Change and Learning: An Advocacy Coalition Approach*. Boulder, Colo.: Westview, 1993. All these works by Paul Sabatier contain efforts to advance the sophistication and usefulness of policy theory. Sabatier's most important contribution to policy studies is his advocacy coalition framework, which has been advanced, tested, and refined for over ten years. At the same time, Sabatier, in his *PS* articles, seeks to locate the advocacy coalition framework in context with other models of the process.

————. "The Advocacy Coalition Framework: An Assessment," in Policy Change and Learning: An Advocacy Coalition Approach, ed. Paul A. Sabatier and Hank C. Jenkins-Smith. Boulder, Colo.: Westview, 1999.

Salamon, Lester M. and Michael S. Lund. "The Tools Approach: Basic Analytics." In *Beyond Privatization: The Tools of Government Action*, ed. Lester M. Salamon. Washington, D.C.: Urban Institute Press, 1989.

Schachter, Hindy Lauer. *Reinventing Government or Reinventing Ourselves: The Role of Citizen Owners in Making a Better Government*. Albany: State University of New York Press, 1997.

Schattschneider, E.E. *The Semisovereign People*. Hinsdale, Ill.: The Dryden Press, [1960] 1975.

Schiavo, Mary. *Flying Blind, Flying Safe*. New York: Avon Books, 1997.

Schlesinger, Arthur M. *The Imperial Presidency*. Boston: Houghton Mifflin, 1973. This book is very much a reflection of the times in which it was written. Schlesinger, writing during the Vietnam and Watergate years, argued that the presidency had gained so much power that it was becoming "imperial" and therefore answerable only to itself. Experience with later administrations has tempered the belief that the presidency is unfettered by other institutions.

Schneider, Anne, and Helen Ingram. "The Social Construction of Target Populations: Implications for Politics and Policy." *American Political Science Review* 87, no. 2 (1993): 334–348.

————. *Policy Design for Democracy*. Lawrence: University Press of Kansas, 1997.

Schulman, Paul R. "Nonincremental Policy Making: Notes Toward an Alternative Paradigm." *American Political Science Review* 69, no. 4 (1975): 1354–1370. Schulman argues that, in many instances, incremental policy making does not explain policy outcomes or cannot work to reach policy goals. He uses NASA's mission to the moon, which started in 1961, as an example of nonincremental policy making.

Smith, Conrad. *Media and Apocalypse: News Coverage of the Yellowstone Forest Fires, Exxon Valdez Oil Spill, and Loma Prieta Earthquake*. Westport, Conn.: Greenwood Press, 1992.

Steinberger, Peter J. "Typologies of Public Policy: Meaning Construction and the Policy Process." *Social Science Quarterly* 61 (September 1980): 185–197. This discusses a way of thinking about policy types that focuses on how participants in policy making attribute meanings to policies, rather than attempting to find objective attributes of policies.

Stillman, Richard J. *The American Bureaucracy*. Chicago: Nelson-Hall, 1996. This is a clearly written and very thorough textbook on the structure and function of the bureaucracy. Unlike many treatments of bureaucracy, this book explains this important part of policy without bogging down in highly technical jargon.

Stokey, Edith, and Richard Zeckhauser. *A Primer for Policy Analysis*. New York: W.W. Norton, 1978. While showing its age, this book remains one of the most useful introductory texts in policy analysis. This book is a good complement to Weimer and Vining's book; Stokey and Zeckhauser rely somewhat less on economic explanations than do Weimer and Vining.

Stone, Deborah A. "Causal Stories and the Formation of Policy Agendas." *Political Science Quarterly* 104, no. 2 (1989): 281–300.

———. *Policy Paradox: The Art of Political Decision Making*. New York: W.W. Norton, 1997. Deborah Stone directly takes on the rationalist approach to policy analysis—she calls this the "rationality project"—in this book. She compares the rationalist notions of society as a market with a more politically and sociologically useful idea of society as the "polis" to illustrate why there are so many paradoxes in politics and policy making that cannot be "rationally" explained.

Tallon Jr., James R., Jr., and Lawrence D. Brown. "Who Gets What? Devolution of Eligibility and Benefits in Medicaid." In *Medicaid and Devolution: A View from the States*, ed. Frank J. Thompson and John J. DiIulio, Jr. Washington, D.C.: Brookings Institution Press, 1998.

Torenvlied, Rene. "Political Control of Implementation Agencies." *Policy Sciences* 8, no. 1 (1996): 25–57.

Tufte, Edward R. *The Visual Display of Quantitative Information*. Cheshire, Conn.: Graphics Press, 1983.

———. *Envisioning Information*. Cheshire, Conn.: Graphics Press, 1990.

———. *Visual Explanations*. Cheshire, Conn.: Graphics Press, 1997. All of Tufte's books are beautifully designed and printed books on information graphics. They are helpful to anyone who wants to honestly present quantitative information,and are useful tools for defense against those who fail, by design or accident, to honestly convey statistical information.

Van Horn, Carl. *Policy Implementation in the Federal System: National Goals and Local Implementers*. Lexington, Mass.: Lexington Books, 1979.

Van Horn, Carl E., and Donald S. Van Meter. "The Implementation of Intergovernmental Policy." In *Public Policy Making in a Federal System*, ed. Charles O. Jones and Robert D. Thomas. Beverly Hills: Sage, 1976.

Vig, Norman, and Michael Kraft. *Environmental Policy in the 1990s*. Washington, D.C.: CQ Press, 1996.

Walker, Jack L. "Setting the Agenda in the U.S. Senate: A Theory of Problem Selection." *British Journal of Political Science* 7 (1977): 423–445. Walker argues that the United States Senate's agenda is heavily influenced by the scarcity of time to deal with every issue. In particular, so many routine or crisis-driven items reach the Senate's agenda that it is very difficult for the Senate to tackle its "chosen problems."

Weber, Max. "Bureaucracy." In *From Max Weber: Essays in Sociology*, ed. and trans. H.H. Gerth and C. Wright Mills. New York: Oxford University Press, [1946] 1973.

Weimer, David, and Aidan Vining. *Policy Analysis: Concepts and Practice*. Englewood Cliffs, N.J.: Prentice Hall, 1992. This book is a standard text on policy analysis, with excellent examples and explanations. Like most policy analysis texts, this book is firmly grounded in economics.

Wheelwright, Jeff. *Degrees of Disaster: Prince William Sound: How Nature Reels and Rebounds*. New York: Simon and Schuster, 1994.

Wholey, Joseph S., Harry P. Hatry, and Kathryn E. Newcomer, eds. *Handbook of Practical Program Evaluation*. San Francisco: Jossey Bass, 1994.

Wildavsky, Aaron. *The New Politics of the Budgetary Process*. New York: HarperCollins, 1992.

Wilson, James Q. *Bureaucracy*. New York: Basic Books, 1989.

———. *Political Organizations*, Princeton, N.J.: Princeton University Press, 1995. In both *Bureaucracy* and *Political Organizations*, Wilson outlines a way of categorizing policies based on the distribution of costs and benefits associated with a policy.

———. "The Rise of the Bureaucratic State," excerpted in *Public Policy: The Essential Reading*, ed. Stella Z. Theodoulou and Matthew A. Cahn. Englewood Cliffs, N.J.: Prentice Hall, 1995. Wilson raises important questions about bureaucratic accountability and discretion, and outlines the circumstances under which bureaucracies become less subject to popular and legislative control.

Wilson, Woodrow. "The Study of Administration." *Political Science Quarterly* 2, no. 2 (June 1887): 197–222.

Wood, B. Dan. "Federalism and Policy Responsiveness: The Clean Air Case." *Journal of Politics* 53, no. 3 (1991): 851–859.

Yiannakis, Diana Evans. "The Grateful Electorate: Casework and Congressional Elections." *American Journal of Political Science* 25, no. 3 (1981): 568–580.

Zahariadis, Nikolaos. "To Sell or Not to Sell? Telecommunications Policy in Britain and France." *Journal of Public Policy* 12, no. 4 (1993): 355–376.

Index

g = glossary

About The Author

Thomas Birkland teaches political science and public administration at the University at Albany, State University of New York. His research focuses on environmental politics and policy, and he is the codirector of the University at Albany's Biodiversity and Conservation Policy Program. Before joining the Albany faculty, Professor Birkland worked for the State of New Jersey in various capacities. His doctorate is from the University of Washington in Seattle.